Achieving
Service
Productivity

Achieving Service Productivity

Lessons from the Best in the World

Edited by
ERIK HÖRNELL
& PER HJELM

in association with Linsey J. Caton

INGENJÖRSVETENSKAPSAKADEMIEN
ROYAL SWEDISH ACADEMY OF ENGINEERING SCIENCES

FINANCIAL TIMES
PITMAN PUBLISHING

PITMAN PUBLISHING
128 Long Acre, London WC2E 9AN

A Division of Longman Group UK Limited

© The Royal Swedish Academy of Engineering Sciences 1994

First published in Great Britain 1994

British Library Cataloguing in Publication Data
A CIP catalogue record for this book can be obtained from the British Library.

ISBN 0 273 60386 8

All rights reserved; no part of this publication may be reproduced, stored in a retrieval system; or transmitted in any form or by any means, electronic, mechanical, photocopying, recording, or otherwise without either the prior written permission of the Publishers or a licence permitting restricted copying in the United Kingdom issued by the Copyright Licensing Agency Ltd, 90 Tottenham Court Road, London W1P 9HE. This book may not be lent, resold, hired out or otherwise disposed of by way of trade in any form of binding or cover other than that in which it is published, without the prior consent of the Publishers.

Typeset by PanTek Arts, Maidstone.
Printed and bound in Great Britain by
Biddles Ltd, Guildford and King's Lynn.

CONTENTS

Foreword   *vii*

1. **THE MODEL FOR THE STUDY**   **1**
2. **RETAIL BANKING**   **4**
3. **COMMERCIAL INSURANCE**   **53**
4. **POSTAL LETTER SERVICES**   **84**
5. **POSTAL GIRO SERVICES**   **120**
6. **SECONDARY SCHOOLS**   **148**
7. **HEALTH CARE**   **170**
8. **CONVENIENCE GOODS DISTRIBUTION AND RETAILING**   **201**
9. **LESSONS FROM THE BEST IN SERVICES**   **223**

Appendix 1 Method and model   *261*

Appendix 2 Steering committee   *281*

Appendix 3 Research associates   *282*

Appendix 4 Executives' commentaries   *285*

Index   *289*

FOREWORD

This book is an independent sequel *Improving Productivity for Competitive Advantage Financial Times* Pitmans Publishing 1992. It is based on a study entitled *Best in Services* conducted by the Royal Swedish Academy of Engineering Science. The main purpose of this was to try to explain what factors have a positive effect on productivity in companies belonging to various service sectors. In the course of our work, we found that negative factors in some service sectors were so interesting and relevant to the trend of productivity that we decided to describe them as well. As in the previous study, our method has been to examine good examples and use this as a basis for learning what we can from successful service-providing organisations and their surroundings.

The research was planned and conducted by the Office of Economic Studies at IVA and supervised by a steering committee chaired by Dr Björn Sprängare. The different case studies were carried out by seven teams – 30 researchers in all. These sectorial studies were extensive, and this book contains only summaries of them. The members of each research team are presented before their respective chapter.

We would like to begin our acknowledgements by thanking all the members of IVA who submitted proposals for suitable organisations to study. This was highly useful, giving us a broad international base to choose from. Anders Wikman of the Swedish Office of Science and Technology in Detroit was very helpful in the task of planning and conducting the U.S. portion of our hospital and banking studies. Phil Beekhuizen of the Australian Manufacturing Council provided invaluable help as our advisor in Australia.

The study would have been impossible to complete without intellectual help from many individuals and generous contributions from numerous sponsors. We thank Skandinaviska Enskilda Banken, the Swedish Employers Confederation (SAF), the Swedish Ministry of Industry and Commerce, the Swedish Association of Local Authorities, the Swedish Working Life Fund, Trygg-Hansa, Bilspedition, the Swedish Work Environment Fund, the Axel Johnson Group and the Swedish Ministry of Health and Social Affairs for sponsoring this project. Special thanks to the Boston Consulting Group, Indevo Partners AB and the Swedish Agency for Administrative Development, which provided top-flight researchers free of charge.

The eighteen organisations that are examined in the book deserve our warm thanks for so generously making their employees available for interviews and analyses. In all cases, their top management participated actively in our analytical task and in lengthy interviews.

We would also like to thank the experts who served as a sounding board for testing our models and evaluating the relevance of the findings from our study. They included Osvald Bjelland and Bjelland Dahl & Partners, Tord Johanson of Sweden Post, Kenneth Synnersten of Arla Plast AB, Jan Edgren of the Swedish Ministry of Industry and Commerce and Professor Gunnar Hedlund of Institute of International Business, Stockholm School of Economics.

We had the pleasure of working for a highly qualified steering committee, consisting of the following members: Björn Sprängare (Chairman), President & CEO, Trygg-Hansa SPP Holding; Professor Pierre Guillet, University of Stockholm; Antonia Ax: son Johnson, Chairman, The Axel Johnson Group; Dr Marin Leimdörfer, President, Industri-Matematik AB; Martin Lundberg, President, Bilspedition; Professor Johan Myhrman, Stockholm School of Economics; Professor Bengt Stymne, IMIT, Stockholm School of Economics; Carl-Johan Åberg, Managing Director, The National Swedish Pension Fund. Our hearty thanks to all members of the steering committee for many inspiring meetings and interesting viewpoints.

We also wish to thank all our researchers, who devoted many years to their analyses and provided us with first-class material, both in the form of summaries and complete reports.

The authors are grateful for helpful discussions and provision of documents from the following persons: Dr. Vinod Sahey, Corporate Vice President Marketing & Planning and Mr. Gail Warden, President and CEO, Henry Ford Health System, Mr. David Sandbach, Chief Executive, Dr. Phil Cartwright, Consultant Anaesthetist, Princess Royal Hospital, Mr. Daniel Holmdahl, Hospital Director, Mr. Olle Saemund, R.N. Anaesthesia, Uddevalla Hospital.

From the field of Food Distribution and Retailing the authors would also like to thank the following: Professor Claes-Robert Julander, The Foundation of Grocery Distribution and Retailing at the Stockholm School of Economics, Mr Kenneth Lilja, President, Liljas Agenturer, Vansbro, Mr Nils-Erik Johansson, President, Mr Bengt Andersson, Marketing Manager, and Mr Kjell Cederlund, Store Manager, Hemköpskedjan, Mr Göran Johansson, President, Mr Hans Hagdahl, Mr Lars Hellström, Mr Stefan Arnberg, DAGAB Nord, Mr Bertil Berndt, Branch Manager, Bilspedition, Östra Skåne, Mr Håkan Engström, General Manager, Coldsped, Mr Harry Watts, President, Mr Peter Walker, Development Manager, Woolworths, Mr Andrew Ward, Warehouse Manager, P&O Cold Storage and Mr John Every, General Marketing Manager, Refrigerated Roadways.

For their contribution to the Retail Banking Section, the authors would like to express their special appreciation to Mr Jan-Gunnar Eurell, Skandinaviska Enskilda Banken, Miss Ingrid Ottoson, Skandinaviska Enskilda Banken, Mr John A. Russel, Banc One, Mr Paul Rhyn, Credit Suisse, Mr Thomas Schneider, Credit Suisse, Mr Erik Ingvarsson, IBM and Mr Sture Bråsjö, Swedish Bankers' Association.

We wish to thank all the people interviewed at Trygg-Hansa SPP Holding and Home Insurance Company for their valuable contributions to our study. A special thanks to: Mr Björn Sprängare, President and CEO, Trygg-Hansa SPP Holding, Mr Lars-Göran Nilsson, Executive Vice President, International Insurance Division, Trygg-Hansa SPP Holding, Mr Lars-Arne Lundholm, Chief Financial Officer, International Insurance Division, Trygg-Hansa SPP Holding, Mr James J. Meenahan, President and CEO, Home Insurance Company, Mr John Tetro, Chief Financial Officer, Home Insurance Company and Mr Gene Ballard, Assistant Chief Financial Officer, Home Insurance Company.

Special thanks to Victor Kaufetz and Jennifer Sundberg, who translated a large proportion of the Swedish-language reports; to Linsey Caton, who edited the book; and to Margareta Janson and Eva Schönning, who assisted us throughout the project.

Finally, we would like to thank our wives Beatrice and Ingalill for their many valuable comments and ideas.

Erik Hörnell and Per Hjelm
Stockholm, September 1993

1

THE MODEL FOR THE STUDY

The purpose of this study was to learn from good examples of others.

- *What can we learn from highly productive companies and organisations?*
- *What internal and external factors create a favourable climate for sustained productivity improvements?*

In selecting companies and organisations for the study, we mainly took into account whether they showed good earnings and enjoyed an outstanding reputation in their respective fields. We relied on assessments from people with professional experience in each sector. We did not try, in the first instance, to measure or classify the potential subjects of our study. We selected leading foreign companies and organisations, and compared them with leading Swedish counterparts in each industry or field. The exception was the insurance industry, where we chose to compare two companies located in different countries but belonging to the same corporate group. We did not examine specific changes resulting from corporate restructuring, for instance, but instead examined long-term programmes aimed at raising productivity and bringing about continuous improvement.

It was natural for us to compare the findings of this study with those of our previous study, which mainly examined manufacturing companies and was organised according to the same model.[1] The question we asked was: 'What distinguishes service-producers from manufacturing companies in terms of their opportunities to achieve high productivity?'

One of our initial theoretical assumptions was that companies that do not palpably experience any resource scarcity find it hard to be efficient. Some degree of external pressure is thus required to motivate employees to be economical with resources. If resource scarcity becomes too confining efficiency declines, because the company lacks sufficient resources to operate efficiently. Resources are defined mainly as the company's supply of capital, labour and input goods.

The degree of resource scarcity is very dependent on the intensity of competition. The stiffer the competition, the scarcer the resources and the greater

[1] Hörnell, 1992, *Improving Productivity for Competitive Advantage*

2 Achieving Service Productivity

a company's efforts to improve efficiency. But other kinds of resources are also significant. For example, the availability of a qualified labour force can offset the scarcity of financial resources.

Our second assumption was that a company that does not face new demands from customers, new actions from competitors, new technology or new input goods has no reason to adapt or be innovative. If the degree of information complexity around the company is too great, however, a company may find it hard to adapt. A high level of uncertainty or chaos in its surroundings can lead to paralysis, since it becomes impossible to adapt. On the other hand, if a company's surroundings are static, there is no reason for it to change. Our hypothesis is thus that the factors behind renewal and innovation are at their most favourable when the company's surroundings are dynamic but not chaotic.

We began our case studies by analysing external pressure for change. First we studied the respective industries or fields in which our companies and organisations operated.

- Who are their competitors, customers and suppliers?
- How do technological advances occur in each industry?
- What institutional frameworks exist?

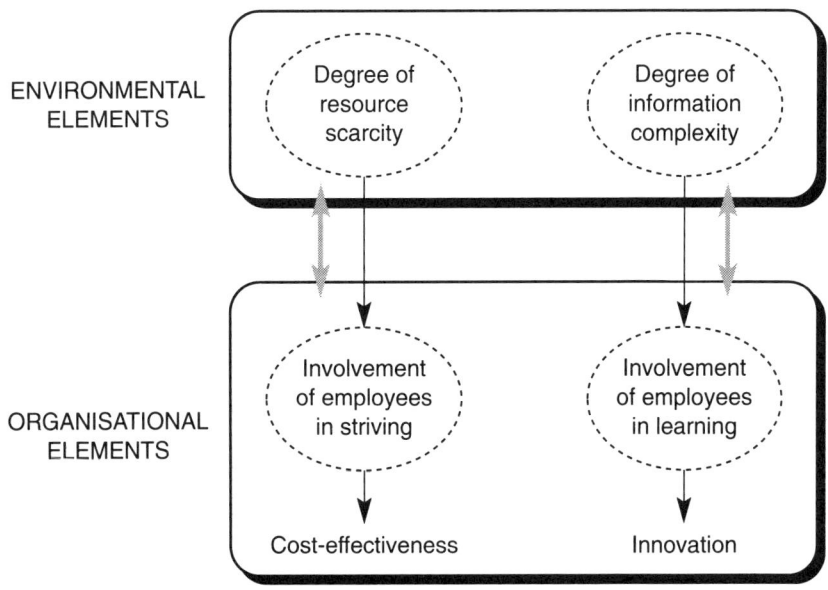

Figure 1.1 Model of cost-effectiveness and innovation

The Model For The Study

Then we gathered information on conditions in the home country of each company or organisation analysed. This included respective labour markets, education and research, and the legal framework.

A suitable level of external pressure for change and information complexity is not sufficient to make a company react, act, innovate or anticipate change. If external pressure for change is actually going to influence the organisation's productivity, three requirements must be fulfilled:

- the company must consciously interact with its surroundings (communication of goals and market demands);
- the company must have the organisational and technical prerequisites to adapt (organisation and technology); and
- human resources must be willing and able to contribute (human resource management).

These three factors were examined by means of interviews in the companies we studied and by reading reports, organisational descriptions, assessment instruments etc.

2

RETAIL BANKING

Authors: Eric Giertz, Erik Grenmark

BANC ONE, Columbus, Ohio, USA
CREDIT SUISSE, Zurich, Switzerland
SKANDINAVISKA ENSKILDA BANKEN, Stockholm, Sweden

Banks the world over are being subjected to growing pressure for change, due to deregulation and increasing internationalisation in the banking industry. New players are entering the once-protected domain of the banks. Meanwhile, advances in information technology (IT) are creating major potential for the streamlining of operations. This new competitive situation is intensifying the need to raise productivity through better profitability monitoring. It will become increasingly important to determine whether customers are willing to pay for the services a bank provides.

Two banks that have firm control over their 'loss leaders and cash cows' in the deposit-taking end of retail banking are Banc One and Credit Suisse. They have become models of market segmentation, offering their various customer categories a differentiated array of standardised products.

Banc One specialises in transaction-intensive accounts maintained by households and small businesses. By acting as the 'McDonald's' of the banking world, Banc One achieves high profitability and rapid growth. Banc One conducts systematic customer and market analyses, and knows what standardised services various customers are willing to pay for. Behind the bank's success is also an efficient production system. Its standardised range of products creates economies of scale and low costs within the framework of a well-developed computer system and distributed data processing. Otherwise the bank operates in a very decentralised environment, combined with detailed monitoring of earnings.

Credit Suisse has taught us the importance of clear customer segmentation. In the household banking market, profitability monitoring showed the bank that it had a small group of profitable customers with large deposits and a large group of unprofitable customers with small deposits in transaction-intensive salary accounts. Credit Suisse thus decided to make these unprofitable customers profitable as well. So, today, it offers different categories of customers different services at different prices.

Today Skandinaviska Enskida Banken (S-E-Banken) is taking clear steps towards more profitability monitoring in the household sector. A differentiated yet standardised range of products and services is being developed for certain designated customer and market segments. The bank is rationalising its production and distribution network, while intensifying active sales work as part of earnings-based decentralisation.

THE RETAIL BANKING SECTOR

Revenues and costs

In principle, the two main functions of a bank are deposits/lending and payment services. Figure 2.1 summarises these functions graphically.[1]

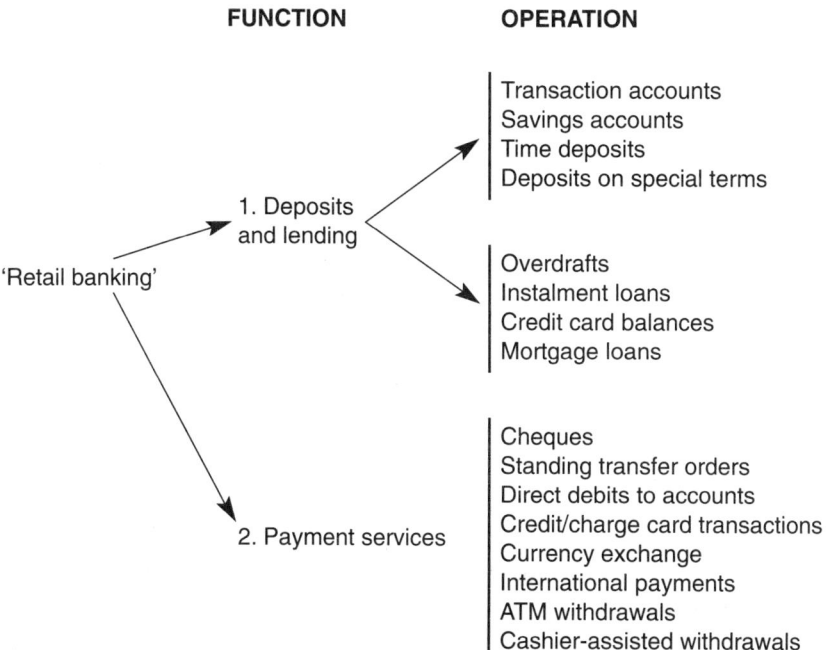

Figure 2.1 Bank functions

[1] Adapted from McKinsey Global Institute, *Service Sector Productivity*, Washington, D.C., 1992.

6 Achieving Service Productivity

Deposits/lending

In principle, this function provides the main source of revenue. The difference between deposit and lending rates, the 'interest margin', creates a net interest income which is traditionally intended to cover operating costs.

Payment services

With cash payments becoming less common, banks are assuming an increasingly important role in payment services, although this function accounts for the bulk of bank costs.Payment services have been viewed as a kind of 'free benefit'. Although practices vary from one country to another, most banks have only charged directly for a few of their services, for example appraisal of collateral, currency exchange, international payments, provision of safe deposit boxes or cashing cheques from other banks.

Net interest income

As shown in Figure 2.2 net interest income remains the dominant source of gross bank revenues, although its share is falling. This decline can be explained by increased international commerce, the wider range of banking services and greater reliance on bank charges as a source of income.

Since 1986, however, the trend in Sweden has been in the opposite direction. In November 1985, the Swedish government abolished its long-time ceiling on bank loans. The resultant battle for market share led to rapid credit market expansion and higher interest income so that between 1985 and 1990, the loan portfolios of commercial banks in Sweden rose by 141 per cent or US$196,000.[2] The limited importance of net interest income in the revenues of Swiss commercial can be explained by Switzerland's large, wide-ranging banking sector and by the significance of international transactions, which provide revenues in the form of foreign exchange profits and commissions.

Personnel costs

While net interest income is the most important source of revenue for banks, personnel costs account for the largest share of total operating costs as Figure 2.3 indicates.[3]

[2] Enskilda Research, *Analys av kreditmarknaden i Sverige* (Analysis of the Swedish Credit Market). Stockholm, 1991.
[3] *OECD, Bank Profitability, Financial Statements of Banks, 1981–1990*, Paris, 1991 (Staff costs/operating expenses, with staff costs as one element of operating expenses).

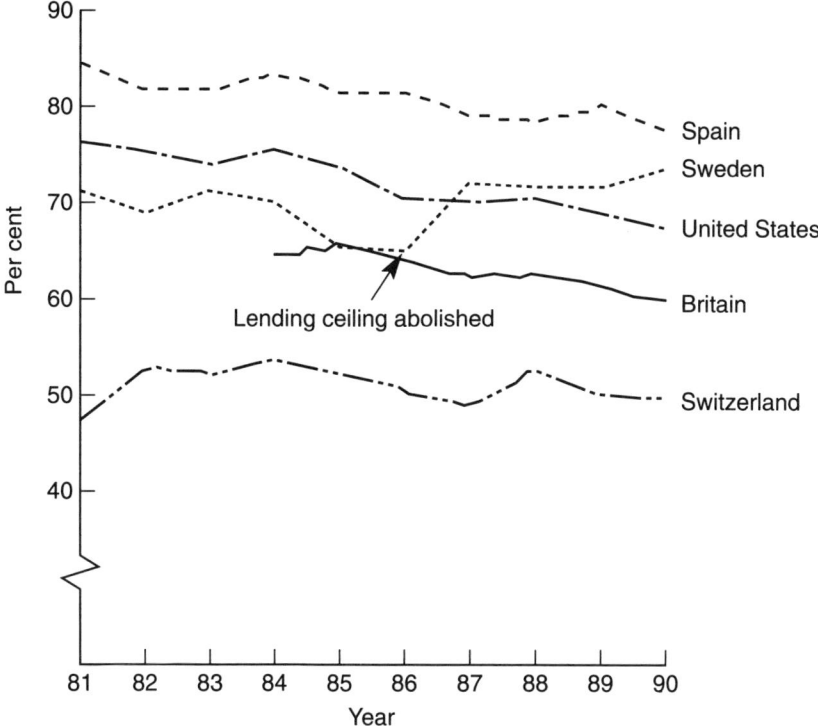

Figure 2.2 Net interest income as a percentage of the gross income of commercial banks

In Switzerland and Spain, personnel costs account for more than two-thirds of total bank operating costs (including costs of premises, computers, loan losses etc.). Although the comparable ratio is lower in the US and in Sweden (personnel costs representing nearly half of operating costs), such costs were still by far the largest single cost item in 1989. (The rapid drop in personnel costs as a percentage of operating costs in Sweden in 1989 is related to accelerating loan losses. In other words, it is not due to lower personnel costs *per se*, but to higher loan losses.)

Correlation between profitability and productivity

Variations in the relative importance of personnel costs largely reflects differences in the use of information technology (IT). Banks in both the US and Sweden are ahead of many other countries in introducing IT, automatic teller machine (ATM) services and electronic payment systems. International

8 Achieving Service Productivity

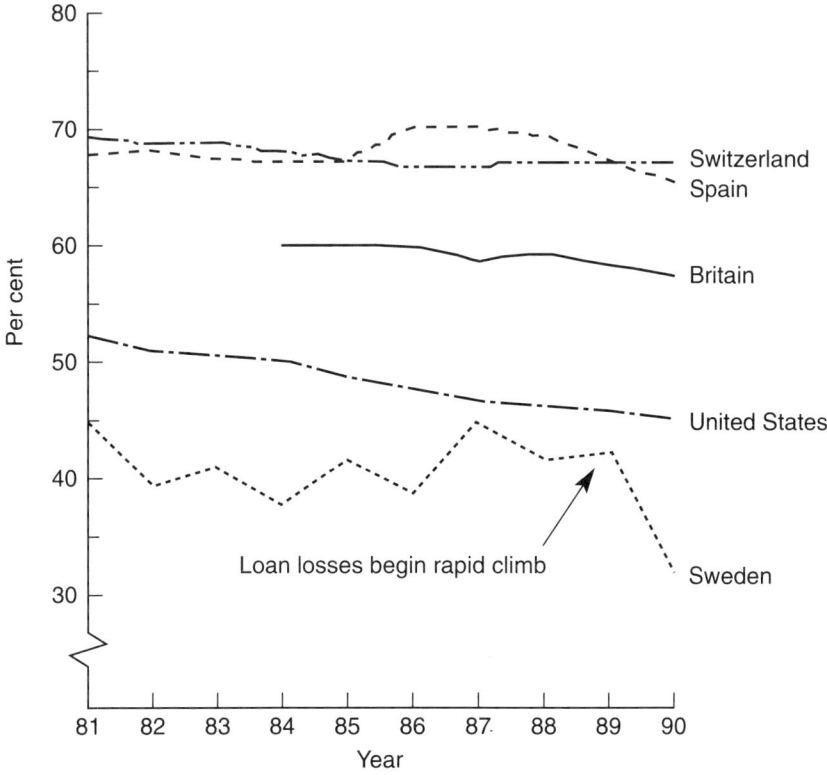

Figure 2.3 Personnel cost as a percentage of operating costs of commercial banks

studies, such as *The Retail Banking Revolution*, also indicate that in international terms, Swedish banks are highly computerised and productive. For example, they have developed efficient joint ventures for cheque processing, clearing and giro payments (inter-account transfers). A comparison between bank branches in Britain and Sweden, for instance, shows that a British branch employs five times as many people as its Swedish counterpart handling the same number of customers and accounts. Table 2.1 below shows that the resultant salary costs (as a percentage of total costs) in Britain are two and a half times those in Sweden.[4]

---

[4] Swedish Bankers' Association, from the film *Banker i Sverige och Europa* (Banks in Sweden and Other European Countries), 1992. Also *OECD, Bank Profitability, Financial Statements of Banks 1981–1990*, Paris, 1992.

Table 2.1 Comparative salary costs

Country	Interest margin in consumer banking [5]	Operating costs as % of total assets	Salaries as % of total assets
Britain	16.4	3.34	1.96
Sweden	8.8	1.97	0.78
Norway	10.0	2.80	1.37
Germany	12.3	2.17	1.41
US	n/a[5]	3.29	1.53
Switzerland	n/a[5]	1.49	0.99

Banks in Britain and Spain exhibit lower productivity but this does not mean that they are not profitable. Spanish banks, which have been operating in a protected oligopolistic national market, are in fact highly profitable in international terms. Of the world's four most profitable banks, for instance, three are Spanish.[6]

MONITORING PROFITABILITY

Traditionally, only in exceptional cases have banks linked a specific cost item to a specific revenue item to monitor the profitability of individual customers, products or services. As noted above, banking remains very labour-intensive and the great majority of employees are found in branch office networks. Traditionally, every branch provides all types of customer with all types of banking service. There has been little systematic monitoring of customers, demand, or the supply of products or services which have generated costs for the bank.

As long as total net interest income (including foreign exchange earnings and service charges) has covered a bank's operating costs, it has obviously earned a profit, but numerous loss leaders and cash cows may have been concealed behind this positive earnings figure.

---

[5] In the film, the interest margin was determined by asking different banks their interest rate for a normal customer who wishes to borrow US$15,000 without collateral. This interest rate was compared with the highest interest rate on a savings account that was not a time deposit. Corresponding figures for the US and Switzerland are not included in the Bankers' Association study. Until 1990 the Sweden interest margin was narrow in international terms, but since then it has also widened.

[6] *Business Week* 'A Nightmare Year – International Bank Scoreboard', 6 July 1992.

Sources of capital

Banks have a pivotal, dominant role in the credit market of all countries, but they are not alone in this marketplace. What distinguishes them from other players is their exclusive right and obligation to perform certain services. In most countries these include.[7]

- accepting account deposits from the general public;
- participating in central bank clearing systems;
- borrowing from the central bank without collateral and depositing money in interest-bearing accounts in the central bank;
- dealing in currencies (foreign exchange privilege).

A bank's operation is based on deposits from the general public. Banks also raise capital through their own borrowings in capital markets. The latter generate smaller costs but also yield a narrower interest margin to the banks. See Figure 2.4.

The comparatively wide interest margin between deposits and lending is, of course, also reflected in the low interest rates paid on customer deposits. If banks offer excessively low interest rates, however, customers will choose other forms of saving. To the banks, borrowing likewise becomes a profitable alternative when their operating costs related to deposits rise very high. Although, theoretically, banks would thus shift to borrowing if operat-

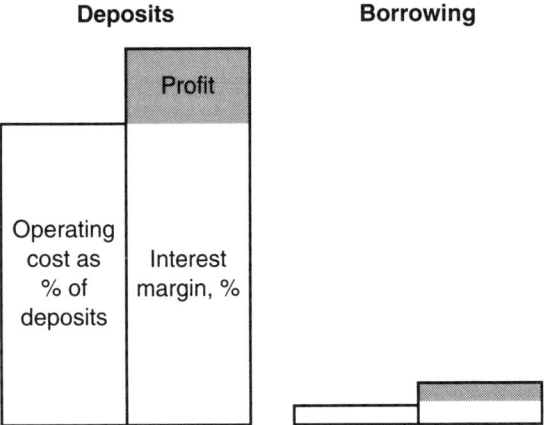

Figure 2.4 Deposits v. borrowing

[7] Lars Wohlin, 'Universalbanken är här för att stanna' (Universal Banking is Here to Stay), *Modern Banking* 1988:1

ing costs on some deposits became too large, in practice they must be able to show the relationship between specific cost items and specific deposits.

Deposit accounts in the consumer banking market can be classified as transaction, savings or special term accounts.

- Transaction accounts are characterised by a large number of transactions. As a rule they are designed to allow withdrawals in a number of different ways, for example cheques or teller withdrawal slips, ATMs or bank cards. A transaction account can also be connected to a giro (inter-account payment) system. Some commercial banks provide a large number of transaction accounts in the consumer market because companies have opened salary accounts for their employees. However, because these accounts are characterised by many withdrawals per month plus low end of the month and average balances, they are often a losing proposition for banks.

- Most deposits by individual customers are instead invested in savings accounts, which are viewed as profitable by the banks. These accounts see fewer transactions and the bank's handling costs are normally low. At Swedish commercial banks, more than half the volume of individual customers' deposits is found in accounts with balances exceeding US$15,000. Account balances are distributed approximately as follows:[8]

Amount	*Number of accounts*	*Deposit volumes*
US$4,000	75%	15%
US$4,000–15,000	15%	30–35%
US$15,000	10%	50–55%

- Individual customers with sizeable funds can also invest money for short or long periods in the money market, which exceed those offered by ordinary savings accounts. The minimum capital required for these special term deposits varies between banks, but is typically around US$75,000.

Deposits

Today, banks actively try to take advantage of the profitability and efficiency-raising potential found in the consumer deposit market. First and foremost, they try to allocate their costs to various products and customers, in order to monitor profitability. They also try to increase their funding in profitable

[8] Sture Bråsjö, *Privatkunden och affärsbankerna* (The Individual Customer and the Commercial Banks), Swedish Bankers' Association, 1989.

12 Achieving Service Productivity

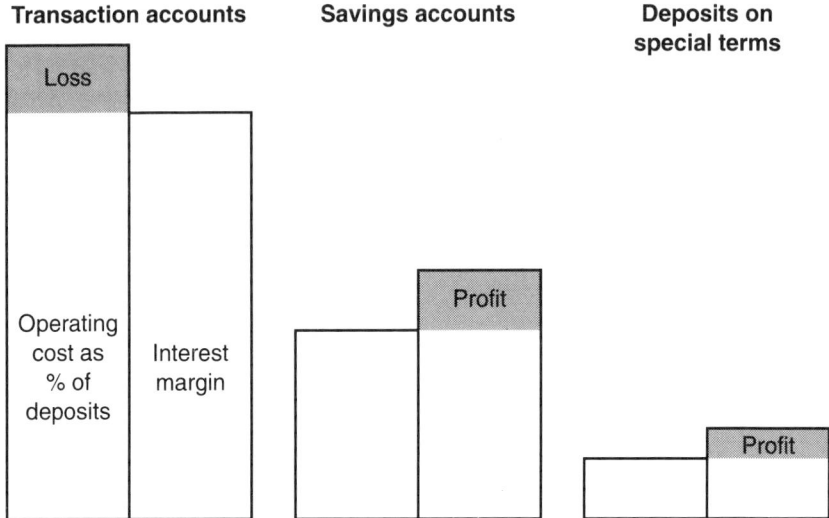

Figure 2.5

segments, or raise efficiency and increase profitability in unprofitable areas. This is because virtually all banks have considerable potential significantly to improve their net interest income by increasing their reliance on deposits from the public. During the second quarter of 1992, for example, the average interest rate paid on deposits from private individuals in Sweden was 7.2 per cent, while the interest rate on six-month treasury discount notes was 11.7 per cent.[9] Banks therefore need to attract funds from the general public without letting their own costs get out of hand. As a result this study focuses on the deposit function of retail banking.

Measures to increase profitability

The principal measures employed by banks to increase their profitability may be summarised as follows:

- to find out what various customers want and are willing to pay for;
- to segment the market and develop a differentiated (but standardised) range of products and services;
- to steer customers towards more efficient and cost-effective behaviour;
- to utilise economies of scale in distribution, first by means of a wider

[9] The Riksbank (Swedish central bank), *Bankernas inlåningsräntor* (Bank Deposit Rates), 10 December 1992.

product range and higher sales volume, and second by means of a more specialised branch network;
- to design distribution systems and methods that ensure that customers receive the right service at the right time and at the right cost;
- to shift sales towards profitable product and customer categories;
- to streamline working methods and systems within production;
- to utilise economies of scale in production and logistics by concentrating these operations at fewer units.

COMPANIES STUDIED

Two respected European commercial banks that took deliberate steps during 1992 to increase their profitability in retail banking systematically were the Zurich-based Credit Suisse and the Stockholm-based Skandinaviska Enskilda Banken (S-E-Banken). Both groups have re-evaluated their organisational and management principles. Their new strategic measures also explain why they have been chosen for this study, although these measures have yet to have any profound impact on visible earnings.

The third bank analysed has deliberately focused on retail banking for a very long time: Banc One, based in Columbus, Ohio (USA) has progressively expanded and shown good profitability for many years. What it has achieved is unique and is forecast to establish precedents for other banks to follow. For this reason the bank is analysed in greater detail than the other two.

Business focus: summary

Banc One

- Retail banking focusing on private individuals and small/medium-sized companies
- No international operations

Credit Suisse

- International focus
- Major corporations
- Small/medium-sized companies and private individuals

14 Achieving Service Productivity

Table 2.2 Comparative key data[10]

1991	Banc One	Credit Suisse	S-E-Banken
Number of employees	27,500	18,900*	10,800*
Number of branches	823	309	326
Total assets	US$46,000 M	US$106,000 M	US$75,000 M
Core capital	US$3,800 M	US$6,100 M	US$3,200 M
Operating income/operating costs, excluding losses	1.76	1.75	1.88
Operating income/operating costs, including losses	1.37	1.35	1.18
Return on equity (ROE)	16.0* %	10.7%*	7.6%*
Return on assets (ROA)	1.6*%	0.6%*	0.4%*
Net interest income as a percentage of gross income	68%	45%	62%
Personnel costs as a percentage of operating costs, excluding loan losses	44%	62%	52%
Deposits as a percentage of capital supply	90%*	63%*	42%*

* = round figure

1990	Banc One	Credit Suisse	S-E-Banken
Return on assets	1.53%	0.38%	0.57%
(Country average)	(0.49%)	(0.40%)	(0.43%)
Personnel costs as a percentage of total assets	1.76%	1.09%	0.91%
(Country average)	(1.55%)	(1.05%)	(0.69%)
Total costs including loan losses as a percentage of total assets	4.93%	2.1 %	2.29 %
(Country average)	(3.46%)	(1.57%)	(2.21%)

[10] IBCA Ltd (rating institute), London, and OECD, *Bank Profitability, Financial Statements of Banks 1981–1990*, Paris, 1992, and annual reports of S-E-Banken, Credit Suisse and Banc One.

S-E-Banken

- International focus
- Major corporations
- Small/medium-sized companies and private individuals, mainly in the Stockholm, Gothenburg and Malmö regions

Table 2.2 summarises the key data for each bank.

Comparative productivity

Number of employees, number of branches and total assets provide some idea about the relative size of each bank and their respective business focus. Banc One, for example, has far more employees and more than twice as many branches as the other banks, despite its smaller total assets. But these differences say nothing about relative productivity. Instead they reflect the fact that while Banc One concentrates on retail banking, the two others focus on the international corporate banking market.

It is also apparent from Table 2.2 that Banc One finances nearly all its lending via deposits, while in the other two banks, a large share of funding is derived from borrowings. Banc One has thus managed to build up a product range as well as production, distribution and sales systems that have attracted funds from households and small businesses. This is reflected in higher operating costs and a wider interest margin – which again says nothing about relative productivity.

However, if the retail banking operations of each bank could be presented separately, the comparative figures would be totally different. For example, rough estimates indicate that in retail banking, S-E-Banken has operating costs (excluding loan losses) as high as Banc One, plus a somewhat wider interest margin. S-E-Banken's retail banking business thus probably enjoys good profitability but, compared with Banc One, this would be more attributable to high prices than high productivity: S-E-Banken has a distinctly upmarket profile in the household banking sector.

Cross-border productivity comparisons are also complicated by national differences. Banks, especially in the retail field, tend to operate in highly regulated, oligopolistic domestic markets while, in some cases, legal differences are also reflected in major disparities between their working methods.

Cheque processing provides an example of how differences in legislation can affect productivity in different countries. In Sweden, cheques are simply stored at the bank where they are cashed. In the US, cashed cheques must be sorted and returned to the issuing banks, which then send the cheque (or a copy of it) to the issuing customer. Since banks cashing cheques are obviously eager to be reimbursed quickly, US banks have invested large sums in cheque-sorting machines; they have also placed great reliance on special airlines and express delivery companies with large trans-shipment centres specialising in dispatching cheques between different banks.

Laws restricting the right of banks to engage in anything besides pure banking – and the right of other companies to offer different types of financial services – also vary from country to country. As banking regulations in Europe have eased, Swedish banks, for instance, have broadened the range of products and services offered by their branch networks. This can obviously lead to higher resource utilisation and productivity in the distribution and sales systems. By contrast, such opportunities remain very restricted in the US.

Comparative organisation and management

Definition and measurement of a number of relevant outputs such as the number of transactions, customers and accounts; number of loans and credit investigations or sales activities of various kinds; and the related number of new customers and/or increase in sales could, in theory, facilitate quantitative comparisons of bank productivity and quality. This kind of traditional benchmarking strategy is found to some extent in the Chapters 4–5 of this book.

It is apparent, however, that in the banking industry, it is neither possible nor desirable to conduct a study along the above lines. Meaningful quantitative comparisons are precluded for a number of reasons: detailed descriptions of various processes are not available, transaction definitions are inconsistent and it is practically impossible to allocate resource inputs among different processes in nearly all banks.

Like many other service companies, today's banks are showing a strong interest in new organisational, management and monitoring principles that might lead to higher productivity and profitability at a time when their industry is facing greater pressure for change. In the light of this, a study focusing on quantitative comparisons of dubious historical data seems less meaningful than a comparison of the new organisational and management principles being put in place. For these reasons,this study makes conceptual comparisons of these principles which are penetrating the banking industry as a consequence of stiffer competition, and of the restructuring programmes attributable to deregulation, internationalisation and technical progress.

These new principles will facilitate future comparisons of processes. Like manufacturing, the banking industry is beginning to study its operations in terms of processes, which can be streamlined and controlled in the pursuit of productivity and quality. Banc One, for example, recently hired production engineers from the manufacturing sector to conduct traditional flow and method studies. Another key element of the new management principles is, of course, profitability monitoring. We can expect that, in future, banks will be able to allocate their costs to different processes, customers, products and profit centres. This will obviously facilitate the comparison of quantitative data.

ORGANISATIONAL/MANAGEMENT PRINCIPLES: GENERAL FINDINGS

Clear business focus

A clear focus on well-defined markets is a characteristic feature of all the banks studied. Banc One, unlike other banks of the same size, has concentrated its entire business on retail banking in the domestic market. The company's motto, 'stick to the nuts and bolts', has a genuine meaning. It is expanding geographically within a very concentrated business area, in which it considers itself to have thorough expertise. The operations of Credit Suisse are more diversified, but by organising itself into several business areas in the mid-1980s, the bank laid the groundwork for well-defined strategies in different markets. The same applies to the divisionalisation that S-E-Banken implemented in January 1993.

Co-ordinated autonomy

The fundamental basis of the organisational structure of all three banks can be summarised as 'co-ordinated autonomy'. Within the framework of a matrix organisation, each combines centralised responsibility for co-ordination, with far-reaching decentralisation to regional and local profit centres.

The centrally co-ordinated activities include systematic customer and market analysis, product development, market differentiation and institutional marketing principles, establishment of quality norms and earnings targets, development of profitability monitoring systems, streamlining and operation of central production units.

Locally decided activities vary from one bank to another, but the fundamental principle is to achieve the greatest possible freedom within the framework of explicit profit centre responsibility. At Banc One, for example, this means that pricing and pay structures are handled on an entirely local basis.

Market analysis, segmentation and differentiation

One significant element of the new management principles is greater market orientation, based on market analyses. These, in turn, provide the basis for market segmentation and the development of a differentiated but standardised range of products and services.

Banc One attaches great importance to systematic customer and market analysis. Such market knowledge controls the development (and discontinuation) of the company's highly standardised product range. The bank combines this standardisation with a far-reaching differentiation that is also reflected among employees at all levels of the company.

General statements, about wealthy private individuals or small businesses for example, are unusual. Descriptions of different customers, their needs and their willingness to pay for services are far more precise. For example, the requirements of wealthy, retired people, working professionals (doctors, lawyers etc.) and busy entrepreneurs are obviously different. It is equally self-evident that the needs of different small companies are based on specific business-related requirements. A real estate broker, a manufacturing company, a local store, a travel agency, a consulting firm and a mail-order business obviously vary greatly in their need for different services and their willingness to pay for them. Various standardised products must therefore be combined, priced and presented in different ways to different customers.

Credit Suisse's market analysis and market segmentation have been possible because the bank can monitor the profitability of individual customers and customer groups. The bank has a small, profitable client base with sizeable deposits and a large number of more or less unprofitable customers with small deposits in transaction-intensive salary accounts. Credit Suisse has therefore tried to persuade previously unprofitable customers to choose less expensive types of transaction or to entrust the bank with a larger share of their assets, thereby increasing the profitability of its customer base.

S-E-Banken, which has a relatively exclusive customer base, is trying to broaden it by developing more standardised services for new, slightly less exclusive customers.

Profitability monitoring

Flexible information systems that make it possible continuously to monitor profitability in various operational areas are an extremely important prerequisite for applying the organisational and management principles of each of the three banks. Both Credit Suisse and Banc One have systems that allow continuous profitability monitoring and analysis of individual customers, customer categories, products or product categories, as well as both horizontal and vertical units in the matrix organisation. At Banc One, all affiliate banks are also measured and evaluated in exactly the same way.

Monitoring of earnings, activities and behaviour

Each bank attaches great importance to steering all employees towards the right goals and subsequently monitoring them. While different sub-goals for different categories of employees are set, the common feature of each is that they reflect what the employee is able to influence. See Figure 2.6 below.

Managers with decentralised profit centre responsibility are monitored using such profitability ratios as return on assets (ROA). Monitoring of non-career track employees, on the other hand, is often related to activities and behaviour that managers believe will lead to good earnings. At Banc One, top executives emphasise the importance of clarifying what good service actually is and may use outside consultants to regularly evaluate its employees' customer service. In one of S-E-Banken's regions, customer service managers must submit reports to the regional manager on the activities they plan during the next two weeks, which are later compared with actual outcomes.

Continuous improvement

Another common feature of all three banks is that they try to organise themselves in ways that allow continuous improvement. The activities of different departments are monitored and compared with each other, a continuous process of internal benchmarking which provides both greater motivation plus the opportunity to learn from each other.

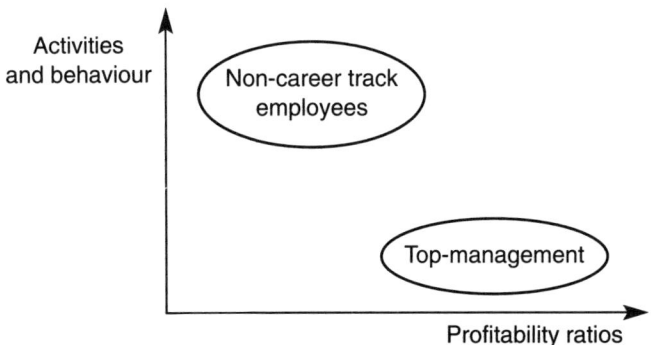

Figure 2.6 Principles for establishing and monitoring goals

Banc One also invests in production techniques specifically designed to facilitate production and flow analyses; another aim is to involve all employees in continuous improvement. Potential improvements are also identified by encouraging customers to complain if they are dissatisfied or have received poor service. The company has also established central telephone complaint lines with significant authority to analyse and correct errors, however serious.

Marketing and business hours

Banc One's desire to provide the best possible service to 'ordinary' Americans is reflected in the way it adapts and differentiates its organisation in a customer-orientated fashion. Customers must be able to do business with the bank when it is convenient for them, which means that Banc One has been a strong advocate of evening and weekend opening hours. In addition, the bank uses unconventional methods and expert systems to maintain and expand existing customer contacts. Credit Suisse, for its part, uses customer segmentation to free up employee resources so that, like S-E-Banken, it can actively market its services to profitable customer segments while steering unprofitable customers towards more cost-effective products. Credit Suisse is eliminating personal teller services for a majority of its customers, but is making the bank accessible by telephone and correspondence. S-E-Banken, too, is heavily committed to streamlining routine services and to transferring some of the work to its customers.

Economies of scale

The three banks studied have all utilised economies of scale by centralising their computer operations and systems development, although Banc One is now investing in 'client-server' technology intended to utilise reverse economies of scale. Credit Suisse and S-E-Banken are now also concentrating other operations at an optimal number of units to provide economies in, for example, payments, cheque processing, and the trust and securities business.

A growing range of products and services, plus the ambition actively to market them to various customer categories, results in a greater need for standardisation. For example, S-E-Banken now allows branch employees to sell products previously handled by separate companies, such as standardised pension insurance policies (deferred annuities). This creates economies of scale in the presentation of products to customers.

Despite its size, Banc One has chosen to work together with Electronic

Data Systems to develop new computer software for its banking operations. In addition, to develop a new credit card system, the bank is working with Andersen Consulting. These systems will allow economies of scale and, because the development costs are shared with other companies, they are more cost-effective. Furthermore, because these systems will also be sold in the outside market, most of the investment can be recouped while, at the same time, Banc One avoids the risk of having a stand-alone system that might not otherwise be generally accepted.

FACTORS INFLUENCING PRODUCTIVITY

External factors

Legal restrictions

Legal obstacles that prevent banks from widening their range of services and expanding their geographic markets hamper competition and ease the pressure for change among existing players: in turn this precludes positive product development. Other laws can also result in sub-optimal behaviour from the standpoint of production technology yet at the same time being profitable. The US, for example, does not allow cheque truncation as in Sweden. Instead, cheques are flown back and forth across the country to the issuing bank. This is expensive, but it enables American banks to earn money on the 'float'.

Collaboration

Collaboration among banks may be either positive or negative. In Sweden, joint ventures such as the bank giro inter-account transfer system and the cheque clearing systems have raised productivity to a greater degree than would have been possible without such co-operation. On the other hand, some banks have cartel-like agreements that are profitable to them but not to their customers. For example, in some countries it frequently takes a long time to send money between banks, even though electronic transfers make faster procedures possible.

Market size

A bank operating in a large market finds it easier to achieve economies of scale than one operating in a smaller market where there are fewer customers to pay for heavy investments. Banks that have previously worked in a limited national market therefore show lower productivity in capital or development intensive functions than their larger competitors in other countries. A larger market also generates better opportunities for risk-spreading.

Internal factors

Customer satisfaction

Only a bank that satisfies the changing needs of different customer segments can be profitable. All the organisations studied give this very high priority.

Product standardisation

Standardised products make it easier for branch employees to undertake more active sales work, and also facilitate economies of scale in information processing and thus product monitoring.

Economies of scale

Thanks to improved information technology, the banking industry has recorded substantial increases in productivity over the past few decades. At the same time, its operations have become more capital-intensive and its product range has broadened, creating new economies of scale in production and distribution.

Decentralised profit centre responsibility

Co-ordinated autonomy is a success. Within certain limits, decentralised profit centre responsibility should be combined with an adequate reward system for the autonomous units.

PRESSURE FOR CHANGE

The traditional banking structure is being subjected to growing pressures, largely attributable to changes in the surrounding environment. Banks face major changes in virtually all areas. Deregulation is eliminating barriers to market entry, other financial institutions are increasing the variety of their products and services, and rivalry within the industry is increasing, as is the negotiating power of suppliers and customers.

Liberalisation and internationalisation

Since the creation of a banking system, the relationship between governments and banks has been characterised by a balance between market freedom and necessary public influence. Support and surveillance by the public sector has been justified in various ways, and the emphasis has shifted over the years. Three important justifications are:

- the need to protect depositors' money;
- fear that foreigners might gain excessive influence and control developments in the country;
- a desire to use the banks as an instrument of Keynesian stabilisation policies.

In most countries, strict government regulation of banking operations is gradually being eased. Banks are being allowed to perform tasks not previously permitted (or only via subsidiaries), such as credit cards, investment counselling, mutual fund management or property appraisals.

The banking sector also became more international during the 1980s. This was partly a consequence of deregulation in various countries, but also reflected other developments: the internationalisation of major corporations, plus increased global trade and travel, plus the parallel development of information technology which created the technical prerequisites for a global money market.

Internationalisation obviously opens national markets to foreign participants. Given the trend towards greater concentration, more business alliances and mergers between banks in different countries may be anticipated.

But internationalisation is not alone in creating new competitors. Another global phenomenon is the blurring of the traditional lines between financial service companies. While banks broaden their field of operations, new competitors are breaking into the financial and capital markets. These include insurance and finance companies, credit and charge card companies, brokerage houses and 'internal banks'. The latter specialise in optimising the capital flows of major corporations, although a number of big companies are considering starting banks of their own to offer bank-like services to their employees.[11]

Information technology

Information technology (IT) has gradually transformed banking. The number of payment transactions used to be small. In Sweden, a typical bank

[11] *Finanstidningen*, Egen bank på Volvo, snart verklighet (In-House Bank at Volvo Soon a Reality) 22 May 1992.

customer received wages in cash, which was used for all current payments. A few times a year, some money may have been deposited in a bank savings account but withdrawals were made even less frequently. Banking, however, was very labour intensive as all bookkeeping and interest calculations were done manually at each branch.

When accounting machines appeared in the late 1920s, the recording of customer transactions became easier, but not interest calculations or the task of producing annual summaries of each depositor's account. These necessitated several weeks' manual work. As a result, during the early weeks of the year, extra shifts and weekend work were the rule at many Swedish banks until well into the 1950s.

In the late 1940s the first teller machines were installed, making the work of bank tellers easier and more efficient. These machines, which became common during the 1950s, enabled tellers to stamp new entries into passbooks, give legible typed receipts to the customer and generate a typed item in a specific space in the bank's accounting system. The latter system enabled tellers to work individually. At around the same time the first punch card machines went into service in major banks. This was the first step towards today's fully computerised, transaction intensive and increasingly capital intensive banking system.

These developments have increased the need for productivity. Banks no longer serve as an intermediary in cash or even paper-based monetary transactions. Instead, they handle electronic information about the movement of money between their own accounts, and other national and global computer networks. Today, withdrawals increasingly take place in entirely paperless fashion via ATMs, autogiro transfers and bank debit cards. This is exemplified in Figure 2.7, which shows the distribution of all payment transactions in the Swedish household banking market during 1990.[12]

The whole banking industry is thus being transformed into a gigantic computer network that makes it technologically possible to send money virtually anywhere in the world in a second. (To banks themselves, however, this is not an entirely positive development, because they used to earn a lot of interest on the float.)

At first, the development of computer systems meant that the task of recording transactions moved from branch offices to centrally located pools of punch card operators. Today, the development of modern terminals has moved the recording of transactions back to the tellers. IT has also gradually made it possible to transfer some banking work to customers. The first step was the growth of ATMs in the late 1970s; banking by telephone is another step in the same direction, as are new recording techniques or optical readers being introduced in giro payment systems.

[12] Sven Eric Jacobsson, S-E-Banken, interview, 24 August 1992.

Credit cards and debit cards US$8.4 bill

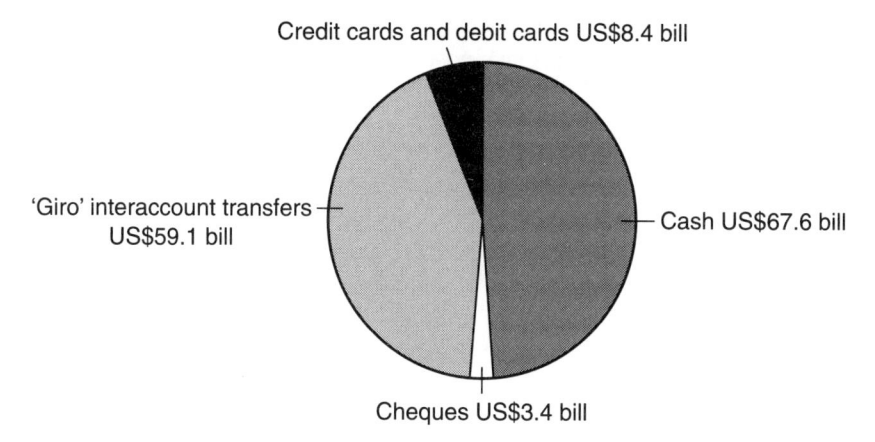

'Giro' interaccount transfers US$59.1 bill

Cash US$67.6 bill

Cheques US$3.4 bill

Figure 2.7 Household payments by type, Sweden 1990

In the corporate banking market, developments have been no less dramatic. Companies can record their own payment orders at ordinary computer terminals or through viewdata systems. Banks can also provide supplementary services, such as cash management or instant updates of customer ledgers when a payment transaction is executed.

Companies that sell to the household market have also become more efficient. For example, department stores can link their cash registers directly to banking systems, so that transfers from a customer's to a department store's account are automatically executed at the point of sale using the customer's bank debit card. Similarly, companies with fixed subscriber or customer lists can streamline their payment systems with the aid of automatic (autogiro) payments at predetermined intervals.

These and other developments put banks under increasing pressure to change. New entrants in financial service markets may be able to offer customers higher interest rates on deposits because they avoid the expensive task of processing payment transactions. Banks must therefore raise the productivity of their payment transactions by using technological advances in ways that benefit customers, yet lower their own costs.

Systems to monitor profitability

Until now, computer payment systems have mainly been designed to make the flow of transactions more efficient. But it has been difficult to monitor the profitability of different customers, products and profit centres. Performing a transaction correctly and at low cost has been more important than billing the actual cost of the transaction to a given customer or profit centre.

26 Achieving Service Productivity

Nowadays banks feel a very strong need to distinguish their 'loss leaders' from their 'cash cows'. This task poses new challenges for information systems. Bank executives are, however, constrained by the original parameters of these systems and the people who designed them. Traditional computer systems are thus gigantic preservation machines in which systems, applications and records are interwoven. It is therefore difficult, time-consuming and expensive to change them, although the list of desired changes and additions gradually grows longer. However, the changes that banks face today in terms of their need for profitability monitoring are triggering radical rethinking in new systems development, as indicated in Figure 2.8.[13]

What is needed to address these new requirements is more database-orientated systems development which recognises that raw data have a relatively long life, whereas procedures, processing and compilations vary for different needs and over time.

Applying a database-orientated perspective to systems development was hardly possible before, but fourth generation programming languages (4GL) and the improved price/performance levels of central units and internal memories are creating new conditions. A 4GL language requires a lot of computer power. At the same time, computer specialists have expanded their sphere of interest to encompass not only administrative data processing, but also PC networks, digital office switchboards and telecommunications links.

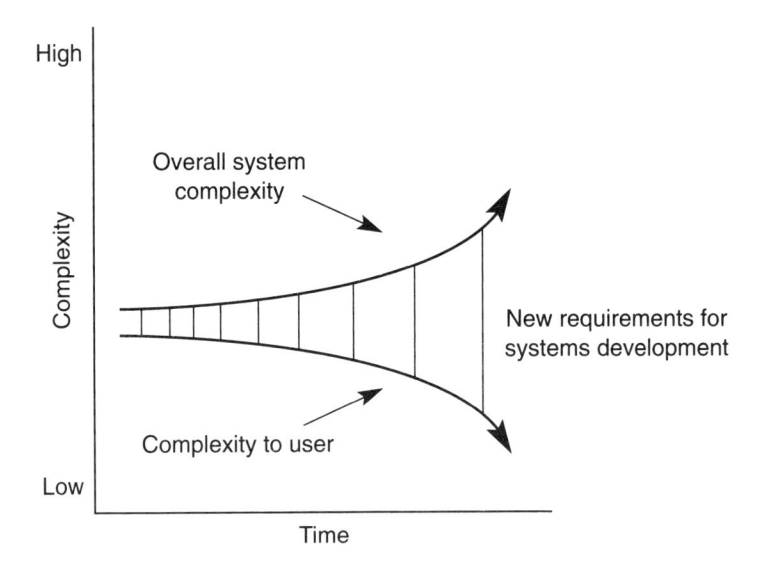

Figure 2.8 Relative complexity of information systems

[13] Adapted from the Gartner Group 1990.

Many companies have also begun a process of decentralisation and visions of distributed flexible data processing are taking shape. In the long term, therefore, the trend is away from the traditional master/slave environment to a client/ server environment.

The old master/slave environment was hierarchical. All data were stored in a mainframe, which was also used for applications. Mid-range mini computers operated as servants to the host computer and masters to the connected terminals. The terminals, in turn, operated as slaves at the bottom of the hierarchy. This also applied to personal computers, which functioned as 'dumb' terminals in relation to the host computers.

The new client/server environment is based on a number of computers, small and large, operating together in networks. The various computers and systems software function as servers for the workstations (clients) at the periphery of the network. Mainframe computers, mini computers and computers in local area networks operate together in such a way that individual users feel as if they are working at their own personal computer, although data are retrieved, and processing takes place, in different computers at different locations.

BANC ONE

Banc One is known as one of the most expansive and strategically successful financial institutions in the US. By acquiring other banks, Banc One has doubled in size every two or three years over a long period. The company has also expanded geographically from its roots in Ohio to other states such as Arizona, Colorado, Indiana and Texas.

At a time when financial systems throughout the world have been shaken to their foundations, Banc One has continued to expand, without harming its return on assets (ROA), return on equity (ROE), equity/assets ratio or earnings per share.

In 1991 its ROA was 1.5 per cent compared to an average of 0.89 per cent among the largest 25 US banks. Over the past 23 years, this ratio has consistently exceeded 1 per cent, while the ROE has been higher than 15 per cent for the past 16 years. In addition, earnings per share have increased for 23 consecutive years and the share dividend for 21 years.

Business focus

Banc One's unparalleled profitability has won it a great deal of attention. On the New York Stock Exchange, its common shares have shot up in value and

28 Achieving Service Productivity

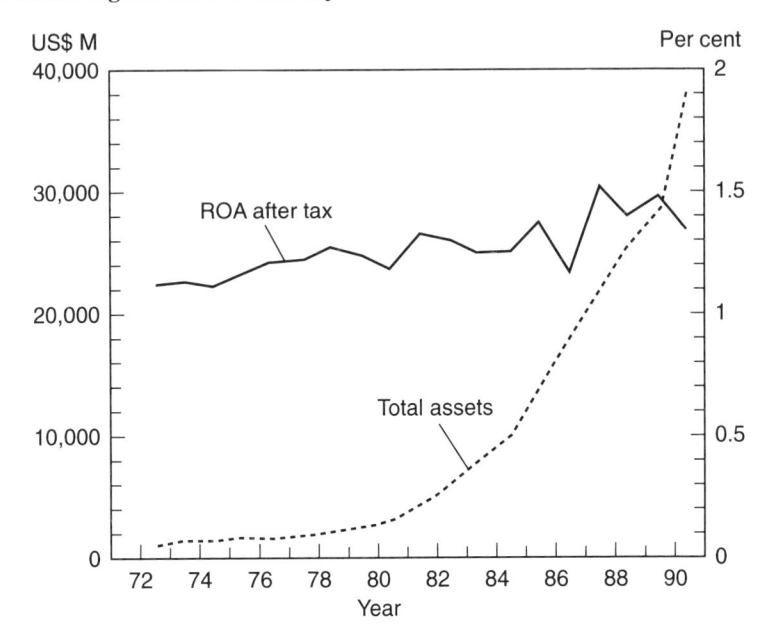

Figure 2.9 Banc One

attracted the interest of speculators. The actual operations of Banc One, however, are anything but speculative. The company has never been drawn into any speculative ventures or exposed itself to major loan or currency risks. Instead, Banc One has stubbornly and deliberately concentrated on the most labour and cost-intensive customer and market segment by aiming at providing the best service to the average American.

The bank has focused entirely on the household banking market, and on small and medium-sized companies. In practice, this has also led to its abstention from operations abroad, despite its size. This strategy even means that Banc One consciously gives up profitable corporate clients that grow too large or international and, as a consequence, few people in the organisation work with foreign exchange.

Its operational focus resembles that of small traditional local banks and savings banks. What is unique is that the company has chosen to grow by 'duplicating' its local business. Banc One has thus grown into a major bank by working in a field that does not normally attract the major US commercial banks.

The bank's firm principle of restricting its operations to domestic retail banking is a clear consequence of the fundamental philosophy that permeates the whole company. Operations have been designed to provide cost-effective service to the American household and small business banking market. Banc One believes it knows what products and services 'ordinary' Americans need at different stages of their lives. It has also used this knowledge to build up its product range, and design its production and distribution network.

The company's motto – 'stick to the nuts and bolts' – has a very real meaning and the message from the bank's top managers is crystal clear: only work with things you know and understand. For example, Banc One has never considered cheap borrowing abroad, since its top executives do not feel that they understand the factors that influence the economies of other countries or the fluctuations in exchange rates. Instead, their task is to serve the American public in such a way that it will entrust its money to the bank.

The message also embodies a conservative credit and lending policy, which emphasises the importance of risk-spreading and achieving a balance between deposits and lending. Profitability must not be based on wheeling and dealing or on fluctuating currency and financial markets. This philosophy is also accompanied by the company's relatively strict moral code. Until recently, for example, employees were not permitted to drink coffee at the workplace or consume any form of alcohol during their lunch break.

Acquisition strategy

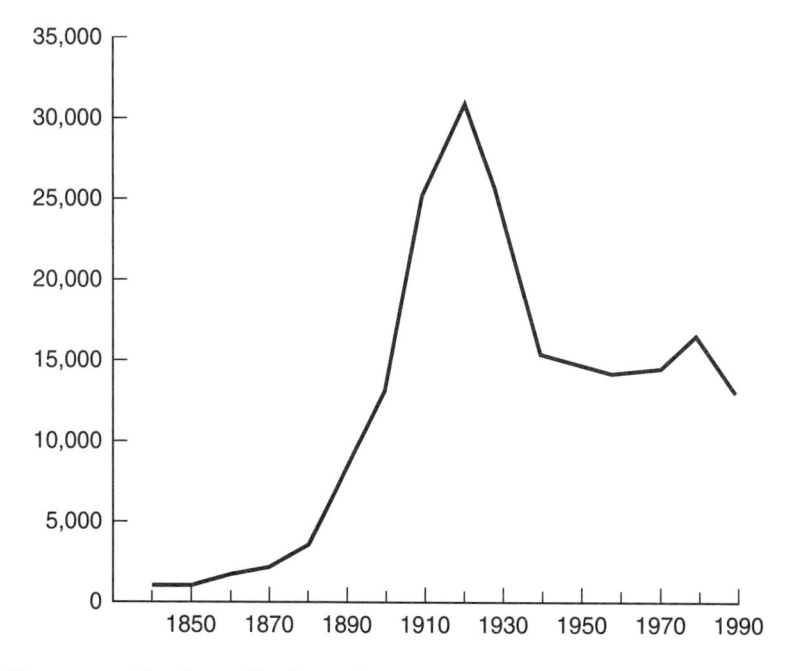

Figure 2.10 Number of banks in the United States

For the past 25 years Banc One has expanded its branch network and geographic coverage via a policy of acquisition.

Between 1968 and 1980, it bought 22 banks in rural areas and small towns, each with less than US$100 million in assets. In 1980 Banc One also began to buy medium-sized banks in major Ohio cities such as Cleveland, Akron and Youngstown so that by 1982 its assets totalled US$5 billion. In June 1983 it bought Winter National Bank of Dayton for US$1.6 billion and subsequently began a new phase in its development; in the mid-1980s the holding company received permission to own banks in other states, something not previously allowed.

Banc One's expansion accelerated and continues at a rapid pace today. Between the beginning of 1991 and the end of 1992, the bank increased its total assets from US$30 billion to more than US$75 billion through acquisitions. The branch network increased from 587 to 1,328 offices, the number of employees from 19,000 to 47,000 and the geographic coverage extended from six to 11 states. Furthermore, this trend is set to continue: by the end of 1993, Banc One will have more than US$100 billion in assets and more than 2,000 branches.

Co-ordinated autonomy

In principle, Banc One only buys banks that are profitable (with an ROA > 1%), and that are less than one-third of its size at the time of acquisition. Its top executives stress that it must never be a matter of merging two cultures, rather to quickly absorb the acquired bank into Banc One's distinctive culture of 'co-ordinated autonomy'.

Banc One's acquisition strategy is accompanied by a management philosophy known internally as 'uncommon partnership'. It combines a very high degree of decentralisation in decision-making with a large proportion of system-wide conformity and monitoring. The bank's executives draw comparisons with franchising in general and McDonald's in particular, when they describe their philosophy. Both Banc One and McDonald's have standardised products and utilise economies of scale. They establish central quality norms and standardised earnings targets, but as long as these are achieved, they offer almost total freedom to local units, for example in terms of pricing and salary structures.

Banc One appears to base its division between matters decided centrally and matters decided locally on the principle that, since market knowledge is local, as much as possible should be decided at that level. It is also difficult to set high earnings targets if the local management cannot make many of its own decisions.

Decided centrally	*Decided locally*
Products	Pricing
Quality norms	Salary structures
Earnings targets	Other matters
Information technology	

Banc One's entire product range of about 200 products is standardised. This means, for example, that all affiliated banks offer the same retirement savings accounts, the same savings accounts with overdraft facilities, the same insurance terms on a given credit card, the same telephone service for payment of bills etc. Pricing, on the other hand, is decentralised and decided at a local level. This means that service charges, deposit rates and lending rates are determined by each individual bank: as soon as Banc One acquires a new affiliate its entire range of products and services is replaced.

Such a standardised range of products and services has also helped keep the training period for new tellers comparatively short. This facilitates their interchangeability, which is important since annual turnover is about 40 per cent in this transitional occupation.

Organisationally, Banc One has amalgamated such functions as systems development and data processing into a single company, Banc One Services Corporation. On the day after an acquisition, the bank's entire computer department is transferred to this service company. The task of absorbing the new affiliate's information system into the parent system begins immediately and possible economies of scale are utilised.

Profitability monitoring

Financial profitability monitoring and profitability measurements are also standardised at Banc One. All affiliates are measured and evaluated in exactly the same way. The system-wide financial management system, called MICS (Management Information and Control System), is installed immediately after an acquisition and is in operation within six months.

MICS is based on monthly reports. Each affiliate must feed its figures into MICS by the fourth banking day of the month. The system supplies more than just final figures, however. Budgeting and planning take place every month, and forecasts for each of the following 12 months are updated continuously.

The most important financial ratio in the system is ROA: the minimum target for all affiliates is 1.35 per cent. Ranking lists are published for different areas to promote internal competition and to encourage each affiliate to improve its relative ranking.

Much time and resources are devoted to financial monitoring and control and, compared to other banks, Banc One has a relatively large number of employees in such functions.

Productivity monitoring

Banc One's operations are largely characterised by a strategy of continuous improvement, a strategy expressed in different ways. Perhaps the most striking is its systematic effort to promote 'friendly competition' among affiliates. Banc One's detailed and uniform income monitoring system tracks differences in the earnings levels of the affiliates, which in turn leads to analyses of the causes. Affiliates that have performed less well than others can improve by studying the routines, methods and work systems of better performers. For example, the central financial management system showed that one branch in Dayton had substantially lower employee costs than other branches of the same size in that region. The reason turned out to be that it used a larger proportion of part-time workers and had streamlined certain transaction routines. The same technique was copied in Columbus, resulting in annual savings of US$3 million.

Standards of customer service are also compared among branches. For example, tellers are expected to provide prompt service, smile when they greet customers, mention the customers' names at some point while serving them, ask if there is anything else they need etc. Customer treatment is scored, with perfect behaviour worth 100 points. Each branch is expected to score an average of 95 points. The managers of branches that repeatedly earn low scores and end up in the bottom third of the ranking list are put under heavy pressure to improve.

To further improve customer service and quality, Banc One also urges its customers to complain when they are dissatisfied or have received improper service. The bank considers complaints very valuable for two reasons. First, a dissatisfied customer whose complaint is promptly and correctly addressed often becomes a satisfied customer. Secondly, complaints can be compiled and analysed, pointing the way to potential improvements. Banc One has also established central telephone complaint lines and delegated substantial authority to them in order to promptly correct serious errors.

Banc One also utilises traditional production engineering methods to identify potential productivity-raising measures. It has hired production engineers from the manufacturing sector to conduct traditional flow and method studies. The aim is to discover and either eliminate or simplify unnecessary or complex flows and work operations, both in the production and distribution systems. In a number of areas, the company has also used frequency studies by which employees record what they are doing every ten minutes. The purpose is to analyse the amount of working time devoted to different activities.

In recent years, Banc One has also tried to involve all its employees in a continuous effort to improve quality and productivity. A chief quality officer with overall responsibility for implementing a kind of quality circle system in the company's regular management work was recently hired by Banc One Services Corporation. The task is to build up an organisation based on work teams, and to generate a team spirit and a capacity to identify potential improvements. These methods were successfully tested in one department of Banc One Services Corporation which was experiencing major problems, i.e. disruptions in production, customer complaints and rapid employee turnover. A process analysis was conducted, followed by the creation of employee groups that received the requisite training and that were then entrusted with implementing changes. Among other things, the department devised better quality monitoring systems that focused on results, not errors. To reduce the risk that employees would relapse into earlier patterns of behaviour, the department attached great importance to letting the entire company know that it was the employees, not their managers, who had changed their work. Error levels fell sharply, disruptions in production largely disappeared and annual turnover dropped from 36 per cent to 10 per cent.

Reward systems

Just over 600 managers are part of a reward system aimed at stimulating earnings growth. The chief executive of a small affiliate can expect a bonus of almost a year's salary if the profitability target is achieved or exceeded. The targets are high, however. For example, no bonus is paid if the ROA ratio is less than 1.1 per cent, an ambitious target considering that only five of the largest US banks had an ROA exceeding this in 1990.

Salary structures for other employees are decentralised. As interest rates and service charges are adapted to local markets, so too are salary systems and levels. Within each affiliate, salaries are treated as an important management tool, even though non-career track employees do not normally receive earnings-related bonuses. In principle, the heads of each profit centre use fixed individual salaries as rewards, based on criteria that may vary from one affiliate to another.

Market communication

Banc One's desire to provide the best possible service to ordinary Americans is reflected in the way it adapts and differentiates its distribution system with the customer in mind. Various categories of wealthy customers such as professionals (doctors, lawyers, consultants etc.) and business owners, receive services specifically adapted to their needs.

The bank has also adapted to the needs of other groups in terms of business hours and time-saving systems. It is no coincidence that Banc One was the first US bank to offer drive-in banking and ATMs – at first simple cash-dispensing machines, but later machines that also accepted deposits. It has not only installed ATMs in supermarkets, but has opened fully equipped mini branches next to the produce counters and shelves of canned goods. These branches actively market their services to grocery store customers who have not yet discovered the advantages of supermarket banking. Banc One has also been leading the move towards evening and weekend banking hours. A type of branch called a 'financial marketplace' is open between 10 a.m. to 7 p.m. on weekdays, 10–5 on Saturdays and noon–5 on Sundays, hours that have turned out to be convenient for customers. At this new type of branch, 37 per cent of new accounts have been opened between 5–7 p.m. In addition, all customers can also contact Banc One 24 hours a day through 'banking by telephone', which is not a computerised voice, but an actual bank employee.

US laws restrict banks to providing classic banking services. But, because Banc One systematically bases its services on customer needs, the company has observed that customers require banking services in connection with other transactions. A financial marketplace therefore offers its customers other banking-related services in an innovative way. Part of such a branch is rented out to other companies, such as subsidiaries selling savings products for example, or unaffiliated travel agencies or real estate brokers. These small boutiques inside the branch live in a kind of symbiosis with Banc One's other operations. For example, it is natural for a real estate broker to ask customers whether they have arranged financing for their house purchase. If not, the broker naturally suggests Banc One. The same is true in reverse if a customer has approached the Banc One counter to discuss mortgages.

The bank also uses unconventional methods to entertain existing customers and recruit new ones. It is not unusual for branches to arrange parties with children's entertainment to attract families. In addition to having a good time, customers can take the opportunity to open a savings account on favourable terms. Marketing activities for specific customer segments are also arranged on a regular basis – for example a fashion show for senior citizens. In themselves, these activities have little to do with banking, but they may be perceived as an extra benefit for Banc One customers compared with other banks.

Banc One's sales strategy is not restricted to these activities. Its information network also includes expert systems that can use information about customers to identify new business opportunities. One example is a system that automatically tracks the ages of bank customers' children. When a child has reached a certain age, the system lets bank employees know that now may be the time to suggest a savings plan for the child's college education. (The need for such reminders is much greater in the US than in Sweden, where people pay for their children's studies and their own financial safety net mainly through taxes.)

Economies of scale

Banc One Services Corporation, whose responsibilities include information processing, plays a pivotal role in implementing the principle of co-ordinated autonomy. This company ensures that the same financial management system and reporting procedures are used at all affiliates. But the company is also entrusted with ensuring that economies of scale are utilised in information processing work and especially in basic banking systems. At one time this might have meant that all data processing was concentrated at centrally located mainframe computers, but today it means that affiliates take advantage of expensive investments in systems development, that data are easily accessible to all Banc One affiliates and that it is possible to adapt products quickly to the changing needs of different markets.

The Services Corporation undoubtedly has a difficult and delicate task, because Banc One's acquisition strategy means that new banks with different computers and systems must continuously be absorbed into a common information structure. Economies of scale must therefore be created within a framework of flexible solutions.

Largely because of these special conditions, Banc One has been a strong advocate of standardisation and 'open systems philosophies'. At an early stage, it also observed the importance of separating raw data (e.g. facts about customers, accounts and transactions) from various applications. This is because raw data are relatively permanent, whereas procedures, processing and compilations vary for different needs and over time.

The Strategic Banking System

Identifying, gathering, structuring and updating relevant customer information, and creating the technical conditions for speeding up the delivery of tailor-made products and services were singled out by Banc One's top management in the mid-1980s as critical factors for success. The company therefore also started a strategic development project in 1986, enabling the first affiliate to convert to a new database-orientated 'Strategic Banking System' five years later. This system has put Banc One at the forefront of a radical change in technology.

To develop this new software system, which reportedly cost at least US$100 million, Banc One established an alliance with Electronic Data Systems (EDS) and another bank holding company, Norwest Corporation. Although the system is strategically important to Banc One, company executives felt that, in the long run, economies of scale make it impossible for every bank to develop its own basic system in such a standardised business as retail banking. EDS is now marketing the system to Banc One's competitors. This will provide royalty income that might eventually reimburse the company's development costs, but that is not the only advantage. The more users the system has, the more funds can be invested in refining it and the greater the chance that, over the long term, it can remain on the cutting edge of the world's banking systems.

One affiliate after another is shifting from the old master/slave systems environment to a client/server environment which, in cost-effective, secure, user-friendly fashion utilises the broad range of technology needed to implement and back up the bank's strategic goals.

The Strategic Banking System makes it possible to store and process data such as price-performance ratios, response times, availability, confidentiality and security at locations best suited to each individual service. Today this means that Banc One can take advantage of the relatively favourable price/performance ratio of personal computers and mini computers. The company has created a kind of reverse economies of scale, which in large systems with shared databases can only be utilised in a client/server environment. All data are constantly updated and are accessible on-line to all users.

Banc One has attached special importance to those databases that describe customers and accounts. The maximum number of information units about each customer has increased from 2,000 in the old system to 12,000 in the new one, including facts about the customer's family, employer, and all products and services the customer uses. Certain data such as account balances are of course generated directly from the transaction systems themselves, while other data are retrieved from other systems or from outside suppliers. Various data can easily be combined and processed in unconventional ways, which is very valuable for profitability analyses, and various campaigns and sales activities.

The Strategic Banking System improves productivity in numerous ways.

- On-line availability of more information means that a number of manual and paper-based processes can be automated or eliminated.
- Investigative and research work is streamlined because all monetary and non-monetary data about customers and accounts are available on-line.

- The system allows bankers to create and change products much faster than before. Every product is assembled from different parameters, enabling Banc One to set uniform, system-wide standards, yet allowing selective changes. Products can thus be customised or changed very quickly for a given market segment or customer.

The system thus uses development tools and techniques that provide the highest possible productivity for:

- systems developers, since it utilises opportunities to automate actual programming work, and since specifications and software modules are reused;
- users, since uniform and user-friendly interfaces are created for the entire range of applications;
- Banc One Corporation, by making data accessible everywhere and by providing options for updating and revising a number of local systems with only one central change function.

The Triumph System

Banc One has long experience of credit cards and other types of plastic bank cards. In 1966 it was the first bank to introduce BankAmericard (later VISA) outside California and in 1970 it initiated the use of plastic cards in ATMs. In 1981 it was also the first bank to process card transactions for outside clients, such as Merrill Lynch.

Today about 14 million cardholders are served by Banc One Financial Card Services. More than half are affiliate customers, while others are customers of other participants in the credit card market that have not built up their own production apparatus for card manufacturing, data processing, high-volume mailings etc.

To date, the evolution of Banc One into a third-party producer has resulted in a near-doubling of its volume in this sector. From a cost standpoint, this is important in a capital-intensive business that is governed by economies of scale. But Banc One is a relatively small third-party producer compared with its largest competitors, which serve two to three times as many cardholders.

Late in the 1980s, Banc One found itself at a crossroads. The company had to decide whether to withdraw from card processing or whether to invest in a world-class system that was superior in quality to those of its competitors. Banc One chose the latter alternative. But to spread the development costs among more users, it again chose to form a strategic alliance with an outside company, in this case Andersen Consulting. Andersen is now marketing the resulting Triumph System both to Banc One's potential customers and competitors.

The Triumph System achieves a unique combination of two different objectives: economies of scale and unique solutions, even for very small customers and groups of cardholders. This is because card programme managers can tailor systems to customers by means of a flexible parameter-controlled product design. The Triumph System also contains unique risk management features which are intended to address increased loan loss risks.

CREDIT SUISSE

Switzerland is a country with many banks and finance companies. The banking business generates no less than 8 per cent of GDP. Credit Suisse is one of four major commercial banks which together accounts for half of all deposits, more than one-fifth of all domestic branches and about half of all bank employees. There are also some 28 cantonal banks of varying sizes, which provide a large share of household and residential financing, and about 170 savings banks, which have a relatively large share of household savings. In addition, there are privately owned banks and co-operative banks, plus other banks and finance companies.

Like other commercial banks, Credit Suisse has primarily focused on the corporate market. Yet it is no accident that the company is now leading the way with a new productivity-orientated approach to profitability in the household banking market with the result that, compared to its counterparts, it has been relatively active in this sector.

Somewhat simplified, Swiss commercial banks have two main types of customer in the household market: very wealthy private customers, all of whose financial activities are related to the bank, and customers with transaction accounts who largely have their savings and mortgage loans at savings banks and cantonal banks. It is therefore an obvious strategy for a commercial bank to aim at improving its profitability in the latter segment by streamlining transaction-intensive systems and acquiring more profitable portions of existing customers' financial activities.

Co-ordinated autonomy

Like Banc One, Credit Suisse has systematically tried to organise its operations in ways that satisfy both the need for centralised co-ordination and decentralisation to autonomous units. In the mid-1980s this resulted in a matrix organisation consisting of several business areas in one dimension and regional responsibility in the other. In 1990 a process of redefining the geographic responsibility to 18 regions was initiated.

Each business area is targeted at a specific customer segment, for example multinational companies or public institutions. The chief executives of each business area systematically focus on the needs, demands, wishes and profitability of their respective customer category and are responsible for strategic functions in each area, for example market strategies and product development. Responsibility for operational sales and production, however, is decentralised to 18 regional managers with profit centre responsibility within a well-defined area.

Within each region, the bank also utilises economies of scale in production by concentrating certain functions from a number of branches – such as appraisal and processing of collateral, foreign exchange trading, recording of payment orders and other back-office processes – at a single unit within each region. Production thus began to shift from bank branches to 15 regional production units, while certain branches became more specialised.

Profitability monitoring

The introduction of management by earnings-related objectives, and of profitability analysis systems that continuously monitor revenues and costs in various units, was a prerequisite for the reorganisation of the mid-1980s. This is because one of the fundamental tenets of the bank's management philosophy is to move profit centre responsibility to the lowest possible level of the organisation.

- At the lowest level, individual bank officers with responsibility for customer relations can continuously monitor the revenues and costs they can influence.
- At the next level, profit centre heads at each branch are monitored. They keep track of final revenues and cost data that they are responsible for and can influence; in addition, they can continuously monitor the total profitability of their unit, because budgeted standard costs are charged to them for items that lie outside their influence and control.
- At the manager level, all costs that the branch manager is responsible for are measured against actual outcomes, while other costs are allocated using budgeted standard costs and measured utilisation.
- At the regional manager level, revenues of branch offices are aggregated and an even larger share of overall costs is measured against actual outcomes when profitability is evaluated.

Profitability can also be continuously analysed for units in the other dimension of the matrix. Thus, for example, heads of central product units and business areas do not merely follow cost trends in the central department. They can also continuously monitor changes in all revenues and costs related to their own product, product category or business area in all regions. In this way, central marketing strategists and product developers also assume a clear responsibility for earnings and profitability.

The reason why Credit Suisse has managed to achieve such a flexible profitability analysis system is that, unlike most other companies, it began to store the raw data in the information system (facts about transactions, customers, costs etc.) at an early stage and in such a way that processing and compilations can be as varied as needed. This gave the bank an almost unique capacity to satisfy the profitability analysis needs of its top executives.

Reward systems

For 900 members of senior management, their profit centre responsibility is accompanied by individually designed salary systems based on merit; packages also include relatively large bonus elements, which depend both on the earnings of the bank and of their own profit centre. In a typical year, up to 50 per cent of an individual senior manager's remuneration may consist of bonuses. The bonus may also be used to buy shares in the company at a discount.

About 5,000 other bank officers (associates) are covered by an earnings-based salary system. The bonus for all associates is directly related to the total earnings of the bank and in a typical year it amounts to about 5 per cent of their aggregate annual salaries. A majority of employees (67 per cent) are below the rank of associate and have fixed salaries, although all managers can give employees 'spontaneous awards' of US$340–3,400 based on merit: about US$1.4 M per year is distributed in this way.

Profitability and market analysis

The division of the bank into business areas meant that centrally placed marketing strategists and product developers, with explicit profit centre responsibility, began to conduct special studies of the needs and demands of different customer categories, and the related revenues and costs.

Two business areas target the household market: private banking and retail banking. Management of an individual's assets in excess of US$140,000 is undertaken by the private banking arm; other individuals belong to the retail banking business area.

For retail banking, the establishment of business areas meant that greater attention was focused on a comparatively unglamorous customer category. Central resources were allocated to this customer segment with the result that new, standardised products and services were developed in more systematic fashion. New principles for improving customer service, and reducing distribution and production costs, have also evolved.

The clear profit orientation of Credit Suisse has also been accompanied by widespread interest in analysing and improving profitability. One important instrument in this context is the flexible information system CRAPA (Customer Relation and Profitability Analysis), which enables the bank to analyse the profitability of individual customers, any customer group and customer segment, or individual products and product groups.

The more or less unique opportunities for profitability analyses provided by CRAPA played a decisive role when Credit Suisse drew up action guidelines for its retail banking business area. The classic 20–225 curve – meaning that 20 per cent of customers account for 225 per cent of annual profit – was found also to apply in principle to retail banking where certain customer groups were actually unprofitable.

The goal of Credit Suisse was to make unprofitable customers profitable, so it followed up its profitability analysis with an extensive market survey. Among other things, the survey indicated that a majority of customers appear to be relatively price-sensitive and cost-conscious, i.e. they are unwilling to pay the actual costs of the services they use and that their behaviour can be influenced by different service charges.

On the basis of its profitability analysis and the market survey, Credit Suisse formulated an extensive programme of change in the retail banking sector which went into effect at the beginning of 1993.

Credit Suisse's action programme to increase the profitability of retail banking rests on three pillars, namely products, distribution and production.

Products

The analysis showed that, in principle, customers with total assets at the bank exceeding US$17,000 are profitable. These customers also demand a broader range of products and services, such as deferred annuities, equity mutual funds and residential mortgages. Credit Suisse therefore decided to split its retail market into two, and to differentiate their product and service range. The aim is to increase benefits to each respective customer category and reduce costs.

For customers in the upper market segment (US$17,000–140,000), it has developed a broad range of products and services. Customers in this segment are considered to have relatively similar needs, which are best satisfied

42 Achieving Service Productivity

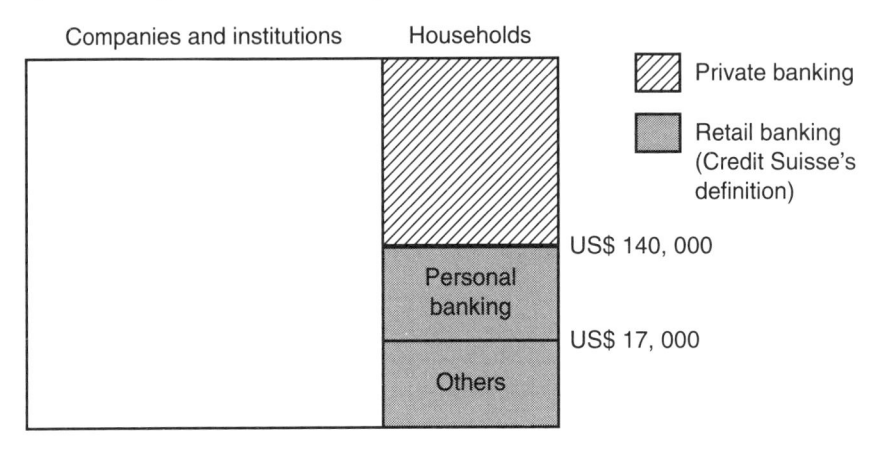

Figure 2.11 Credit Suisse: market segmentation

with standardised products such as equity mutual funds instead of investment counselling, and standard insurance policies instead of specially designed ones. Because these customers are already profitable to the bank, Credit Suisse also waives any charges on normal banking services.

The customers in the lower market segment should be offered adequate banking services in a cost-effective way. In practice, this means that they are steered to ATMs when they wish to make withdrawals or find out their account balances. One way of doing this is to charge for teller-assisted services. The comparatively cost-effective ATM withdrawals are free of charge, at least for large amounts or a certain number of withdrawals per month.

Distribution

Credit Suisse serves the two retail banking customer segments through separate distribution systems.

In the private banking business area, every customer has a personal counsellor, called a private banker. Each private banker is responsible for about 200 customers. Similarly, each customer in the upper customer segment of retail banking is allocated a personal banker, with a good overview and knowledge of the bank's products and services. Each personal banker is assigned about 700 customers.

A personal banker should be available when customers contact the bank but the banker should also acquaint themselves with their customers' needs and actively market the bank's products and services.

In keeping with the general management philosophy of Credit Suisse, profit-orientated management by objectives is also employed in this context. Each personal banker receives profit points based on the profitability of their customers but also receives extra points if these customers entrust such large assets to the bank that they are transferred to private banking. Obviously it is also equally important to market the bank's services to customers in the lower segment who keep their savings elsewhere.

Customers in the lower retail banking segment will be served according to entirely new principles. They will only be offered the three services of deposits, currency exchanges and safe deposit boxes: teller services will be kept to a minimum. The customer is expected to handle all other bank business via ATMs and viewdata systems, or by phone and correspondence.

Many customers in the lower segment may view the new system favourably. This is because in every region, Credit Suisse is establishing central offices to provide personal telephone services to customers. These offices will have about one employee per 2,500 customers and will be open on weekdays between 8 a.m. and 6.30 p.m. The bank is also devising new and more efficient methods for banking by correspondence.

A majority of customers in the lower segment, or nearly 90 per cent of all household customers, mostly perform simple banking transactions. The new system gives them easier access to the bank. But those who are dissatisfied with the system can pay an annual fee and receive the same service as customers in the upper segment.

These changes in the distribution system will improve productivity and will be reflected by staff movements. Credit Suisse currently has about 1,000 tellers and while some will stay, others will be offered positions as personal bankers or in the central telephone service; the bank expects to need about 200 fewer employees even in the initial phase of the changes.

Production

Production offers the greatest potential for raising productivity. Credit Suisse is currently implementing extensive automation and streamlining of working methods. These steps have the potential to raise productivity three or four times more than the changes under way at the distribution level of the bank's regional production units. But as production is automated, new economies of scale emerge.

Labour-intensive tasks are being transformed into capital-intensive tasks, making further concentration of production necessary in the future. Credit Suisse is therefore preparing a far-reaching, organisational reform which will completely detach the regional sales and distribution network from the production system.

Computer operations and systems development are concentrated at one unit outside Zurich. Other production, which now takes place in each region, is also being further concentrated to utilise economies of scale. Every production area should be concentrated at the economically optimal number of units for that type of operation. For payment services, this may be three to seven units, for cheque processing one to two units, for trust and securities processing two units etc. The potential productivity improvements from such streamlining far exceed those now being implemented in the existing structure.

SKANDINAVISKA ENSKILDA BANKEN (S-E-BANKEN)

S-E-Banken was established in 1972 through a merger between Skandinaviska Banken and Stockholms Enskilda Bank. At the time it was formed, the new bank – the largest in the Nordic countries – had about 6,600 employees and accounted for nearly one-third of total assets in the Swedish banking system.

Despite its size, however, the merged bank had a limited scope of operation. Stockholm's Enskilda Bank had focused on major international corporations and private banking, and had only a tiny branch network, concentrated in Sweden's two largest cities, Stockholm and Gothenburg. Expanding its branch network to gain access to more deposits from the increasingly important household banking market was one of Stockholm Enskilda Bank's main motives for the merger. Skandinaviska Banken, for its part, had about 300 branches under its three central offices in Gothenburg, Stockholm and Malmö. Thus, despite its expanded branch network, even the merged S-E-Banken was a commercial bank whose customer base consisted largely of international corporations and wealthy private banking customers in Sweden's three biggest metropolitan areas.

Its three central offices in Stockholm, Gothenburg and Malmö operated relatively autonomously until 1991. They even had their own boards of directors. In some ways, the bank resembled a chamber of commerce rather than a business. Large stockholders and representatives of major S-E-Banken clients have also been very active as directors, both on the boards of the bank and on the boards of its largest client companies. Some of the major owners of S-E-Banken have also played a central role in Sweden's industrial development.

Co-ordinated autonomy

Major reorganisations have begun at S-E-Banken and the emergent structure seeks to achieve both central co-ordination and greater decentralisation.

Retail Banking

The bank took its first tentative steps toward divisionalisation as early as 1982, when the Stockholm central office split its operations into two. One part served major international corporations, and its responsibilities included the bank's representative offices abroad; the other was in charge of the branch network and was responsible for households and small/medium-sized companies, i.e. retail banking in a broad sense.

Since the early 1990s, however, the central offices have been gradually dismantled. In 1992 S-E-Banken halved the number of its central board of directors and in early 1993 it unanimously approved the elimination of the central offices as organisational units. Directly below the group chief executive are two divisional managers, responsible for major corporations (the Enskilda Corporate Division) and domestic retail banking (the S-E-Banken Division) respectively. There is also a unit for computer production (SEB Data). These units comprise about 2,000, 7,500 and 500 people respectively.

The bank has a group executive committee and a headquarters staff, plus two divisional managements with central responsibility for different market segments. The latter facilitates efforts to achieve more in-depth analysis of various customer needs plus a differentiated and standardised range of products and services. At the same time, it creates new opportunities to utilise economies of scale, and improve productivity in production and distribution.

The Enskilda Corporate Division has taken over the corporate contact units of the former central offices, which have been responsible for maintaining the bank's relationships with major corporations. It has also taken over the international branch network and certain production units, such as foreign exchange trading.

The S-E-Banken Division, which specialises in small/medium-sized companies and household customers, is taking over the entire Swedish branch network, which is under the supervision of six regional managers. The division is also taking over Enskilda Asset Management and most centralised production functions such as payments, trust and securities business and credit/charge cards. Certain subsidiaries dealing with mortgage loans, leasing/factoring and life insurance and retirement annuities are also part of the new S-E-Banken Division. They are being more closely integrated largely because new banking legislation allows banks to broaden their operations.

The operations of the S-E-Banken Group were previously organised into separate corporations, partly for legal reasons. Many of these companies provided the public with products and services that supplemented traditional banking, for example financial advisory services, investment management, investment and capital goods financing, mortgage loans for one person households, co-operative apartments and commercial properties, real estate appraisals, credit and charge cards, and trading in foreign equities.

In principle, each subsidiary company built up its own sales and distribution organisation, but during the 1990s these sales operations have been increasingly integrated into the regular branch network.

Market analysis and segmentation

Since the mid-1970s, S-E-Banken has regularly monitored the attitudes of both its own and its competitors' customers. Every two years, it commissions a survey of the consumer banking market, asking certain standard questions that make it possible to monitor changes over time. In recent years, these surveys have been supplemented with lifestyle questions that have enabled the bank to segment customers.

These surveys confirm that S-E-Banken has a reputation for expertise in corporate banking and parts of the private banking sectors. But in the S-E-Banken Division's market, there is a need for systematic customer and market analysis to provide the basis for developing products, services, pricing and marketing. This is one of the most important tasks facing the division's management.

These surveys are now being supplemented by qualitative studies, i.e. in-depth interviews or group discussions to gain a deeper knowledge of customer needs and attitudes. The findings are being used in strategy discussions, product development and target group determination. Where development of specific products is considered, and in special decision-making situations, additional studies are conducted, for example product and advertising tests and impact surveys.

During 1992 the bank ran a major quality-raising campaign and conducted a large-scale survey to assess customer perceptions of quality. Every branch was told how customers perceived its service, proficiency, office hours etc. Branches were also allowed to compare their scores, not only with other S-E-Banken branches, but also with competitors. Every branch had to produce an action plan to improve its level of quality in the most critical areas. Subsidiaries and central units of the bank also conducted similar quality surveys. The bank intends to follow up these findings with new surveys every two years.

Product range and service

Unlike Credit Suisse and some other commercial banks, S-E-Banken does not have large numbers of household banking customers who only have transaction-intensive salary accounts. But like Credit Suisse, S-E-Banken is

Retail Banking 47

intensifying its efforts to recruit relatively affluent Swedes, mainly in the three biggest metropolitan areas. Pension insurance policies (deferred annuities) are a particularly important element of this effort. But at the same time, top executives of S-E-Banken stress the importance of standardisation. People with relatively simple needs will not receive the best quality at the lowest cost if tailor-made solutions are created for each. Instead, unique combinations of standard packages should be assembled for individual customers. It is thus possible to utilise economies of scale while requiring only a reasonable level of expertise from employees in the distribution system.

In the corporate banking field, S-E-Banken has relatively well-developed systems for analysing the profitability of different customers. Pure transaction costs, for example, can be allocated to the individual client, and bank employees can 'debit' especially heavy work inputs. In the household sector, however, the situation is different. All of the bank's relationships with a given customer can be aggregated, and net interest income and other revenues can be calculated per customer, although it has not normally been possible to allocate costs. Consequently, S-E-Banken does not yet have the same capability as Banc One and Credit Suisse to analyse the profitability of individual customers, customer categories or products. Yet obviously there are both 'loss leaders' and 'cash cows', and S-E-Banken is equipping itself to respond appropriately to market trends.

Figure 2.12 shows that there have been dramatic changes in transaction services at S-E-Banken, as at many other banks.

The bank has tried to use simple methods to lower its costs by steering customer behaviour. For example, its ATMs have preselection buttons for amounts from US$50 upwards. This is not only intended as a convenience to customers, but is also a way of persuading them to withdraw larger amounts each time, resulting in fewer withdrawals and lower overall costs. S-E-Banken's customers are also unique in Sweden in that they can make inter-account transfers not only by telephone but also via ATMs. Older, wealthy customers are declining in number and being replaced by younger clients with different priorities. The bank is therefore trying to be more proactive and is now aiming its campaigns at ordinary big-city dwellers with access to a certain amount of capital. This category is expected to be interested primarily in standardised products, but also in financial advisory services.

Decentralisation

The centralisation of the S-E-Banken Division is accompanied by a clear decentralisation of authority to the six new regions. Independent regional

48 Achieving Service Productivity

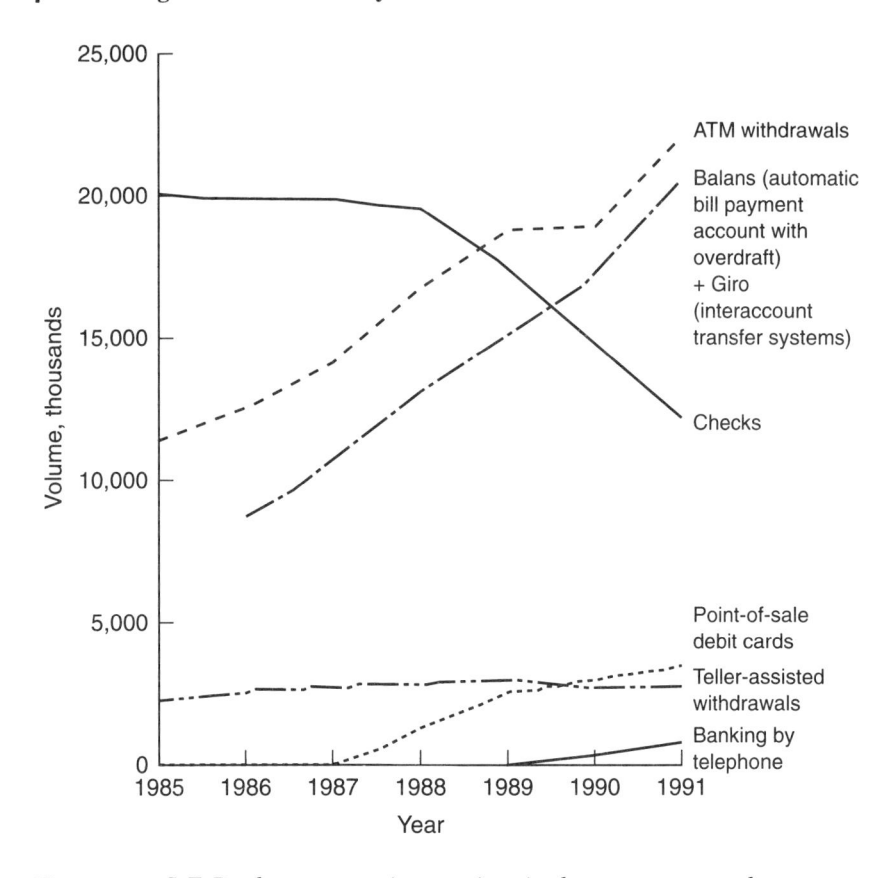

Figure 2.12 S-E-Banken transaction services in the consumer market

managers with clearly formulated profit centre responsibility are expected to develop regional sales organisations representing the collective product and service range of the entire S-E-Banken Group. In building up their distribution systems and sales operations, the regional managers are being given a substantial degree of freedom. They are expected to segment their own markets in accordance with central guidelines. All regions thus have certain common factors, but by necessity they also show differences, especially in speed of development.

The process of change

One region that is far ahead in the process of change is Central Stockholm, ('Stockholm City'), which has about 700 employees. The changes under way there will probably spread to other regions.

Market segmentation

Exactly like Credit Suisse and Banc One, S-E-Banken has traditionally offered very wealthy customers special services, i.e. private banking. These people are rather few in number, but their percentage of overall deposits has been significant. Now the Central Stockholm region is proceeding with a concept that resembles Credit Suisse's personal banking. In each of the five districts in Central Stockholm, the bank has opened a specialist unit for specifically identified customers. The exact criteria have not yet been established but, in principle, companies in this new category should provide a certain profit contribution to the bank while private individuals should have a certain level of assets in the bank. Some of the private banking customers previously handled by the bank's trust and securities business offices are also being transferred to these new specialist offices, which feature financial advisers who are personally responsible for their customers. They work in small teams so that in the course of their work they will learn and be able to benefit from each other's knowledge. At the same time, there is a manager for the consumer banking market and a manager for the small/medium-sized company market.

Financial advisers working at the specialist offices are expected to operate more independently and actively than their counterparts handling routine matters at regular branches. This is also the reason why the profitability analysis systems for regular branches and specialist offices focus on different things. Financial advisers at the specialist offices are rated primarily on the basis of their activities. This can be measured in terms of number of customer visits or price quotations delivered. Specialist advisers submit regular reports to the regional manager on their planned activities for the next two weeks, which are then compared with actual outcomes. Every four months they submit more detailed reports, including profitability figures, and summaries of past and planned activities. Starting in 1994, resources will be allocated mainly to those who demonstrate that they have an active portfolio.

The other 38 Central Stockholm branches that have lost some of their profitable customers because of this segmentation are thus generating reduced earnings in their operations. In spite of this, similar profitability targets are being set for the managers of these branches, in an effort to force them to think along new lines and generate good earnings from the remaining customer base. In practice, this means that working methods, service levels and staffing must be reviewed to ensure that costs are covered by revenues from the traditional banking services provided to the remaining household customers. The focus of this analysis is not the level of activity but financial ratios such as profit contribution per employee.

Specialised working structure

The Central Stockholm region's specialisation of its branch network is aimed at raising the quality of marketing to customers while achieving higher profitability for all customer segments. The idea is that a more specialised structure will make it possible to redeploy employees from routine daily transactions to aggressive marketing at all branches. Transaction services and financial advisory services will be more clearly separated. To see an adviser, it will be necessary to make an appointment. This allows advisers to shoulder a heavier workload and also enables them to plan active sales promotions. One overall goal of the region's efficiency-raising programme is to redistribute 10–15 per cent of existing costs to this type of activity. Every branch must produce an action plan specifying its target market, its service level and what service routines can be streamlined or automated.

Management development

These changes pose new and sometimes more difficult demands on employees. The classic branch manager, a generalist with many years of service and who knows everything about branch activities, is no longer as necessary as in the past. Instead it is important for the manager to be an inspiring team leader, in turn increasing the need for training in management and working methods. The Central Stockholm region is focusing more attention on such qualities, as evidenced by the regular meetings between the regional manager and branch managers, where both sides complete personal assessment forms about themselves and each other. They are asked to rate themselves and their colleagues on a five-point scale in terms of drive, independence, interpersonal skills, analytical ability etc. The meetings also provide an opportunity to discuss career development plans, willingness to relocate etc.

Longer business hours

Like Banc One, S-E-Banken is beginning to adapt its business hours to the needs of customers. Led by the Central Stockholm region, all branches are extending their Monday to Thursday hours to 4.30 p.m. and, when negotiations with the Bank Employees' Union are completed, hours will be further extended.

Customer input

The Central Stockholm region has begun to apply something that is referred to internally as the 'drugstore model'. The idea is to increase the level of

Retail Banking 51

self-service inside the branch by, for example, installing customer-operated coin-counting machines that dispense banknotes. Customers can also complete cheque reorder or other forms, leave them in a box, and return a day or so later to pick up the finished documents. This enables branch employees to perform these tasks when their workload is less and it is also more convenient for the customer.

There are also some bold ideas that have not yet become a reality. For example, the Central Stockholm regional manager is considering letting small/medium-sized companies service ATMs. These machines are normally serviced by special employees who are responsible for ensuring that they contain enough cash. This is also true of ATMs located on the premises of the bank's customers, for example at one Metro supermarket. This supermarket regularly carries its cash dispensing cassettes to the bank. The bank is considering letting the supermarket take responsibility for keeping the ATM filled with cash: this would not only save the bank money, but would also be easier for Metro employees.

Economies of scale in production

S-E-Banken is trying to take greater advantage of economies of scale in production. Just as Credit Suisse did in the mid-1980s, each region is gradually concentrating certain types of production, such as back-office operations and the processing of company computer tapes, into a single unit. In the Central Stockholm region, for example, back-office operations have been concentrated into a single centre, the bank's new 1,600-employee administration building in Rissne.

Current changes in the company's structure also create opportunities to apply new economies of scale at the national level. Such functions as payment services, and trust and securities business that were previously under the jurisdiction of the three central offices have now been organised into nationwide units. The payments unit, for example, has about 400 employees, of which about 200 work in Stockholm, 125 in Gothenburg and about 75 in Malmö. About half of these employees are engaged full time in recording transactions. In the relatively near future, this task can be automated or eliminated with the aid of such systems as autogiro, optical character reading of documents and electronic transfers of payment orders directly from the customer.

Systems development and computer operations have been concentrated for many years in a single unit, SEB Data. The unit employs about 500 people and has revenues of about US$120 M. (The cost of all data processing at S-E-Banken is about US$80 M higher per year, because some of the bank's data processing costs are not reported via SEB Data.)

S-E-Banken's basic banking systems, which are linked to about 8,000 terminals and 400 ATMs, remain very cost-effective although most of them were designed more than 20 years ago. They perform about 2.5 million transactions each day, and print out about 175 million lines of text and about 1.5 million letters each month. Yet S-E-Banken is at a crossroads. There is a growing need for more management information of the type generated by Banc One's Strategic Banking System and Credit Suisse's Customer Relation and Control System. There is also reason to utilise the reverse economies of scale offered by distributed data processing in a client/server environment. S-E-Banken is currently taking some small steps in this direction, but when and how the bank will take a larger strategic development leap remains to be seen.

3
COMMERCIAL INSURANCE

Authors: Alarik Arthur, Fredrik Lennartsson

HOME INSURANCE CO., New York, NY, USA
TRYGG-HANSA SPP INTERNATIONAL INSURANCE, Stockholm, Sweden

Home, a US company, is a subsidiary of Sweden's Trygg-Hansa. Both companies are successful in the field of industrial insurance.

At the heart of an insurance policy is a promise by the insurance company that, in the event of damage, it will compensate the policyholder for the costs resulting from this damage. The company receives a premium in exchange for its promise. The overall cost to companies that transfer risks to insurance companies is about 30 per cent of the premiums. This is the average operating cost of insurance companies. It covers underwriting – i.e. risk selection and pricing – as well as marketing, production, reinsurance, investment, service and claims adjustment. Standardisation of insurance products can potentially lead to major productivity increases.

There are sizeable economies of scale in the insurance business. If these were fully utilised, some observers believe that a dozen insurance companies could dominate the world market.

In Sweden, large corporate customers have been the driving force behind the trend toward lower costs and deregulation in industrial insurance. Trygg-Hansa tries to improve its earnings by focusing on operating costs. There is major potential to improve productivity with the aid of new user-friendly information systems. Trygg-Hansa uses a team approach to risk selection and price-setting.

In the US, industrial insurance is usually sold through brokers. Home's priority is to become more skilful in making good risk selections. Because the American market is so much larger than the Swedish market, there are greater opportunities for segmentation. Home's risk selection and pricing are decided by underwriters, who enjoy a strong position in the organisation.

54 Achieving Service Productivity

Underwriters are individually evaluated in a monthly basis and are rewarded or reprimanded depending on the financial outcome of their respective policy portfolios.

In Sweden the insurance market is regulated by general principles, while the US uses detailed regulation. In Sweden, the government agency that oversees insurance matters has some 30 employees. By way of comparison, the State of New York, which has one of the most liberal rule systems in the US, employs about 1,400 people to keep track of insurance matters. Another factor that makes the relative cost of insurance much higher in the US than in Sweden is the volume of civil litigation related to insurance claims.

THE INSURANCE SECTOR

In 1989, global premiums for all types of insurance amounted to the astronomical sum of US$1.2 billion. The United States is by far the largest market, with a total market share of 37 per cent, or US$450 billion; Europe and Japan account for a further 30 per cent and 22 per cent of the global market respectively. In order to examine the business more closely, it may be useful to divide it into two main sectors: life and health insurance, and property and casualty insurance. The relative importance of each of these sectors varies significantly between countries. For example, the American market is characterised by a high proportion of casualty insurance (which accounts for 60 per cent of the total property and casualty insurance market), while in Japan, life and health insurance accounts for as much as 75 per cent of total premiums.

Table 3.1 The World Market for Insurance: spending as a % of GDP, 1989

	Non-Life		Life		Total	
	% of World Market	% GDP	% of World Market	% GDP	% of World Market	% GDP
US	44.8	5.5	30.4	3.6	37.5	8.8
Japan	11.1	2.4	32.2	7.2	21.9	9.6
W. Ger.	8.0	4.7	2.8	6.3	6.3	7.5
GB	4.7	3.4	7.9	6.0	6.3	9.4
France	5.0	2.8	5.5	3.2	5.2	6.0
Sweden	1.1	3.2	1.2	3.8	1.1	7.0
Total	74.7		81.9		78.3	

The following facts about a Swedish multinational company with activities all over the world will further illustrate the composition of the global insurance market.While the company has 25 per cent of its revenue and activities in the US, 90 per cent of its risk costs originate there. The difference in these ratios primarily reflects differences in the relative importance of product liability insurance and workers' compensation. In other parts of the world the cost of insurance is seen as being an almost negligible part of the company's costs. In the US, on the other hand, risk costs solely for product liability amount to 2.5 per cent of the company's gross margins.

Commercial insurance

Another useful way of categorising the insurance business is according to the type of client. Insurance clients are either private individuals or companies. Company insurance accounts for more than half of the US property and casualty market. It can generally be said that risks insured in the company insurance market are larger, fewer in number and display more variation than risks insured in the private market. Consequently, insurance products are characterised by a low degree of standardisation. Each insurance policy is priced individually and its terms, conditions and coverage may vary infinitely in order to satisfy customer needs. It is clearly much more difficult to calculate the risk premium for insurance against production stoppages in the processing industry than to calculate car insurance for a private individual.

The low degree of standardisation affects the way business activities are run. Setting prices for insurance services differs markedly from other lines of business where it is normally possible to base price calculations on known costs, such as raw materials, salaries, machinery etc. In the case of insurance, the insurance company must predict and estimate the probability and extent of future events which it may, at best, only be able to influence to a limited degree. As far as possible, statistics and the laws of probability are used to support price setting; the greater the number of observations and the number of risks of the same type, the more certain the conclusions that can be drawn. Greater reliability in the prediction of future events means that the company requires smaller margins in its premiums in order to cover possible future losses.

The amount insured and the size of the premium do not present any significant problems for industrial insurance companies. The only limitation is the company's ability to take on risks over a certain size according to its capital base. If a risk is too large for a company to retain it, reinsurance can be purchased.

Insurance – idea and application

An insurance company is a company that, in exchange for taking on the potential financial consequences associated with a risk, receives a relatively small, predetermined premium. This reduces financial uncertainty for the policyholder and risks are manageable. At the same time, the total risk cost is reduced since the risk is transferred from the party who puts a high price on carrying it to a party that demands a lower remuneration for accepting that risk. The key characteristic of an insurance product is therefore a promise to compensate the policyholder for the costs associated with an unknown future. The basis for this promise is the company's credibility, which in turn is based on its financial ability to fulfil its promises and its demonstrated willingness to do so.

Insurance is therefore quite simple in concept, and in theory it should be possible to handle insurance in precisely the same way as, for example, foreign currency or shares, i.e. to buy and sell products via a computerised network where sellers meet buyers. However, while this type of market is primarily characterised by low transaction costs, such costs in today's insurance market are high. Generally speaking, when a business wants to transfer risk to an insurance company, the cost is 30 per cent of the premium paid. This is the amount that disappears in operation costs for the insurance company. Thus although the principle of insurance is simple, its application is often very complicated.

So what does an insurance company do?

Its activities are wide-ranging and include marketing, underwriting, production, reinsurance, investment, service and processing of claims:

- marketing is what a company does to establish contact with potential customers and to persuade them to buy its products;
- production refers to the issue of the insurance policy and the processing of information;
- reinsurance is the process by which the insurance company accepts a risk but, because of its insufficient capacity, limits its exposure to risk;
- investment is the purchase of assets to earn income from premiums and reserves;
- service can, for example, be in the areas of engineering and loss control;
- processing of claims is the receiving, investigation and settlement of claims. All insurance companies have to develop systems for handling these processes and it is by carrying these out effectively that an insurance company can make a profit.

Uncertainty, risk and insurance

This study focuses on commercial insurance, primarily property and casualty insurance. Risks are normally divided into three categories: business risks, financial risks and loss risks.

- Business risks are those that a company is exposed to in the normal course of business. It is unusual to buy insurance to cover this type of risk, although examples do exist.
- Financial risks are the risks associated with the company's financial situation and the supply of capital. A company handles this risk with the help of the mechanisms provided by the banking system, and the debt and the equity markets. This area of risk has not traditionally been an object for insurance either.
- Loss risks can only have negative consequences. A company's risk of accident can be divided into five distinct categories: personal injury, damage to goods, damage to property, third-party liability and damage which is the result of an earlier accident. On the whole, a company can handle this type of risk in three different ways. First, it can take preventative measures, to minimise the likelihood and effect of accidents should they occur. Examples are installing a sprinkler system, improving the work environment or adapting products. Secondly, all or part of the financial consequences of accidents to may be transferred to an insurance company, in return for a premium. A third course of action is to build up reserves for dealing with accidents when they occur.

As a result of the various types of risk a company is exposed to, an insurance package will include a range of different insurance services such as: fire insurance, insurance against stoppages in production, transport insurance, car insurance, pension insurance (deferred annuities), product liability insurance, environmental liability insurance etc.

THE COMPANIES STUDIED

This study covers the industrial insurance activities within the Home Insurance Company (from now on described as Home) with its head office in New York City, and Trygg-Hansa SPP International Insurance (from now on described as Trygg-Hansa) with its head office in Stockholm.

While not leaders, both companies are successful in their respective markets, which makes them worth studying. Another interesting aspect is that they operate in two very different markets, with differing structures and institutional environments. The ownership connection between Trygg-Hansa and

Home (the former owns 60 per cent of the latter) also made it possible to study what each company can learn from the other, what common efforts are and will be relevant, plus the potential for synergy which may result from co-operation between the two.

Home Insurance Company

There are 3,900 companies in the US active in the field of property and casualty insurance. Nine hundred of these are responsible for insurance activities in all 50 states. No company has a market share of more than 10 per cent, and the ten largest companies' aggregate share is less than 40 per cent.

In 1991 net premium volume for Home was US$1.7 billion. This included all areas of activity: major accounts, commercial lines, speciality lines, personal lines, reinsurance, international and investments. Home has 4,400 employees and is the US's twenty-third largest insurance company; it is also one of the ten largest companies in the field of commercial insurance. With the stronger capital base it gained from Trygg-Hansa's shareholding, Home's aim is to catch up with leading US industrial insurance companies such as American International Group (AIG) and Chubb. AIG is one of the world's largest insurance companies, with 32,000 employees in 130 countries and a premium volume of over US$9 billion (net premiums written) within the property and casualty insurance field: one-third of total premiums is generated outside the US. Chubb has a premium volume of US$3.1 billion within the property and casualty insurance field, mainly generated in the US, and has approximately 9,000 employees.

Trygg-Hansa Group

Employing 14,600 people, the total premium revenue for the Trygg-Hansa SPP Group amounted to US$7.2 billion in 1991, making it the twelfth largest insurance group in Europe. Measured in terms of capital under management, however, the group ranks fifth in Europe. Premium revenue in the Trygg-Hansa SPP holding group amounted to US$1,285 million and operating income to US$92 million, including profit shares in associated companies.

Insurance activities of the holding group were primarily within Trygg-Hansa Forsakrings AB, which consists of two main divisions: the Swedish Market Division and International Insurance.

The Swedish Market Division is divided into three business areas: Direct Market, Partner Market and Companies, the latter targeting small and medium-sized companies, where the insurance requirements of the company, the employees and the owner are interlinked. The division's 1991 revenue was US$685 million and the net income was US$150 million.

Table 3.2 Comparative financial data: Home and Trygg-Hansa 1991

(US$ million) (SEK/$:5.55)	Home Insurance	Trygg-Hansa International
Premiums earned (Net reinsurance ceded)	1,705	236
Net investment return	331	47
Losses		−200
Losses and loss adjustment Expenses	−1,389	
Operating expenses	−518	−61
Insurance result	129	22
Ratios:		
Loss	64.8	76.6
Loss adjustment expense	15.2	
Expense	28.0	23.2
Combined (Net reinsurance ceded)	109.5	109.3
Number of employees	4,440	340

Trygg-Hansa International Insurance offers property and casualty insurance for large and medium-sized Swedish companies, i.e. companies with a revenue of more than SKr200 million, or with an insurance risk (EML) exceeding SKr50 million: it also offers insurance to municipalities and county councils. The division's premium volume for 1991 was US$236 million and net income was US$22 million. The number of employees was 340.

The largest player in the Swedish industrial insurance market is Skandia, with a market share of approximately 25 per cent. Trygg-Hansa's market share in 1991 was 19 per cent. The five largest companies had a market share of over 90 per cent.

Processes

The range of processes an insurance company has to be able to handle is outlined above. How the two companies have chosen to organise and work with these processes is summarised below.

Marketing

Marketing is of relatively greater importance for Home in the US than for Trygg Hansa in Sweden. This is partly because the American market is larger, more complex and more competitive, and because Home, like most other companies, is trying to specialise in certain types of insurance and cus-

60 Achieving Service Productivity

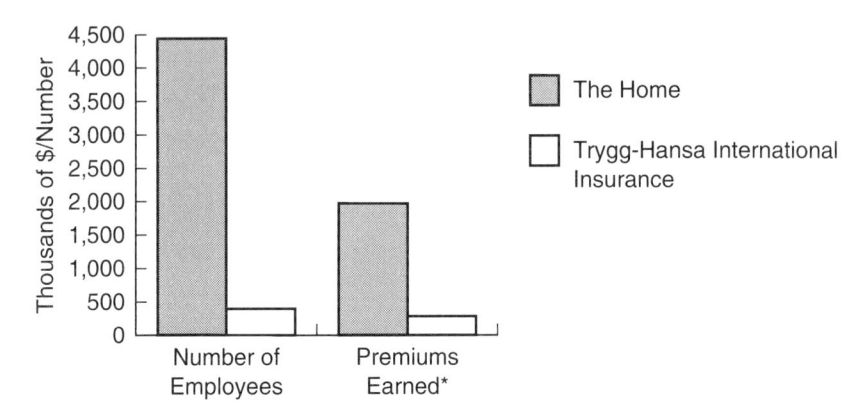

[Bar chart comparing The Home and Trygg-Hansa International Insurance by Number of Employees and Premiums Earned, with y-axis "Thousands of $/Number" ranging 0 to 4,500]

Figure 3.1 Comparative size

tomers, a strategy that necessitates a high profile. Trygg-Hansa, on the other hand, is already very well known in the Swedish market and offers, in principle, all types of insurance to all types of customers. The higher importance accorded to marketing in the US reflects two other factors. First, in a market where companies regularly go bankrupt, financial strength has for a long time been important in attracting customers (the same pattern is however now emerging in Sweden) and secondly Home, like most US commercial insurance companies, sells all of its policies through insurance brokers and agents. Brokers do not have the same strong position in Sweden, where 85 per cent of Trygg-Hansa's sales are made by its own sales force.

Underwriting

Individual underwriters have a very strong position at Home. As long as a risk can be classified as larger, and more complex, and falls under one of the business areas of major accounts, commercial lines or speciality lines, the underwriter selects the risk and sets the price. The underwriter receives the data for the evaluation on paper from the broker and the price is set by classifying the risk in accordance with the rating system. The underwriter then adds 'debits' and 'credits' to this rating to arrive at the price quoted to the customer. This price may be higher or lower than the rating price since, in practice, the price may only be set by the underwriter after assessing the market rate. The rating department then has to 'reverse' the risk into the system in order to arrive at the price that has already been set. It is very unusual for underwriters to meet the customer, but they have a great deal of contact with brokers. Underwriters are evaluated on a monthly basis, and their personal compensation and rewards are tightly linked to their portfolio results. If the portfolio shows a negative result for several months in a row, particularly with regard to small frequency claims, the underwriter will be transferred or dismissed.

All risks are quoted in principle at Trygg-Hansa, apart from those not taken on as a matter of policy. The individual underwriter, however, does not enjoy the same strong position as at Home and more work is carried out in groups. The contact person, the risk engineer and the underwriter work together on risk selection and price-setting. Although the underwriter formally has the final authority, the contact person and the risk engineer may have more experience, and thus greater influence. The data for assessment are collected by the contact person and the risk engineer, who are often in close touch with the policyholder. The price is set by classifying the risk according to objective factors and feeding them into the system. The underwriter and the contact person, working in co-operation, then offer discounts which may sometimes be as much as 50 per cent. This can be explained by the fact that the tariffs are out of date and do not bear much relation to the current market situation. Again, unlike Home, individual underwriters and their results are not evaluated very often.

Production

The production process in both companies is, on the whole, sequential and involves a great many people. In both firms, the same information is fed into different systems, at different times. The system has little relevance for price-setting. At Home, insurance policies are issued by the 27 field offices, but they are then sent in centrally for registration in the system: at Trygg-Hansa, policies are issued centrally.

Reinsurance

Both companies have a central reinsurance department. Home places responsibility for the reinsurance of a risk on the underwriter. If a risk needs to be reinsured, it is never approved until this has been done. Responsibility at Trygg-Hansa is divided between the underwriter, the production department and the reinsurance department. Sometimes, however, there are breakdowns in communication and reinsurance is not completed until after the policy has been issued.

Investment

Investment activities fall outside the terms of reference of the Trygg-Hansa International Insurance Division studied here, and have therefore also been excluded from the Home study.

62 Achieving Service Productivity

Service

Answering enquiries about insurance, terms and conditions and coverage are important service functions at both companies. This is done by underwriters at Home and by the contact person at Trygg-Hansa. Risk engineers and their work represent another important category of service. They may, for example, offer advice on risk prevention. As the large US brokers have their own engineers, this work is less important at Home. In Sweden, and at Trygg-Hansa, it is almost taken for granted that risk engineer services will be included in insurance packages offered by the company.

Claims handling

Processing of claims is defined by both companies as an important service function. Studies performed at each firm have shown that customers put a very strong emphasis on claims handling when forming an opinion about the company. The speed at which claims are settled shows a high correlation both with favourable customer opinion and low dollar claims. Home consciously works towards improving its service in the processing of claims.It aims to contact customers within 24 hours (at the latest) after a claim has been made and to pay compensation within 48 hours after the amount has been determined. Independent claims processing companies exist in the US market, and some brokers also offer this service, so it is not certain that an insurance package will include processing of claims by Home. Many of the Home staff who work with processing claims have legal training. External legal advisers also represent a considerable proportion of the cost of processing claims. In 1991, Home spent nearly US$170 million on outside legal services.

Trygg-Hansa also invests in offering a good claims processing service. The risk engineers, who have been in contact with policyholders earlier, play an important role here, but with support and control from the central claims processing department. Services for processing claims in the field are also purchased from the Swedish Market Division.

FACTORS INFLUENCING PRODUCTIVITY

External factors

Efficiency

The three financial ratios which are most commonly used to measure efficiency in the insurance industry are:

- loss ratio;
- expense ratio;
- combined loss and expense ratio (combined ratio).

The loss ratio indicates how well the company has performed in order to:

- select risks;
- quote premiums;
- assist the insured to prevent losses;
- handle incurred losses from a qualitative and quantitative point of view.

The expense ratio indicates how well the company has performed in order to:

- market the business;
- select risks;
- quote premiums;
- manage the production process, i.e. issue policies, invoice, provide service to customers.

Thus the combined ratio is a measurement of the company's overall performance, investment income excluded.

Another financial ratio frequently used within the insurance industry is the solvency margin which indicates an insurance company's ability to stand extraordinary operating losses. Comparative ratios for some leading international companies are given in Table 3.3

Table 3.3 Comparative ratios

	Combined ratio, non life (%)	Solvency margin
Allianz	104.0	185.0
Zurich	110.0	84.0
UAP	118.0	60.0
AIG	100.4	180.0
Trygg-Hansa SPP Group	109.0	176.0

Most insurance companies have a combined ratio exceeding 100 per cent but still make a profit. One of the reasons for this is that the premiums are paid in advance before the losses occur, i.e. the insurance company receives investment income on the premiums less operating costs and indemnities paid. The insurance companies often have a significant portfolio of assets to manage which yield substantial investment income. Thus another important standard for measuring business performance is the rate of return on invested assets. When comparing different insurance companies it is premium income, net profit, equity and funds managed which are measured in conjunction with the above ratios. See Table 3.4.

Table 3.4 Financial data: International insurance companies (US$ billion)

	Premium Income Total	Premium Income Non-Life	Net Profit	Net Equity	Assets Managed
Allianz	23.7	13.9	0.61	8.5	85
Zurich	11.3	8.7	0.26	4.0	39
UAP	17.5	9.7	0.76	6.1	63
AIG	16.7	12.0	1.55	11.5	70
Trygg-Hansa SPP Group	7.0	3.5	0.22	2.4	44

Efficiency at a national level

Is it possible to compare the industrial insurance industry in different countries in the same way as it is possible to compare efficiency and productivity within the motor industry and many other manufacturing sectors? The answer is that the insurance industry is often heavily regulated at a national level rendering internationally fair comparisons difficult. Furthermore, the product *per se* is often quite different, i.e. the risk of theft, fire and natural disaster can vary significantly from country to country and also within each country, for example between big cities and small villages.

Despite differences in the relative size of each market (the Swedish market is approximately equal to that of a medium-sized American state such as Illinois), certain other external factors affect efficiency and productivity on a national level:

- the influence and power of the buyers;
- degree of competition;
- economies of scale;
- an efficient capital market.

Commercial Insurance 65

Buyer power

To illustrate the impact of buyer power on a national level, the situation in Sweden from the early 1970s may be analysed. Until the end of the 70s, the Swedish industrial insurance market was an oligopoly with Skandia totally dominant. Skandia, one of the Wallenberg group's more important companies, enjoyed a market share of approximately 45 per cent and it was quite obvious within the Wallenberg group that Skandia was the most suitable insurance company for the group's firms. New establishment and pricing were regulated by the authorities and also within the industry itself, and other players including Trygg-Hansa received the market share Skandia found appropriate. Industrial insurance was a most profitable operation for the insurance industry as a whole and Skandia in particular.

The buyers, including the Swedish multinational companies, therefore began to question both the costs and the structure of the industry. Several companies, among them AGA and SKF, started their own captive insurance companies to handle their international reinsurance and thereby reduce insurance costs. At the same time, more and more international companies centralised their insurance purchases and employed experienced risk managers to control the companies' total risk exposure. As the buyers became more and more sophisticated their demands for internationally competitive prices, quality and new areas of insurance increased.

The other Swedish insurance companies, particularly Trygg-Hansa, also started to question Skandia's dominant position. Earlier co-operation ceased and in the mid-1980s buyers persuaded the authorities to change the existing regulations for operating insurance companies. Previously when applying for a licence to start a business, an insurance company had to provide proof of the demand for another player in the market, which, for obvious reasons, was impossible. In 1985, however, this requirement was abolished. The legislation now states that a licence must be granted unless it can be proven that it will have a negative effect on the competition, i.e. in direct contrast to earlier legislation. As a consequence, several international companies started up operations in Sweden and brokers have secured a stronger foothold in the market, to the extent that they are now procuring 15 per cent of industrial insurance business.

Swedish multinationals are the driving force behind the deregulation of the Swedish insurance market. Buyer pressure has also led to increased competition, lower prices, the development of new insurance solutions and improved quality. The buyers, particularly the big multinational companies, will remain the most important force influencing change in the industrial insurance sector. For one thing they are increasingly purchasing insurance in the international market (one of the reasons behind Trygg-Hansa's internationalisation strategy) and for another buyers' demands for a more efficient business structure will lead to simplified products and greater standardisation. From a buyer's point of view it still costs approximately 30 per cent of the premium to transfer a risk to an insurance company. The insurance company, in turn, often has to transfer part of the risk to the reinsurance market. In the end up to 40 per cent of the premium will be expenses, profit margin and commissions.

One of the strongest players in the American insurance market is the broker and, traditionally, brokers and agents provide the dominant distribution channel for industrial insurance. This extra link in the channel reflects the complexity and greater specialisation (segments and risks) of the market, making it essential that someone represent the buyers against the sophisticated sellers on a professional basis. Thus, American brokers perform many of the functions normally regarded as part of the insurance company's responsibilities in Sweden. They help the client identify and analyse risks: they propose the mixture of insurance, loss-preventive steps and self-insurance that is the most appropriate, and they assist in the selection of insurance company and the purchasing process. Brokers also use their expertise to advise on what companies to contact for a specific risk. Without this competence, the tender process would easily be prolonged and the final price/quality ratio would be too high.

Do brokers increase or decrease efficiency in the industrial insurance sector? Some argue that brokers have a very positive influence. They are forcing the industry to increase productivity and efficiency by intensified competition, more rapid product development and by increasing freedom of choice for the customer. Others have a more ambivalent attitude. They regard the brokers as an extra link, not adding any extra value to the product yet costing a lot of money. While initially they may contribute to increased competition and lower prices, over the longer term the broker is regarded as a conservative force which does not help the simplification of the insurance product.

In the US moves towards greater competition started much earlier than in Sweden. As a result the American market has a much broader range of insurance products, particularly within casualty insurance. At the same time, the power of an American buyer towards an individual insurance company is strong, thanks to the large number of competing firms. However, American buyers have not achieved the same degree of market deregulation as in other countries including Sweden. Regulation of the insurance system is a state concern, not a federal one and this legislation at a state level is regarded by many as a great obstacle to increased efficiency in the sector as a whole. The American civil justice system, with different laws in different states when it comes to handling matters such as indemnification claims, leads to a low degree of standardisation. By contrast, a high degree of standardisation and deregulation is considered to enhance the effectiveness of the insurance system. A proposal for federal liability, backed up many of the dominant insurance buyers (IBM for instance), was voted down by the Senate in September 1992.

According to well-informed observers, the influence exerted by American buyers on state legislation and the civil justice system is much less than in Sweden. In addition, the fact that Sweden as a small and extremely export-orientated country, is more dependent on the competitiveness of its export industry means that this industry's wishes usually enjoy a greater political impact.

Competition

The cartels started to break down in the US in the 1950s and 1960s and the influence of cartel or collective pricing has steadily fallen ever since. As a consequence competition has progressively increased. The market is highly fragmented due to state regulation, different civil justice systems and the competition presented by almost 1,000 nationwide companies.

There is also great competitive pressure from alternative markets. In the US the chief threat for the insurance companies in most cases is self-insurance, i.e. the company takes out no insurance at all or when it does the excess is very high. Self-insurance now accounts for approximately 30 per cent of the total market for industrial insurance, a share that is increasing. This leads to diminishing premiums and the frequent result is that the risks with the lowest claim costs disappear, leaving fewer and worse risks for which to compete.

At the same time there is a danger in excessive price competition, as insurance is a promise of future payment of all or part of the costs if a certain event occurs. A low price on a policy can indicate that the insurance company is not fully aware of the inherent risk. Furthermore if a company takes too many bad risks, there is an obvious danger that it will not be able to fulfil its commitments towards the buyer. In the US, insurance companies are collectively liable to fulfil the commitments of an insurance company going bankrupt. This might well lead to hazardous underwriting because both the seller and the buyer of the policy know that at the end of the day someone else will eventually pay for the losses incurred.

Among the reasons behind the extensive legislation controlling the property and casualty sector of the insurance industry is the desire to preserve competition and influence the pricing of the product, while at the same time ensuring that the insurance companies have made sufficiently safe risk assessments and loss reservations. Describing the US insurance system, one observer has stated: 'We [the American insurance industry] are handling an inefficient system in an efficient way'.

As noted above, competition in the Swedish market was, until the mid-1970s, fairly restricted due to Skandia's dominant position, regulation and the profitability of the industrial insurance industry. The main reason why Trygg-Hansa began to challenge Skandia in industrial insurance was that it found itself attacked in its core business (personal lines) by Skandia. The challenge was effected by way of price competition which led to rapidly falling prices: for example, the premiums paid by one of Sweden's leading forest companies fell by two-thirds between 1976 and 1981. It was also effected by new insurance applications and other solutions such as the establishment of so-called captives, retrospective rating etc. Increasingly demanding buyers asked for new insurance products and the traditional risk/fire engineer's role as a contact person *vis-à-vis* the customer was replaced by economists or technicians with financial competence.

The present competition in Sweden will be intensified with the ratification of the European Economic Area (EEA) agreement on international trade. This implies that European Community (EC) regulations for a single financial market will apply. It is based on the twin principles of one authorisation and home country supervision. Essentially this means that a company authorised in one country can operate in all other countries without further authorisation. Home country supervision means that wherever operations are carried out they shall be supervised by the home country's authorities. As the Swedish insurance companies consider their premiums low by international standards, they do not fear their market shares will be eroded due to the ratification of the EEA agreement. (Foreign insurance companies operating in Sweden currently have a 6 per cent market share compared to an EC average of 15 per cent.)

Economies of scale

Insurance is to some extent a commodity: this implies that the factor costs to deliver the product are of great importance. Three of the main cost components in an insurance product are:

- capital costs;
- salaries;
- technology.

What economies of scale are inherent within these three categories? One of the principal economies of scale is the size of funds managed: financial strength and financial issues such as quality of assets, data processing, leverage and adequacy of loss reserves are critical and will become even more so in the future. In fact the current direction and momentum of state and possible federal regulation, the pronouncements of politicians and the emergence of risk-based capital concepts, all suggest that we will see an even more rapid separation of the 'haves' from the 'have nots'. There are some that argue that financial strength and power will be the **only** determinant of success in the 1990s. They predict that in ten years the world insurance market will be dominated by a dozen international mega companies.

One of the foremost strengths of the Trygg-Hansa SPP Group is the size of funds managed. Totalling some SKr265 billion, Trygg-Hansa is one of the 20 largest insurance companies in the world and one of the five largest in Europe.

The acquisition of Home by Trygg-Hansa and the subsequent consolidation of its capital base provided Home with financial strength. S&P upgraded Home's rating for claims paying ability in 1991, a move which aroused great attention within the US insurance community in a year which saw very few upgradings and many downgradings. Furthermore, Home's upgrading was probably the largest S&P has effected for any one insurance company. It resulted in improved financial conditions and increased order volume, reflecting improved buyer confidence in Home's financial strength.

There are several other economies of scale such as those embodied in:

- information technology;
- marketing organisation;
- competence.

One of the main reasons why Home withdrew from personal lines was that it did not have sufficiently competitive information technology for standardised personal lines nor the financial resources to build up the extensive information systems needed for the huge personal lines business in the US. Trygg-Hansa, on the other hand, has, as one of the leading providers of personal lines in Sweden, committed significant resources to develop market-orientated information technology for personal and commercial lines.

The two companies are now devoting large resources to building up new information systems for increased efficiency and productivity within the production process for commercial lines. As commercial lines are generally a local business, a good distribution network is a prerequisite. For instance, Home has 30 regional offices throughout the US. Trygg-Hansa has four regional headquarters with a great number of smaller local offices. A geographically widespread organisation provides an important economy of scale, a necessity in order to reach the profitable and less competition-intense, medium-sized companies.

Both Trygg-Hansa's and Home's internationalisation strategy is also aimed at building up a global marketing network cost-effectively. This is to be achieved by seeking co-operation with companies with a similar marketing and management philosophy: in a later phase acquisitions/mergers will be considered. This strategy has already been fulfilled by AIG and Allianz which have established global networks within the industrial insurance sector, much in the same way as international accountants Arthur Andersen and Ernst & Young have done.

In a large organisation economies of scale in competence are obtained by employing expertise (e.g. underwriting) in many related areas. Similarly, training, information systems and international insurance competence etc. can be developed in a cost-effective manner.

The focus of Trygg-Hansa is to take advantage of prevailing economies of scale. The company is strongly committed to achieving a target expense ratio of 19 per cent. This is to be achieved by low operating costs via efficient use of modern information technology, and other resources such as a well-developed marketing network and a strong balance sheet facilitating prudent risk selection, i.e. a low-cost strategy to achieve cost superiority.

An efficient capital market

As the insurance industry often makes a technical (underwriting) loss, it is essential that it make a substantial profit on investment assets. Over the last 25 years in the US the technical income of the property and casualty insurance industry has been positive for only five years while the industry has made a net loss for three years. This implies that for 17 years, investment income has been sufficiently high to offset underwriting losses.

The presence of an efficient and profitable financial market is an external factor which strongly influences the pricing of insurance lines. Even in a year like 1991 when companies recorded a total underwriting loss of approximately US$20 billion, an investment income of US$32 billion outweighed this loss, resulting in a net profit of US$12 billion or 5.5 per cent of total premium volume. Similarly, Swedish insurance companies have, for several years, offset underwriting losses with a high investment income, generally resulting in a positive net income.

What influence a high capital yield will have on the efficiency of the insurance industry is much debated. Some argue that the intense price competition which has prevailed for many years is a consequence of a high capital yield. On the other hand, it can be asserted that for a long period the industry has not been forced to rationalise or increase productivity because the high capital yield has allowed the existence of low insurance premiums and high operating/claims costs at the same time.

Internal factors

As discussed earlier the financial ratios used to measure efficiency are the loss, expense and combined ratios. Which internal factors allow an insurance company to achieve a high premium income combined with a low loss and expense ratio?

The four principal internal efficiency-promoting factors are:

- vigorous and visionary leadership;
- a clear market strategy combined with focus on internal efficiency;
- competence;
- a financially strong, investment-orientated owner.

Leadership

AIG, the foremost international company in industrial insurance has, for 25 years, been managed by the legendary 67-year-old Hank Greenberg. He is viewed by many as a combination of a very vigorous visionary, entrepreneur and cost-cutter. But he is also acknowledged worldwide as one of the sharpest underwriters around. Members of AIG's management team generally have a long career within the company, a fundamental knowledge of the business and relatively high average age. Looking at Trygg-Hansa and Home, the same pattern can be observed although the average age of their managers is somewhat lower. In much the same way as Hank Greenberg, Lars-Göran Nilsson (Trygg-Hansa) and Jim Meenaghan (Home) are regarded as two of the most innovative and knowledgeable experts within their companies, and each has an extensive career in industrial insurance.

Apart from a profound knowledge of insurance the management style must also be vigorous, inspiring and strong. At the same time the environment must be stimulating, not too restricted or dominated by management, factors that can encourage employees to move to competitors. The management teams of Home and Trygg-Hansa are somewhat differently structured. Home's management team is fairly large: 15 vice-presidents reporting to the president, all of whom have a solid career in industrial insurance. Trygg-

Hansa the management team is considerably smaller, comprising individuals with more varied backgrounds, from big Swedish multinationals like Electrolux and Saab-Scania, for example. These different management structures can partly be explained by the respective strategies of the two companies. At Trygg-Hansa, Lars-Göran Nilsson holds overall responsibility for the group's internationalisation strategy, a strategy which demands visionary management. At Home, Jim Meenaghan's overall responsibility is to develop the company into one of the leading industrial insurance companies in the US, a task equally as challenging but leading to a more consolidated and structured management style.

Market strategy combined with internal efficiency

For Trygg-Hansa, with a large market share of the relatively homogeneous Swedish market, sophisticated market segmentation is not that important. Although they can and do exclude certain defined segments such as small, privately-owned saw-mills, some municipal real estate and certain types of industries, maintenance of their high market share (and the low share held by foreign competitors) necessitates their quoting on most types of business. However, while it is essential to underwrite good risks within large parts of the total market, the possibilities of underwriting only the good risks will diminish, the higher the market share the company achieves. One of the reasons for Trygg-Hansa's internationalisation strategy is that the management judges global expansion to be more profitable than an increased market share in Sweden. The acquisition of Home, a focus on overseas expansion, and the development of new products and services are thus some of the most important aims of the Trygg-Hansa SPP Group.

Precise (international) market segmentation and suitable partners will be two key components of this global strategy. Trygg-Hansa and Home's global market shares in industrial insurance are approximately 0.6 per cent: in order to be considered as one of the ten leading international insurance companies it is estimated that net premiums need to increase by a minimum of two to three times.

For Home however, precise market segmentation is essential due to the complexity of the market. The company's overall domestic market share in commercial lines is around 1.0 per cent, but within certain segments Home is the market leader. When Jim Meenaghan joined the company as president in 1986 one of his first moves was to change the firm's strategy. Whereas it had previously been an insurance company covering all types of risks for all kinds of corporations and individuals, the new strategy focuses on large, complex risks for large and medium-sized corporations: speciality lines covering complex risks for defined market segments such as doctors (medical malpractice), lawyers etc. (areas where true underwriting skill is needed) are also offered.

The strategy of focusing on specific market segments has been successful and the company's combined ratio has improved considerably from around 138 in 1985 (compared to an industry average of 117) to 109 in 1991, also better than the industry average. Through Trygg-Hansa's acquisition of Home, the ability to focus on large complex risks and speciality lines increased considerably, principally because of the improved capital base. Home's segmentation strategy fitted in well with Trygg-Hansa's internationalisation strategy. Furthermore, the interest expressed by potential European partners to co-operate with Trygg-Hansa in building a global industrial insurance network has increased considerably as a result of the acquisition of Home.

Regarding internal efficiency, and looking to the future, Home predicts that the 1990s will witness 'a game of margins', and that both producers and customers will, as in other industries, place more attention on cost-effectiveness.

Home has now left the personal lines market. Instead, it aims to be one of the leading players in commercial property and casualty insurance alongside AIG and Chubb. AIG and Chubb, however, have different market strategies. Chubb is investing in very sophisticated market segmentation and a high-class service, while AIG although not investing as much in services, is famous for its underwriting capability. It is regarded as a highly innovative company providing solutions to complicated insurance problems that no other company can or dares to solve. Both AIG and Chubb have a low combined ratio compared to the industry average, but they achieve it in different ways. Chubb does it via a low loss ratio but a fairly high expense ratio (35 per cent), AIG via a low expense ratio (22 per cent) but, compared to Chubb, a higher loss ratio. Both companies had a combined ratio just below 100 for the period 1987–1991, compared to an industry average of approximately 108. Home intends to position its business between these two. It has deliberately recruited underwriters from AIG and other aggressive companies and has recruited several top managers from Chubb and other companies with a high service standard for their service department.

Competence

The third factor promoting efficiency is competence development, a factor that will become an increasingly important asset in the future. To a large extent, market segmentation is a reflection of competence within the company. Home has pursued a systematic recruitment policy in both its underwriting and service departments. The manager for major accounts and commercial lines was recruited from AIG, and the manager for the service division (accounting for 55 per cent of total employees) was recruited from Chubb. Home's mission is to be pre-eminent in underwriting skill, and to provide cost-effective and quality services to support this strategy. Underwriting skill has two key components: technical skill and social skill. Social skill is important in that the underwriter acts as a salesperson towards brokers. A skilled underwriter ensures that the broker offers business in which he or she is interested. If a company wants to start a new business they must either have or recruit the required competence. Within Home there are several underwriters who have worked in AIG's international operations, which is consistent with Trygg-Hansa's globalisation strategy.

Competence development was described by Jim Meenaghan in a typically American way at a National Insurance Leadership Conference:

> The best companies in the 1990s will be those companies that have the best people, the best trained, best paid, most highly motivated people. Not only in New York but across the country in all field offices. People with knowledge, skill and authority to make decisions. There's no secret having superior people. You hire the brighter people, you pay them more than your competitors, you train them in a technical way on a continuing basis, you bonus them if they beat specific business objectives, you truly reward those that make money for you and in the end you dismiss those that can't or won't perform at a superior level. An organisation cannot rise above the level of its people.

Home has an extensive individual training programme for underwriters and other key knowledge workers. Linked to this is a monthly follow up of key knowledge workers' achievements regarding quality of work but also interpersonal skills, leadership qualities etc.

Within Trygg-Hansa international insurance competence is now being built up by training and recruitment. Together with Cranfield School of Management, a one-year international management training programme has started. The group is also running an extensive internal training scheme where employees receive an average of seven days' training each year. In the past Swedish insurance companies had plenty of joint training but this has now largely been replaced by in-house education. In co-operation with firms such as ABB and Volvo, a far-reaching project is also under way within Trygg-Hansa to identify and measure those intangible facets of leadership and competence development, leading to both improved commitment and results. A reward system is linked to the measurement of both hard and soft data, which will lead to a combination of increased efficiency and personal development.

In many of the interviews conducted for this study it was stated that knowledge of the distinctive character of insurance and the regulations in each market is of the utmost importance. As an example Home said they were pleased that Trygg-Hansa was their majority owner for several reasons: its strong balance sheet, knowledge of the American market and interest in discussing overall goals and strategy without wishing at the same time to interfere with daily operations. This is in contrast to several other foreign insurance companies who have acquired American firms, yet have insufficient knowledge of how the US market functions. They have run into serious financial problems because they have tried to introduce their own corporate management philosophy and method of operation into the American market.

Ownership structure

The ownership structure at both Trygg-Hansa and Home has changed, and the consequences for Home of Trygg-Hansa's acquisition have already been discussed above. In summary, however, the total financial investment for the Trygg-Hansa group in Home corresponds to US$700 million, making it one of the biggest US investments ever for a Swedish company. Through a special issue of new shares, equity was increased, loans taken over or replaced, and long-term investments in market development and information technology are in progress.

For the Industrial Insurance Division in Trygg-Hansa the situation is somewhat different. The division is part of Trygg-Hansa SPP Holding, a listed company with the two mutual life companies Trygg-Hansa Liv and SPP holding shares corresponding to 30 per cent of the voting rights. The other shares are owned by 800,000 shareholders, making Trygg-Hansa's share capital the most fragmented in Sweden. Discussions are now taking place as to whether this ownership structure is ideal. For a successful strategy of internationalisation it might be necessary to have a different structure. The present organisation is most convenient for Trygg-Hansa SPP Holding's operations on the Swedish market, but is not ideal for long term and financially demanding investments in global industrial insurance. At the same time one of the group's major strengths is the size of funds managed, totalling US$45 billion.

Together with some other well-known Swedish companies including Volvo, Trygg-Hansa is regarded as a management-controlled company where no single owner/group of owners has a distinct influence on the operations. It has also been stated by Trygg-Hansa that a financially strong national or international owner could be a suitable complement to the present ownership structure.

BARRIERS TO PRODUCTIVITY

As we have seen, some observers argue that within ten years the world market for insurance will be dominated by half a dozen to a dozen globally active giants. Accordingly, insurance companies must define their strategies. New competitive advantages in the marketplace need to be found, the potential benefits of information technology need to be utilised and, not least, companies must become more cost-effective. A far-reaching rationalisation is expected in which the largest companies will increase their market share at the expense of small and medium-sized groups. Trygg-Hansa estimates that in both Sweden and the EC the number of companies will shrink to around a third of the current total over the next few years.

External factors

Regulation

Institutional conditions can have a strong negative effect on efficiency: certainly the institutional framework of industrial insurance restricted competition and efficiency in Sweden until the 1980s. Today, however, the Swedish regulation system can be regarded as very liberal, essentially regulated by principles of financial strength, legitimacy and soundness. The principle of financial strength indicates, among other things, how claims reserves, deficiency reserves etc. shall be calculated and the margin by which a company's assets must exceed the technical reserves. (The latter is a collective term for the premium reserve, claims reserve and claims adjustment reserve.) The principle of legitimacy covers some common rules about premium legitimacy in terms of insured risk, company expenses and how claims should be handled and settled etc. The principle of soundness is linked to the licence to operate an insurance company: a licence is granted unless the planned enterprise is considered not to be consistent with the sound development of the insurance business. One main mission of the Financial Supervisory Authority is to grant licences, supervise and stipulate the rules for the insurance industry.

In principle there is no significant difference between insurance regulation in the US and Sweden. What differs is how these principles are applied in the two countries. In the US the authorities regulate the industry to a much higher degree, and in some cases stipulate and control the pricing of the product. As regulation is enforced at a state level a national insurance company has to adapt to 50 separate systems. As a result there is an ongoing battle between those who want regulation of at least commercial property and casualty insurance to be a federal concern and those who consider that increased efficiency is best achieved within the present state regulatory system. AIG has described the present state regulatory system in the following way:

> On the subject of insurance regulation the current state by state regulatory system is an expensive anachronism with little relevance for today's global insurance industry. In contrast to the fragmented regulatory climate we face in the United States, in the new European Single Market home country regulation and mutual recognition will be the rule. In our view a federal charter for commercial insurers with regulation limited to solvency only is a preferred option.

Advocates of the present system point to voluntary co-operation between some states (on reform and standardisation) and fear that federal legislation, together with modified legislation at state level, will lead to a more complicated legal structure than the present one.

One problem for authorities who wish to reform the regulatory system, however, is that it is politically very popular to propose more detailed rules for the insurance industry: it is also popular to interfere with the pricing of car and property insurance, for instance, particularly when there is a forthcoming election. The American state supervisory authorities employ many more civil servants for detailed supervision than their Swedish counterparts. In the state of New York, for example, which has one of the most liberal state regulatory systems, 1,400 civil servants are working to supervise and give information about insurance companies and insurance services. In Sweden, the government agency that oversees insurance matters has some 30 employees.

The legal environment

Litigation processes in the US are becoming more and more of a problem. The American preference for consumer activism and lawyers' contingency fees has taken many complicated cases of indemnification to the courts where the jury invariably decides that higher and higher indemnification costs should be paid. There is intense debate about the reform of the civil justice system. Referring to a five-year study commissioned by the American Law Institute, former Vice-President Dan Quayle stated in a speech to the American Bar Association's annual meeting in 1991.

The exorbitant costs of litigation is a drain on the US economy. Excessive litigation and its costs have a detrimental effect on the ability of US business to operate competitively with foreign business. The civil justice system is, at times, at a self-inflicted competitive disadvantage. Every year individuals and businesses spend more than US$80 billion on direct litigation costs and higher insurance premiums. When indirect costs are included the costs may add up to more than US$300 billion. If a portion of these billions of dollars now spent on litigation was redirected to develop and expand more income-producing segments of business, American business and eventually the consumer would benefit.

The same study also found that the US liability system penalises corporations by way of inconsistent and excessive awards for non-economic losses. It concluded that the civil justice system has to be reformed in many respects. Among the recommendations were the limiting of awards for pain and suffering to only the most severely injured plaintiffs, providing a scale to juries that could be used to determine dollar awards and having the legal fees of a successful plaintiff paid by the defendant. Another recommendation from the president's council on the competitiveness of the civil justice system was the use of alternatives to traditional litigation to settle a dispute, such as early neutral evaluation, mediation, arbitration and summary judgement trials.

Market fragmentation

Different state regulations and the civil justice system make the US insurance market highly fragmented. Insurance companies can select niches for property and casualty insurance in a much more sophisticated way than if there were common and simplified rules for handling casualty claims in particular. Even so, few changes are taking place, a situation which largely reflects the fact that those who earn a living from the prevailing system are numerous and influential, e.g. politicians, employees in state supervisory authorities, insurance companies, brokers, lawyers etc. The total number of employees working directly or indirectly for the insurance industry is approximately 2.1 million (including agents, brokers and service personnel).

Thus, far-reaching standardisation would lead to a more homogeneous market with a considerable reduction in employment. The individuals and organisations that would benefit from standardisation (the insurance buyers) are not a homogeneous group and, for them, insurance cost is a high though not a crucial expense. (In the US, expenditure for all kinds of insurance represents 5.6 per cent of all household spending.) At the same time, even if the large national insurance companies favoured standardisation of the different state regulations and a modernisation of the civil justice system, they have limited power to influence legislation, regulatory systems etc.

Internal factors

What internal factors are restraining Trygg-Hansa and Home from finding new competitive advantages, from using the *opportunities* afforded by IT and from becoming more cost-effective? There are three principal factors:

- the structure of the production process;
- departmentalisation;
- internal regulatory systems.

The production process

Certain insurance products are standardised where the statistical basis is solid and consequently premium quotations, risk provisions, the issuance of insurance policies and invoicing are automated to a large extent. In the case of a global insurance programme for a big multinational, however, the complexity is great – premium quotations etc. must be based on many individual and detailed calculations. Quotations are, in many cases, based upon intuitive judgements and the final price is settled after prolonged negotiations. The elapsed time between the first enquiry and the closing of the deal can be very long in cases where the matter is dealt with by several departments and people.

There are some explanations for this time-consuming procedure. Certain matters are complicated and need thorough investigation, calculation and negotiation. Another explanation is that the information technology prevalent in the 1970s and the 1980s has now become fairly obsolete and in many cases there exists little or no integration between different systems. A third reason is that in some cases the rating and tariff systems are based on obsolete or non-adapted statistics, and thus provide an insufficient foundation for risk assessment or premium quotation. Questioning the necessity of involving so many steps and people, however, is typically countered by the legitimate demands (in many cases) of precision and accuracy in risk selection, premium quotation etc.

Underwriting skill is also, to some extent, intuitive. Evaluation of the work of an underwriter or a risk engineer is difficult as results are not immediate: a rapid increase in market share can be a sign of bad underwriting. Both Trygg-Hansa and Home state that they have a conservative risk-assessment policy and give priority to profitability at the expense of market share. Because of the qualitative character of industrial insurance, those who are directly involved in the decision-making process (key knowledge workers) enjoy high status, whether the assessment is complicated or not, and cases are often handled much the same way in the production process. Renewals for instance will, in many cases, take almost as long as new contracts, despite the fact that 80 per cent of all contracts are renewals. In some extreme cases the time spent on marketing and investigations can cost as much as the premium. Efforts towards standardisation have sometimes met with great resistance because of a simplified product and production attitude from external data-processing experts with limited understanding of the qualitative art of industrial insurance. On the other hand it is obvious that many of the functions that are carried out manually today, or are processed in separate systems, can be automated and integrated.

Trygg-Hansa and Home are pursuing extensive IT projects to automate, integrate and increase efficiency in the production process. Home is working with a bench-marking IT project where the target is to match or even excel best industrial practice. Through ongoing projects, lead times will be shortened, quality improved and cost reductions made. Some of the changes in the production process are as follows:

Today	*Tomorrow*
Departmentalised assembly-line proccessing	Self-directed teams focused on outcomes
No integrated quality system	Quality integrated into processes and systems
Limited emphasis on issues that impact external sources	Non value added activities eliminated
No external communication	Communication with external sources

In a similar way Trygg-Hansa manages projects aimed at simplifying the production process, diminishing the number of process steps and shortening the lead times from request to issuance of an insurance policy. The problems are similar, i.e.:

- the different electronic data-processing systems are not integrated;
- the production process is sequential and extended in time;
- several departments and officers are involved;

- the tariff and rating systems are weakly linked and have little relevance to the premium quotation.

An interesting example of restructuring the production process is being implemented in one of Trygg-Hansa's European subsidairies. There they start from scratch building up new IT systems without consideration of existing systems within the group. The target is that immediately after closing the contract with the buyer, the salesperson/underwriter issues insurance policies, invoices etc. on his or her own portable terminal, resulting in considerable time savings.

Departmentalisation

Within an insurance company there are many specialists with different skills and aims. Underwriters often have an academic background in law, economics or technology. Risk and fire engineers generally have a technical background, while to handle the massive flows of information, highly skilled information experts are required. Furthermore, as the product itself is complex and the external and internal regulatory systems extensive, a high degree of inter-departmental understanding is required.

There are many examples of how insurance companies with a simplified view of industrial insurance have run into big financial problems as a result of not having correctly estimated the necessity of detailed underwriting: instead they have adopted inadequate rules of thumb. This can be devastating, particularly in the US, with its complex civil justice system. At the same time it is tempting for a specialist sector to constantly point out bad examples of standardisation because of complacency, and a fear of automation and simplification. None the less to an outsider it seems that many of the more standardised operations of an underwriter or other key knowledge workers could be automated with substantial gains in time and efficiency, and that the purely qualitative work involved in underwriting, claims control and customer service can be improved by IT. Different skills in different departments, however, can induce departments to focus on their own interests, resulting in much vertical, but inadequate horizontal, communication.

At Trygg-Hansa there was a dispute in the early 1980s between the traditional risk/fire engineers and some new more financially-orientated business people within the company. The dispute centred on whether insurance operations should be based on rules and tariffs established in the insurance industry or the customers' total need for insurance coverage including all kinds of risks. The businesspeople won the battle and several of them now make up the present management team within industrial insurance.

Both Trygg-Hansa and Home are aware of the potential problems associated with departmentalisation. They work actively to promote co-operation and understanding between the different departments. This is achieved by joint project teams working towards common goals, strategies, IT and training. Both companies are trying to transfer parts of the American or Swedish way of operating to the other company. One of the major advantages of the 'American way of operating' is said to be a greater focus on individual achievements, which among other things makes it easier to get things done according to plan and as agreed. The advantages of the 'Swedish way of operating' are said to include a less hierarchical working climate which leads to better co-operation in project and management teams, and a more open and innovative climate.

Within Home it is stated that the working climate will, to a greater extent, be more long term, team-orientated and based on common goals and values than was previously the case. In Trygg-Hansa there is a corresponding move towards 'individualisation' through increased focusing on individual goals and individual development.

Regulatory systems

In businesses which, to a great extent, are influenced by external regulations, there must also be internal regulations to adapt to external demands. It is necessary to create internal guidelines for underwriters' and risk engineers' authority and responsibility. It is also essential to continuously update, modernise and, if possible, simplify internal regulations and guidelines. To achieve this a general knowledge of insurance is needed. In the early 1980s Home had a top management team from other industries. They rationalised heavily according to their own experience and the result was devastating. Home's combined ratio rose drastically and its financial situation became considerably weaker. They rationalised the wrong way.

Within the industrial insurance sector it is a genuine problem to determine objective insurance grounds, particularly for casualty insurance in the US. How can the casualty premium for a prominent financial adviser or lawyer in New York be determined, for example?

Taken together, this implies that the internal regulatory system which is necessary and essential is easily achieved with rules and guidelines that are superfluous, unnecessary or obsolete. The very nature of insurance means it is easier to pay attention to one case that is improperly treated than perhaps ten cases where there has been too high a degree of caution. In this way an internal regulatory system can be created in much the same way as an external system. Tradition is important in this respect. Security and confidence are highly valued and are two of the key qualities of an insurance company. Cost-effectiveness, which is decisive in the long run and one of the cornerstones of the company's business, is looked upon by many as a more abstract virtue and not that important for the customer or the company. The tradition in many international manufacturing companies of continuously making comparisons with the best within the same and other lines of business – benchmarking – does not have the same tradition and impact in the insurance business.

4

POSTAL LETTER SERVICES

Authors: Claes Fritsch, Sven Söderberg

PTT POST, The Hague, The Netherlands
POSTEN BREV, Stockholm, Sweden

Two of the worlds's leading postal services in terms of quality and profitability are PTT Post in The Netherlands and Posten Brev, the letter-carrying unit of Sweden Post. Both countries have maintained price controls on postage and the operations of both companies are separate from the national telecommunications authority. In recent years both post offices have experienced stagnating letter volume and mounting competition, mainly from fax and electronic mail. The Swedish letter monopoly was recently abolished and the Dutch monopoly will be abolished too. Both companies have taken steps to lower their costs, improve their organisational structure and enter the electronic mail market.

Postal service is a very labour-intensive business, where one goal is to achieve economies of scale and therefore lower the cost per item. Productivity can be defined as the volume of mail per full-time equivalent employee, in relation to costs. Calculated in this way, PTT Post delivers 171,000 pieces of mail per employee, Posten Brev 147,000. One reason is that a larger share of the services provided by Sweden Post are of a more sophisticated kind. Another explanation is that Sweden is a sparsely populated country, while The Netherlands is densely populated.

About half the costs in both companies are generated by outbound mail shipments. Mail delivery costs are about twice as high in Sweden as in The Netherlands. In The Netherlands, households are closer together, and in apartment buildings the letter carrier leaves the mail in boxes inside the main door. Swedish households get their mail delivered through a slot in each apartment door. About one-third of mail distribution costs are attributable to sorting. Both companies are improving their productivity in this area by stepping up their use of automation.

Part of the cost difference is due to the more centralised organisational structure of PTT Post, with clearer profitability monitoring and more thorough measurements of operations. PTT Post knows how far its letter carriers walk, where they are etc. PTT Post is also willing to adopt scientific models to improve its operations. Sweden Post has a more decentralised organisation, with independent profit centres.

THE LETTER POST SECTOR

Information provision is of vital importance to national economies and, as a result, postal services are a public utility in most countries. Most governments find it necessary that every inhabitant and every company, including non-profitable thinly populated areas, has access to a reasonably priced postal system.

Postal services normally comprise:

- a collecting operation made by a network of mainly post offices and letter-boxes;
- a sorting operation, normally highly sophisticated technically;
- a distribution network, from letter-boxes to mail delivery;
- a network of post offices.

Services are generally provided in a monopolistic market structure. However, even monopolies are forced to change in response to:

- technical development of sorting machines, faxes etc;
- changes in customer demands, structure, urbanisation, the increase in mass mailings from big organisations etc;
- political decisions, for instance the regulation of postal rates has, in practice, decreased the rates in real terms, forcing the organisations in question to increase their productivity.

This chapter focuses on letter mail comprising:

- private mail;
- business mail;
- addressed direct mail;
- unaddressed direct mail;
- magazines and journals;
- newspapers.

In both countries the market for letters can still be seen as monopolistic although, as in the rest of the EC, the trend is towards greater competition. In The Netherlands there are a few small city postal organisations distributing letters, but their market share is less than 1 per cent. In Sweden a small company – City Mail – started to compete with Posten Brev in 1991 on written business messages in the central parts of Stockholm. The company's market share is hard to estimate but, in relation to total market volume, it is very low.

Licences

Postal services in almost every country are based on obligations and exclusive rights or licences.

PTT Post is the holder of the licence in The Netherlands.

Obligations

- to carry addressed postal items weighing up to 10 kg;
- to provide a daily nationwide service at uniform prices;
- to make tariff modifications within the tariff control system;
- to provide a national network of service points, including post offices;
- to form links with international postal networks.

Exclusive rights

- the distribution of letters weighing up to 500 g;
- the placing of letter-boxes in public places;
- the issuing and commercialisation of 'official' postage stamps.

Besides the services provided within the delivery, PTT Post is free to provide other services or products. Such services (logistics and courier services, for example) have to be supplied in a competitive market situation. In general, however, postal services cover collecting and sorting operations, a distribution network and a network of post offices.

Until December 1992, Sweden Post had a licence covering the following obligations and exclusive rights.

Obligations

- to carry addressed postal items up to 20 kg;
- to provide a daily nationwide service for mail, parcels and payments at uniform prices;

- to provide a national network for mail, parcels and payments;
- to form links with international postal networks;
- to make tariff modifications for 20 g letters in accordance with the resolutions of the government.

Exclusive right

- to provide regular distribution of letters and written or partly written messages at a fee, including extensive rights for stamps and letter-boxes.

In January 1993, however, this exclusive monopoly was abolished. This puts Sweden Post, as the first former monopoly post company in the world, in a fully competitive market position. A new law on postal services is planned by parliament late in 1993.

However, although its exclusive monopoly rights have been abolished, Sweden Post still has the same obligations, without any compensation from the government for maintaining a nationwide network.

The monopoly

In both countries the monopoly has a positive and a negative side. It is easy to be complacent in a monopoly situation which is, of course, negative. Lack of pressure for change makes it relatively easy for substitute products to enter the market, as for example the fax. Traditionally, public businesses in a monopolistic situation have not been particularly meticulous in measuring cost structures, normally due to the lack of pressure for change from the owners.

Another negative aspect due to cost structure obligations is, at least for Sweden, the fact that Sweden Post is obliged to guarantee postal services to all parts of the country – a vast area. This can also in some respects of course be regarded as a positive aspect for both society and for the image of the business; it may also be seen as an advantage from a competitive point of view.

On the positive side, monopolies facilitate the establishment of a financially and technically strong organisation, since competitors face a strong barrier to entry in order to build their initial distribution and sorting centre network.

Both Posten Brev and PTT Post are expecting, and working towards, a future without a monopoly or a reduced monopoly in conjunction with full competition for licences in either end of the mail distribution processes. Both organisations have devoted resources to survive and thrive in a future where new products and new businesses have taken over parts of the classic postal services.

88 Achieving Service Productivity

Cost structure

A company can choose a low cost strategy or a differentiation strategy to achieve sustainable competitive advantage. In a differentiation strategy, the focus is on achieving added value and therefore higher prices as well as higher margins, instead of increased volumes. In a low cost strategy, the goal is to achieve economies of scale with high volumes and therefore lower costs per item. (See Figure 4.1 below.)

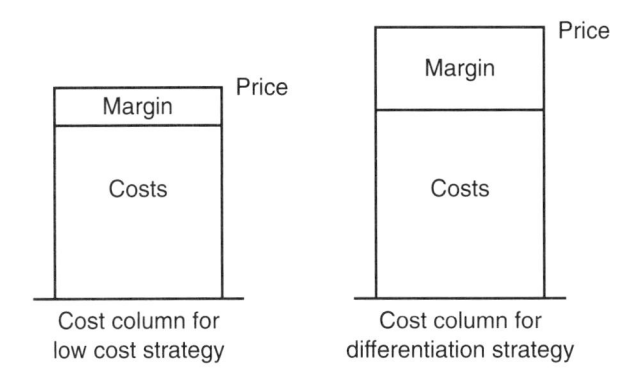

Figure 4.1 Strategy effects on costs and margins

Postal services are supplied according to a low cost strategy by which it is necessary to generate a high volume of mail. The focus is firmly on the process.

The position of PTT Post and Posten Brev on the cost curve in Figure 4.2 is somewhere on the right side of the curve where it is almost horizontal. A marginal increase or decrease in volume has little impact on the cost per item.

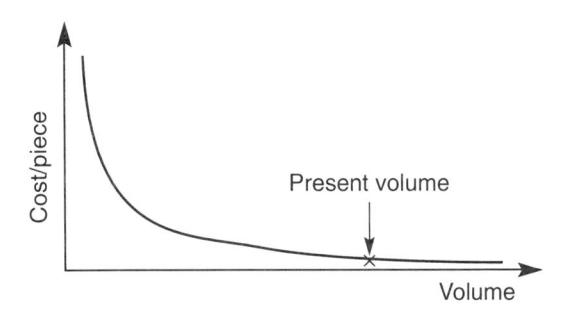

Figure 4.2 Cost/item and volumes in postal services

Traffic-related costs

The mail business is characterised by an infrastructure that can manage large volumes every day. It therefore has a cost structure that differs from 'normal' cost rules of economics. The cost behaviour in the mail business is dependent on how costs relate to traffic. 'Traffic-related' costs will differ from normal changes in volume.

Traffic-related costs refer to changes in fixed and variable costs at a micro level – the production process; they will differ from normal changes in volume.

For instance, given that around 85 per cent of all addresses receive mail each day, the cost of delivery will not increase very much with an increase in the volume of mail. The cost driver in that respect is if the number of delivery points increases.

As shown in Figure 4.3, as long as the actual volume of mail is within a certain band width, an increase in volume will have a minor effect on total costs and profitability increases will be almost proportional to volume increases. However, this also works in the opposite way; a decrease in volume of mail will have a strong negative influence on profitability.

This relationship can be illustrated by the following formula:

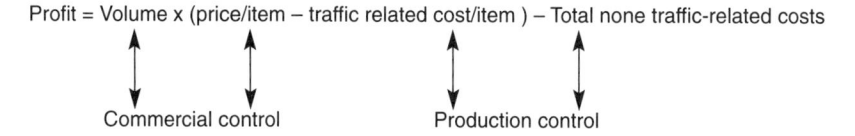

Profit = Volume x (price/item – traffic related cost/item) – Total none traffic-related costs

Commercial control ↕ Production control ↕

From a strategic point of view, a situation with increasing volumes means that the traffic-related cost per item has to be as low as possible, although

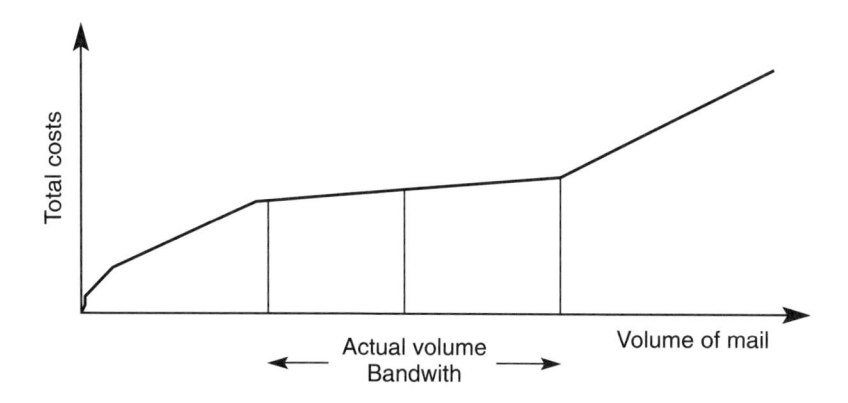

Figure 4.3 Total costs in relation to volume

total non-traffic-related costs can be relatively high. With declining volumes, total non-traffic-related costs must be reduced.

Price structure

During the 1980s real postage prices for 20 g letters in both Sweden and The Netherlands increased at a slower rate than prices overall.

In Sweden the price structure has been based on:

- content – until 1980;
- service level – since 1980;
- weight and shape.

Until 1 January 1993, postage rates were controlled by the government. Since that date Posten Brev has been free to modify tariffs in accordance with an upper limit related to inflation. Before forming the limited company this was also the situation in The Netherlands, but since 1989, PTT Post has been free to modify tariffs within limits set by the so-called tariff control system (TBS). The letter postage in Sweden was 2.80 Swedish Crowns (US$ 0.48) in 1992 and in The Netherlands slightly lower (approx. 2.70 SwCr).

Definitions

Productivity

Productivity is defined as volume of mail per full-time equivalent (FTE) in relation to costs. Differentiation can be made between sorting and delivering mail so that it is possible to see in which part of the production process improvements are made.

Quality

Quality may be assessed in different ways. It may be technical, objective quality which can be measured in processes. Examples are the percentage of mail that is delivered on time to the right address and the percentage of mail that is not damaged.

But there is more than technical quality. The objective of business is to satisfy customers, so it is necessary to know what aspects customers find important in judging the performance of the postal service. The scores on these aspects give a measure of customer satisfaction.

COMPANIES STUDIED

Historical development

PTT Post

The national decree establishing the postal service was not issued until 1799. Prior to this there were only regional postal services. The first Dutch Post Office Act was passed in 1807, making provisions for a monopoly to collect, transport and deliver mail, and stipulating that a single tariff should apply throughout the country. The result was considerably lower rates and a postal service which came to be regarded less as a source of revenue and more as a social institution. However, the poor state of government finances soon forced a change. Rates rose, services were cut and revenue once again became all-important.

The 1848 revolution led to a change of thinking, with the interests of the public assuming greater importance. This was reflected in the Post Office Act of 1850 which introduced a simpler and cheaper system of postal rates. Stamps were introduced in 1852 to cover delivery costs, the number of post offices and sub-offices rose sharply, and dispatch offices were set up in smaller towns.

The distribution network also expanded as increased use was made of the railways and the net effect was an increase in the number of letters from 5 million to almost 30 million between 1850 and 1870. The next two decades saw the introduction of new services such as postcards and parcel post and, in 1925, the postal service launched a completely new service: house-to-house delivery of unaddressed printed matter.

After the Second World War the organisation concentrated on becoming more commercial and less centralised. Part of the new commercial direction was the drive to monitor and improve efficiency. The level of mechanisation and automation increased, but most significant of all was the changed attitude towards the customer. In the past, customers had been offered a uniform product at a fixed price, regardless of whether they tendered one postal item or many. This changed in 1970 when varying products and rates were introduced for different customers.

This market segmentation confirmed that the postal service had evolved from a government service to a fully-fledged business. The shift in emphasis has been reflected in the formal status of the postal service since 1 January 1989, when the postal side of the state-owned enterprise became PTT Post BV, an operating company of Royal PTT Nederland NV.

Sweden Post

The origins of Sweden Post can be traced back to the seventeenth century, while the eighteenth and the nineteenth centuries saw the gradual introduction of restrictions in the rights to distribute letters. In 1947 Sweden Post was granted the exclusive right to distribute letters.

The 1950s and 1960s saw a number of changes reflecting increased urbanisation and efforts to reduce costs. For example, a large number of post offices were closed and replaced by rural postmen.

The 1970s saw further rationalisation, and a programme of productivity and quality improvements was implemented. During this period Sweden Post changed from an authority to a customer-orientated company, a change expressed in the division of the Post into the distribution business and the counter, bank and giro business.

More recently, the development of printing and copying techniques made it increasingly difficult to regulate the monopoly, and in 1981 pricing in accordance with content was abolished and replaced by pricing in accordance with service levels. Such developments have been influenced by requirements that Sweden Post earn a profit and that investments be financed with assets generated by the business itself.

During this century volume has steadily increased by an average of 3–4 per cent per year. At the beginning of the 1950s Swedish Post distributed about 1,500 million items per year and, by 1991, volume had risen to 4,277 million items.

Mission statements

PTT Post aims to provide a collection, sorting and distribution network for mail, goods, services, security items, and related products and services for national and international private and business customers. Transport services required for the collection and distribution network is a derived product and does not constitute core business. The company provides a service partly as a unique obligation – including exclusive rights – and partly in competition with private carriers.

Sweden Post's business concept is to deliver letters, parcels and payments throughout Sweden and internationally, and to offer financial services to enable everyone to reach everyone else, and to support the businesses of its customers.

Revenue trends

Despite predictions of a paperless office in future, mail volume has increased in recent years.

The revenue of PTT Post has increased, not only because of the increase in volume, but also due to higher prices. In 1991, for example, there was a general rise in postal rates, while revenue increased by 5 per cent in the same year. Business mail (excluding financial institutions) and Direct Mail experienced the largest growth.

The revenue of the mail service in 1991 was US$170 M: mail services account for 65 per cent of the revenue of PTT Post.

The following medium-term developments are predicted.

- Replacement of business correspondence by fax and Electronic Data Interchange (EDI).
- A stagnation and decline in financial traffic, reflecting fewer statements and the placing of statement printers in bank branches. As a result, customers have to collect their statement from the branch rather than receiving it through the post.
- Continued expansion of the direct mail market, but at a slower rate; opportunities for further growth will be limited by tough competition. It is expected that there will be a lot of small, high-quality mailings instead of fewer, bulk mailings.
- Saturation in the magazine market, plus, as a result of a fall in advertising revenue, a lower average weight per periodical.
- The development of new products. For instance EDI provides the opportunity to supply services for distributed printing. This means that a customer delivers the mail in an electronic format and PTT Post handles the printing, enveloping and, of course, the delivery. In this way the postal service can add value to products.

In the late 1980s the demand for Posten Brev services increased by 5 per cent per year, but now it is stagnating. In 1991 there was zero growth in letter volume and a 2 per cent decrease in revenues (fixed prices). The recession, increased use of the fax and the collapse of the Swedish financial and real estate markets are the main reasons behind this trend. Furthermore, because of the continuing recession during 1992 and 1993, Posten Brev is expecting a continued fall in sales.

The revenue of the mail service in 1991 was US$150 M. Posten Brev accounted for 63.5 per cent of the revenue of Sweden Post that year.

The following medium-term developments are predicted.

- Increased use of fax and EDI (indirect competition) which will affect the market for Posten Brev negatively, plus deregulation which will increase direct competition.

94 Achieving Service Productivity

- New product development, for example EDI as described above. In Sweden electronic mail is called ePost and has already been implemented by Posten Brev.
- Greater mail volume due to increased use of marketing mail and address databases.
- Deregulation of the TV and radio business which will generate more mail due to greater commercial activity in the media.
- Increased competition in the bank and insurance businesses, deregulation of the social insurance systems and a larger role for trade unions during the 1990s will generate more commercial mail.

Personnel

PTT Post

The postal service is a very labour-intensive business. PTT Post employs 62,000 people, who are equivalent in working hours to 36,400 full-time equivalents (FTE). The letter division employs 53,600 people, in 33,600 FTE. Absence through illness is higher than the national average, but is declining: hours lost due to illness accounted for 7.2 per cent of total working hours in 1991. In the same year, the average cost per FTE was US$26,600 per year, while the average cost for an employee in the production process was US$25,700. These figures include salaries, taxes and costs of commuting.

Gross working hours at PTT Post amount to 2,087 hours per year of which two-thirds (1,382) constitute net productive hours. This breaks down as follows.

Table 4.1 Working hours at PTT Post

Items	1991 average Number of hours reduction	Total figure
Working hours per year		2,087
Reduction in hours[1]	104	
Illness	151	
Holidays/public holidays/special leave	260	
Training/work meetings/planning etc.	60	
Total number of unproductive hours	705	
Net productive hours		1,382

[1] The reduction of working hours at PTT Post is called ATV. In the negotiations with the unions companies in The Netherlands have decided that their employees have to work 38 hours per week, although they get paid for 40 hours per week. The objective is to create more jobs because then each FTE is 13 days less per year.

Posten Brev

Sweden Post employed a total of 67,300 people in 1991 in 56,400 FTE; Posten Brev employed 40,100 in 29,100 FTE. The average costs for a FTE in Posten Brev in 1991 was US$39,200, including salary and general payroll taxes. In contrast to PTT Post, however, absence through illness is lower than the national average; it is also declining. As a percentage of total working hours, however, the proportion lost to illness is higher at 8.6 per cent.

The gross working hours at Posten Brev have been defined as 2,087 hours per year to make the figures comparable with the Dutch figures. This breaks down as follows.

Table 4.2 Working hours at Posten Brev

Items	1991 average Number of hours reduction	Total figure
Working hours per year		2,087
Illness less than 14 days	100	
Illness above 14 days	80	
Total illness	180	
Childcare	52	
Holidays and public holidays	321	
Training etc.[1]	64	
Total number of unproductive hours	617	
Net productive hours		1,470

[1] The training figure is probably too low.

Comparison of the above two tables highlights certain differences. For example:

- in a labour-intensive industry like the mail business, a difference of more than 6 per cent in the amount of net productive hours (1,470 at Posten Brev, 1,382 at PTT Post) is significant;
- differences in absence due to illness are quite high (8.6 per cent at Posten Brev, 7.2 per cent at PTT Post), which can be partly explained by social welfare regulations.

However, the above should be considered in the light of differences in definitions and how personnel productivity is measured. At Posten Brev, in particular, there are opportunities to improve the personnel data-collecting process to make the data a better tool for cost and productivity control. It is also impossible to make conclusions as to how the two organisations utilise their net productive hours, i.e. the proportion that is actually used for direct labour.

Profitability

PTT Post is a profitable company; in 1991 profits were 7.3 per cent of turnover. The letter division, which is directly comparable to Posten Brev, accounts for the major share of the profit.

Posten Brev is also a profitable business; 1991 profits were 6.7 per cent of turnover.

Distribution network

PTT Post has a very dense distribution network, as reflected in the following figures:

- 2,373 post offices of which 1,162 are sub-post offices. The number of post offices includes 45–50 mobile facilities which offer almost all PTT Post services one or more times a week in the areas they serve;
- 6,225,000 delivery points, of which 1,530,000 are in apartment buildings;
- 19,000 postal rounds;
- 672 delivery offices, including 168 presorting centres and 12 mail interchange centres;
- 275,000 PO boxes in over 2,000 locations and 18,350 letter-boxes;
- 4,500 motor vehicles, 33 trains and 66 mail wagons.

Posten Brev has a very extensive network of distribution channels, including the following:

- 1,800 post offices, and about 200 entrepreneur post offices. The post offices are a part of the business area known as bank and counter services. Posten Brev buys services from bank and counter services;
- 2,700 rural delivery routes. The rural delivery routes offer almost all postal services, e.g. bank and counter services, postal giro services and parcels;
- 8,300 city postal districts;
- 4,200,000 delivery points;
- 240,000 post office boxes and about 40,000 letter-boxes;
- 12,000 city postmen and 4,000 rural postmen;
- 8,000 motor vehicles, 29 mail wagons and three aeroplanes, which are owned by Sweden Post. In addition, Posten Brev buys services from Swedish Railways (SJ) and airline companies

FACTORS INFLUENCING PRODUCTIVITY

External factors

New technology

Technological developments provide both opportunities and threats. The opportunities lie mainly in the optimisation of the production process. New technologies (e.g. optical character recognition) can create cost savings, while more advanced databases detailing current and potential customers provide opportunities for direct mail promotions.

But there are also serious threats. The introduction of the fax, electronic banking, E-mail and EDI, have increased the use of electronic information while growth in the volume of physical information has stagnated. Furthermore, the use of the fax is increasingly a substitute for letters. Posten Brev has taken advantage of this technical development and has introduced a hybrid product, ePost. The ePost product is a letter, transported via a modem to a local printing centre, where it is printed, put in an envelope and distributed.

Regulations

In The Netherlands, postal services are bound by strict regulations detailed under the obligations and exclusive rights itemised above. In Sweden the monopoly for letters has been abolished, but the obligations still remain.

The European Commission has issued a document on the development of the single market for postal services: its aim is to stimulate discussion about postal services. It represents the opinion of the EC countries, although there is no official regulation concerning the issues as yet.

The main theme of the document is harmonisation and liberalisation. It calls for a *universal service* to be defined and safeguarded, enabling postal administrations to fulfil their public obligation to provide a good postal service between all citizens and businesses, both within each country and across borders. It would allow the establishment of a range of *reserved services* conferring exclusive rights on national postal administrations. These would broadly include personal and business correspondence, with clear limits defining the precise scope of the reserved area in terms of weight and price. The scope of the reserved area would have to be strictly proportional to the need to maintain a universal service. Other postal services would be outside the reserved area and will be opened to competitors in future.

National importance

The national importance of the postal service has had both a positive and a negative impact in the two countries. It was probably the first infrastructure to be built up, is highly visible and, as a result, the emphasis is on ensuring service levels rather than increasing profit. On the negative side there is a built-in tendency to disregard facts on the cost side, and a reluctance to create new business and revenues. Being highly visible has meant that both post offices have not been able to differentiate prices. Private letters have a limited influence on revenue but a significant influence on creating the image of the business. Hence pressure for change on the cost side of the letter business.

The positive side, as mentioned above, started with the drive towards monopoly. But a monopoly does not encourage a mean and lean organisation. As a result, this positive driver turns, over time, into the seed of its own destruction.

Market share

There are several different types of mail. For some products PTT Post and Posten Brev are the only official supplier in each country, but other products face serious competition.

For example, in the private and business mail sectors, the market share of PTT Post should be 100 per cent, but because of the existence of city delivery services and self delivering it is slightly less. In the case of magazines and journals, while PTT Post and Posten Brev are the main distributors in each country, there are some strong competitors.

Respective market shares in the newspaper sector, however, are much lower. In The Netherlands newspapers are mainly distributed by the publisher,

Table 4.3 Estimated market share

Estimated market share of Posten Brev and PTT Post and the share of revenue for each product segment 1991

Market segment	Estimated market share in % Posten Brev	PTT Post	% revenue in the letter business Posten Brev	PTT Post
Private mail	100	98	9	7
Business mail	99	98	61	63
Direct mail	98	98	15	18
Unaddressed mail	55	19	7	2
Magazines and journals	98	62	6	9
Newspapers	10	4	2	1
			100	100

while in Sweden, they are mainly distributed by newspaper delivery firms in urban areas to ensure early morning delivery: in rural areas newspapers are delivered by Posten Brev.

Competition

Competition will increase in future due to changes in and liberalisation of regulations, the disappearance of borders within the EC and because of an increase in the relative importance of non-licence/substitute products (fax, EDI etc.) and the growth of city delivery services.

There are about 100 city delivery services registered in The Netherlands. The companies change frequently but a hard-core of 25 per cent account for less than 1 per cent of mail traffic nationwide. They operate mainly at the local or regional level and their customers are usually local institutions and small businesses. With the exception of the Christmas/New Year period, private individuals make only sporadic use of city delivery services. The remaining 75 per cent of these operators are active on an irregular basis or restrict themselves to courier services and one-off campaigns.

In Sweden a small company – Citymail – with approximately 200 employees established itself in Stockholm in 1991 and started to attack the market for computer-generated business letters. Citymail operated only within Stockholm and had about 4 per cent of the market within that area before it went bankrupt in 1992. It has since been reorganised, but its current market share is not known.

Customer satisfaction

There have been major changes in customer behaviour in the 1980s and 1990s: customers are becoming more critical and want more choice. In the 1970s the supply of postal services was very limited, but increased customer demand has led to substitutes and competing services.

In a monopolistic market, however, customer retention is not a good indicator of customer satisfaction, although as competition in the market increases, retention will probably become a good future indicator.

Both organisations have introduced systems for measuring customer satisfaction. At PTT Post the system is called the Quality Meter and at Posten Brev, the Customer Satisfaction Index.

At PTT Post, the major factor determining private customer satisfaction is delivery, specifically delivery at the right address, reliability, the number of letter-boxes and the percentage of damaged mail. Other less important factors include information supply, complaints handling and the post offices.

100 Achieving Service Productivity

The major factors accounting for business customer satisfaction include delivery, information supply and complaints handling. Other specific factors include reliability of delivery, delivery at the right address, number of days between collection and distribution, billing and clarity of information. Less important are business counters, post offices and staff behaviour.

At Posten Brev the major factors accounting for private customer satisfaction are, in rank order: reliability; price; delivery; information; supplied services; availability; stamps; mail shop.

The major factors accounting for business customer satisfaction are, in rank order: reliability; enquiries; price; service levels; availability; supplied services; mail shop; information.

Macro factors

The key data summarised in Table 4.4 affect both the productivity and quality of the letter service in each country.

Table 4.4 Key figures: external factors

Key figures: 1991	The Netherlands	Sweden
Area in km^2	41,500	410,900
Inhabitants per km^2	446	21
Population (million)	15	8.6
% of inhabitants in the three largest urban areas	18.6%	31%
Number of companies	713,000	568,000
GNP per capita	US$19,300	US$25,900
Number of households	6,185,000	3,670,000
One person households	30%	36%
% of inhabitants in workforce[1]	43%	52%
Unemployment rate (mid-1992)	4.4%	4.4%
Volume of mail per inhabitant	383	498
Volume of mail per household	966	1,165

[1] Workforce – The Netherlands: 15–64 years of age
 Workforce – Sweden: 20–64 years of age.

The effect of these macro, external factors is summarised below.

- Significant differences in population density gives PTT Post the advantage concerning network productivity – organisation of sorting centres and delivery etc. – in comparison with Posten Brev.

- The geographic distances in Sweden also put Posten Brev at a disadvantage since it is forced to use air transport for overnight delivery, increasing relative production costs. By contrast, the longest distance in The Netherlands takes only three hours by train.

- Volumes of mail per inhabitant and per household are higher in Sweden (30 per cent and 20 per cent respectively): this might reflect higher usage of direct mail and mail order, but there are no figures to confirm this. If this is true, however, it means that in this case geographic distance is an advantage to Posten Brev, as customers have a longer distance to travel to the shops. The higher volume of mail per household in Sweden also gives Posten Brev a relative advantage in delivery costs.

Process issues

In addition to the above, macro, factors a number of external process issues also affect productivity and quality.

Table 4.5 Process issues; external factors

Extrenal process issue	PTT Post	Posten Brev
1. Regulations Higher pressure for renewal at Posten Brev	Regulated	Deregulated since January 1, 1993
2. New Technologies Higher utilisation of new technology for product development at Posten Brev	Moderate stake on electronic data interchange. New technology used mainly for increasing internal efficiency	High stakes on EDI and hybrid mail due to competition from substitutes
3. National importance Pressure for efficiency that gives low costs. Conservative effects, especially in Sweden on changes in the postal infrastructure	High visibility	High visibility
4. Customer needs	Highly standardised products with local variations in secondary service.	High market orientation due to decentralised responsibility for customers, but still a need for using highly standardised products.

The effect of the above factors may be summarised as follows:

- Posten Brev has been completely deregulated, while retaining responsibility for keeping the infrastructure. This should increase the pressure for change compared to PTT Post;
- it appears that PTT Post has used new technology mainly for increasing internal efficiency;
- utilisation of new technologies in product development appears to be higher at Posten Brev;
- both organisations are highly visible locally;
- it appears that Posten Brev has developed a high sensitivity market orientation with decentralised responsibility for customers, but still using highly standardised products. PTT Post uses highly standardised products.

INTERNAL FACTORS

Cost analysis of the value chain

PTT Post

Depending on the type of customer – private or business – mail is collected from postboxes, business counters at the sorting centres, post offices or from customer sites. Mail posted in a postbox must be prepaid with stamps. Mail delivered by business customers at the post office or at the business counter does not have to be prepaid. Payment can be made later on account.

After collection the mail is transported via presorting centres to 12 mail interchange centres where it is sorted automatically and/or by hand for delivery to households, postboxes and businesses.

The costs of this process are broken down in Table 4.6.

Table 4.6 Cost distribution in the production process at PTT Post

	Transport (5%)	
Collection (10%)	Sorting (35%)	Delivery (50%)
Inbound shipments	Operations	Outbound shipments

Posten Brev

The company serves private customers, small and medium-sized companies, and big enterprises. The mail is collected from postboxes, post offices,

Postal Letter Services

business counters at sorting centres and from customer sites. The payment systems used are stamps, postage-paid and postage-free marks or postal franking machines. The mail is transported to outward centres where it is sorted according to the first two digits of the postal code. Mail which is not local is transported to other parts of the country while local mail is transported to inward sorting centres for delivery to post offices. Table 4.7 provides a breakdown of these component costs.

Table 4.7 Cost distribution in the production process at Posten Brev

	Transport (9%)	
Collection (12%)	Sorting (28%)	Delivery (51%)
Inbound shipments	Operations	Outbound shipments

As can be seen from Tables 4.6 and 4.7, transport costs incurred by Posten Brev are almost double those at PTT Post. The figures also stress the need to focus on the delivery side, which accounts for about half of total costs in both organisations. There are, however, substantial differences between PTT Post and Posten Brev in the relative costs for specific operations in the process:

- payment with franking machines is five times more expensive at PTT Post;
- collection from postboxes is 70 per cent more expensive at Posten Brev;
- intermediate regional transport is nine times more expensive at Posten Brev;
- manual sorting for delivery is approximately twice as expensive at PTT Post;
- the urban delivery operation is twice as expensive at Posten Brev;
- delivery at post office boxes is approximately twice as expensive at PTT Post.

There are, of course, some very obvious explanations for these differences. For example, in The Netherlands, 85 per cent of the delivery points in apartment buildings are downstairs, which explains part of the difference in the cost of urban delivery. Some of the difference could also be explained by different methods of measuring costs and also quality in the two organisations.

Quality management

Posten Brev and PTT Post have long striven hard for high quality in their operations. The quality approach helps people to focus on the important

104 Achieving Service Productivity

issues when the operations affect customer values (externally and internally) as well as costs.

The data in Table 4.8 illustrate a single important measure – the percentage of first-class/24-hour mail delivered on time to the right address.

Table 4.8 Change in technical quality first-class/24-hour mail delivered on time

Change in technical quality: first-class/24-hour mail delivered on time to the right address

Year Measure	1991 S	NL	1990 S	NL	1989 S	NL
National letters	95.6%	88%	94.7%	87%	92%	91%
Regional letters	98.1%	93%	98%	92%	97.2%	95%
Average national and regional letters	96.6%	90%	96%	89%	94.1%	93%

It is apparent that whereas quality (according to this measure) has been improving in Sweden similar progress has not been achieved in The Netherlands.

In comparison with manufacturing industries this performance is not particularly impressive; however industrial processes are, to a large extent, deterministic and machine controlled. By contrast, a service industry relies on the human element whose flexibility at best absorbs failures and at worst aggregates them along a value chain. Additional issues affecting mail distribution in this context are circumstances outside the control of the business, for example delayed and cancelled airline flights due to bad weather.

PTT Post

Sorting and distribution: until recently PTT Post used a quality measurement system that took only objective facts into account. This was done by a market research agency and/or PTT Post itself. Variables that were measured were:

- mail delivered on time;
- mail delivered to the right address;
- mail delivered on time – specified by product segments;
- percentage of damaged mail.

Analysis of the first two criteria is summarised in Table 4.9.

Table 4.9 Mail delivery quality and mail delivered to right address: PTT Post

Mail delivered on time – by product: PTT Post (%)

	1990	1991
Financial institutions	93	94
Remaining business mail	92	92
Private mail	90	89
Magazine market	99	96

Mail delivered to right address (%)

	1990	1991
Delivered to right address	99	99

Customer satisfaction/quality: from 1993, PTT Post will conduct surveys of customer satisfaction (ratings will be published quarterly in the form of a Quality Meter), while to increase the quality of the process and the organisation, it is going to work according to international quality standard ISO 9002.

The International Standardisation Organisation drafted standards in the 1980s and The Netherlands has used ISO 9002 since 1985. Companies with this certificate comply with internationally accepted quality standards. If an office of PTT Post (pre-sorting centre, sorting centre, delivery office etc.) meets the standard, PTT Post employees from the region award it an internal PTT Post certificate. If all post offices receive the certificate, PTT Post will apply for the official ISO 9002 designation. In addition a quality training programme has been implemented.

Posten Brev

Sorting and distribution: quality in the sorting and distribution processes is checked with test letters and resultant measurements are published internally. Some interesting measurements, besides first-class/24-hour mail delivered on time, are presented overleaf.

Other systems used for measuring and monitoring quality in the distribution processes are as follows.

- Cost of quality – a system for measuring and budgeting a limited number of the most serious quality failure cost elements. The system is integrated with financial monitoring procedures.

Table 4.10 Mail delivered on time, by product: Posten Brev

Second-class mail delivered on time to the right address: Posten Brev (%)

Type	1990	1991	1992
National letters	89.7	91.9	94.7
Regional letters	97.8	98.3	97.9
Average of national and regional letters	93.6	95.0	96.2

First-class mail with handwritten addresses delivered on time to right address

Type	1992
Weighted average	96.5
National	95.4
Regional	98.0

- On-line quality report systems – covers delays in transport, mail remaining and sorting errors.

In addition to the above measures, Posten Brev has devised a Customer Satisfaction Index to set objectives and monitor the degree of customer satisfaction. Quality training has been conducted since 1988 and quality audits are conducted in the regions as well as at headquarters.

Posten Brev has also initiated a process aimed at building up and documenting its quality system in accordance with ISO 9001 and the National Award of Quality.

Organisation

The organisational concept by which people's efforts are directed towards a common goal tells a lot about how the organisation wants to achieve its mission and objectives. A highly decentralised organisation tries to maximise local initiative and enthusiasm in contacts with customers. A highly centralised organisation tries to keep control over important aspects of their products or services.

To understand variations in productivity, quality and effectiveness, it is important to analyse differences in organisational development and structures.

Table 4.11 Overview of the organisational changes at PTT Post

Organisational development: PTT Post

Period	Main problem	Solution
To 1945	Lack of efficiency in daily operations	Taylorism (harder work and detailed planning in processes). Introduction of night transports by train and truck
The 1950s	Lack of business control	Formation of 12 postal regions
The 1960s	Lack of cost control	Cut back in delivery from twice a day and automation in the production process
The 1970s	Growing market but no pay off	Differentiation of products and tariffs for different customers
The 1980s	Business differentiation creating cost of complexity	Volume orientation and focus on revenue
1986–1989	Not enough freedom for policy-making	Formation of state-owned limited company
1990s	Declining volumes and rising costs. Risk for decreasing profit	Formation of business units to increase market orientation and apply better cost control

Table 4.12 Overview of organisational changes at Sweden Post

Organisational development: Sweden Post

Period	Main problem	Solution
To 1965	No real cost control related to output. Need for structural changes in the network	Establishment of the commercial bureau. Decentralised budgeting process. Monitoring of earnings. Structural changes in the network
1965–1976	'Business as usual'	–
1976–1979	Lack of financial control	7 districts -> 7 regions. 60 postal areas with responsibility for production costs and productivity improvement
1979	Complexity of financial results	Division of accountability for financial results between distribution and counter services.
1983	Lack of focus in business operations. Need to get closer to the market and push responsibility downwards	Decentralisation by eliminating one level of organisation. 7 regions -> 33 regions. Earnings analysed according to product areas.

108 Achieving Service Productivity

Period	Main problem	Solution
1987	Complex situation of management from HQ-level point of view. Quality problems	2 business areas -> 5 business areas. Introduction of a new business planning tool (LOTS) and total quality management
1991	Unsatisfactory productivity improvement	Formation of regions in each business area to get closer to the customer and to keep cost control within each business
Future trends	Competition in a deregulated market. Adaptability Market and earnings orientation	Formation of a limited corporation, living under 'normal' market conditions

Restructuring

PTT Post

To further improve productivity an extensive reorganisation of the letter division has been planned. The sorting of letter post will undergo major changes to be more efficient, a process that must be finished by the end of 1998. More than half of all processing and sorting is currently done by hand which, combined with annual wage increases and rising inflation, means that the profit of PTT Post will decrease over time. In the longer term, fewer and fewer letters will be sent, and the mail-sorting process will require fewer people using less space. Savings generated by the new sorting method will be 'enormous': 175 MUS$ per year, plus 5,150 jobs, most of which can be achieved by means of natural attrition. In addition, space required to process mail will decrease from 530,000 m^2 to 380,000 m^2.

After 1998, all letter mail will be sorted to the level of the postal round at one of the six hubs – large mail interchange centres with fully automatic sorting for 98 per cent of mail. Reorganisation will eliminate the need for presorting. The present sorting and cancelling machines will be adapted to meet the new requirements and OVIS machines (OCR Video Indexing Systems) will read and index standard and non-standard mail.

Posten Brev

The pressures for productivity increases are very heavy. The main changes are as follows.

- Restructuring of the terminal network: the number of sorting centres will be reduced from 56 to approximately 15 which will be very dependent on modern production and planning systems. Other prerequisites are machine sorting, high logistical focus and quality control systems to minimise cycle times and quality failure costs in the sorting and transport activities. The network of 15 sorting centres plus increased machine sorting will make it possible to rationalise the sorting processes substantially.

- Profit centres: Posten Brev is planning to organise most of its activities into decentralised profit centres. This will (in theory) give staff financial inducements and the motivation to work more efficiently.
- Restructuring the transport network: parcel and letter flows will be separated, which will affect the transport organisation substantially, as well as the restructuring of the terminal network.
- Implementing ePost production: the ePost product will be further developed, affecting the production system and making it possible to rationalise the sorting and transport processes in the future.
- Changing the piecework system in the delivery operation: Posten Brev is changing the piecework system and working time calculations in the delivery operation to raise productivity.
- Reducing quality failure costs: by monitoring quality failure costs, productivity and quality will be improved.

Headquarters restructuring

At PTT Post, indirect costs account for around 25 per cent of total costs. These include all the costs that are not directly attributable to the production process, for instance the cost of headquarters, regional offices and all other administration.

The formation of business units will have implications for the role and organisation of the head office. A small headquarters with 75 to 100 employees will be established and the remaining employees – approximately 1,000 at present – will be transferred to other parts of the organisation, including the business units. The headquarters will assume the role of strategic controller – monitoring the operation of and relationship between the business units.

At Posten Brev the percentage of administrative working hours in relation to net productive hours in 1991 was about 10 per cent; this includes the headquarters and regional offices. In addition, there are other activities which are administrative, but current monitoring systems do not provide appropriate information regarding true indirect costs.

The implementation of business areas has also affected headquarters organisation in Sweden Post. Responsibility for product development, finan-

110 Achieving Service Productivity

cial control, production structure and quality control lies in each business area. In addition there are corporate units that co-ordinate financial control, information (communication), strategy development, security, insurance, personnel and quality management.

A rationalisation project was conducted at Sweden Post headquarters, the central units for each business area, the corporate units and central service units (data processing, payroll etc.) during 1992. A new organisation was implemented at the beginning of 1993 which will involve a reduction in headquarters staff by approximately 25 per cent.

Other internal factors

The data in the table below summarise the key internal measures affecting productivity in each company.

Table 4.13 Financial ratios: internal factors

Key figure – 1991	PTT Post	Posten Brev
Net productive hours	66.2%	70.4%
Average cost per employee	US$26,600	US$39,200
Labour cost per productive hour	US$19.30	US$26.60
Average labour cost per item	US$0.16	US$0.27
Profit as a percentage of revenue	Not available for the letter business, but it is positive	6.7%
Revenue per full-time equivalent	US$50,600	US$75,900
Number of employees per FTE	1.6	1.38
Sick leave[1]	7.2%	8.6%
Mail delivered on time[2]		
– First-class/24-hour mail	90%	96.6%
– Second-class mail/48-hour mail[3]	96%	95.0%

[1] Based on 2,087 working hours per year.
[2] The figures for Sweden cover delivery on time as well as to the right address. The Dutch figures only cover delivery on time, i.e. the figures are not directly comparable. The Dutch results are too 'high' or the Swedish are too 'low'.
[3] The service level for second-class mail in Sweden is 72 hours (0–3), in The Netherlands 48 hours.

The data may be summarised as follows.

- Average cost per employee is about 50 per cent higher in Posten Brev, which can partly be explained by the higher relative cost of labour and higher relative price levels in Sweden in general.
- The differences in average labour cost per item can be explained by

higher labour costs in Sweden, the greater use of machine sorting at PTT Post and differences in product structure.
- By using more part-time workers, PTT Post has a more flexible work system, which may affect the cost structure.
- The ratio of net productive hours is higher in Posten Brev, which partly can be explained by differences in systems and definitions used for the personnel data.
- The differences in the percentage of mail delivered on time can probably be explained by the high focus on overnight delivery and the extensive total quality programme at Posten Brev.

The companies operate in different national environments. Therefore a direct comparison between absolute figures can be rather misleading, i.e. further analysis is required. However, if we relate revenue to the following:

- labour cost per productive hour,
- average labour cost per item,
- average cost per employee,

and relate the ratios to each company's respective strategy, an interesting conclusion can be made as follows.

1. PTT Post has a low cost strategy, reflected in lower costs.
2. Posten Brev has a differentiation strategy, reflected in higher costs and higher average prices per item. These findings indicate that both companies could learn from each other.

Process issues

The following internal process issues also affect productivity and quality.

Table 4.14 Process issues: internal factors

Internal process issue	PTT Post	Posten Brev
1. The value chain Marginal differences in the cost distribution between the main activities, but substantial differences in relative cost per activity	Focus on sorting	Focus on transport High relative costs in transport and delivery operations
2. Productivity management PTT Post appears to have more economical practices	Strong focus on knowledge of key figures. Big increases of productivity at mail interchange centres	Focus on earnings rather than productivity. Increasing focus on productivity control.

112 Achieving Service Productivity

Internal process issue	PTT Post	Posten Brev
3. Quality management Both appears to be very competent in measuring what they have chosen to measure	Focus on right address and delivery on time. From 1993 focus is also on customer satisfaction	Focus on end to end reliability (on time and to right address). Focus on customer needs and satisfaction
4. Organisational issues	Centralised organisation but moving towards a more decentralised organisation	Decentralised organisation

COMPARATIVE PRODUCTIVITY

The most obvious productivity measure is the number of mail items/number of FTE. That ratio, however, while a useful initial indicator, cannot be used for any objective interpretation of productivity performance, without further analysis. Inter-country comparison must also include product structure, cost structure and volume per product. Other issues that must be analysed are geography, the infrastructure, and the operating and financial costs incurred in the distribution of mail.

Table 4.15 Mail per FTE on yearly basis

Mail per FTE (1991)	PTT Post	Posten Brev
Number of items annually per FTE	171,000	147,000

Taking the above data at face value it would appear that PTT enjoys a 16.3 per cent productivity advantage. However, behind this figure are the effects of geographic differences in distance and differences in the mail structure, the effect of which has not been analysed. Another factor is that PTT Post has 36,400 FTE and Posten Brev 29,100 FTE. Given that The Netherlands has about double the population of Sweden this is interesting and strongly suggests higher productivity in PTT Post mail operations. Levels of productivity, in Posten Brev are unsatisfactory so the corporate strategy is to increase productivity by 10 per cent over the next three years.

Productivity measurement

PTT Post

In the management of the postal regions, a distinction is made between management areas (MAs) and mail interchange centres (MICs), using the 'globalisation' management model. The work done at a mail interchange centre is mainly sorting, while in a management area work focuses on collection and distribution. In the globalisation management model, units are compared in an identical fashion and average productivity is calculated using regression analysis. A precondition is that the units are comparable, so that labour capacity can be corrected for work which does not occur in all units.

An indicator, the number of items per hour, is used for 117 management areas nationwide. This indicator is calculated using the following formula: average weekly pigeon-hole count in a year divided by the average labour capacity × 40 hours.

For the mail interchange centres, of which there are 12 nationally, calculations are also based on the number of items per hour. The production figures required are expressed in a weighted production figure (__w__eighted __t__otal __m__achine and __m__anual __p__rocessing – wtmmp). This refers to the various flows and processes that mail passes through (e.g. machine and/or manual processing). The indicator is calculated using the following formula: average weekly wtmmp in a year, divided by average labour capacity × 40 hours.

The productivity figures are shown in Table 4.16 below:

Table 4.16 Productivity figures: PTT Post

Productivity figures: PTT Post			
Productivity figures	1990	1991	1992 (estimate)
MA Productivity			
Items/hour	71.1	71.9	71.8
In %	–	+ 1.1	–0.1
MIC Productivity			
Items/hour	168.4	178.1	194.5
In %	–	+ 5.8	+ 9.2

In the above indicators, part of the traffic refers to the total labour capacity. This method works quite well when determining policy and objectives at a regional level. At the unit level, however, such global comparisons provide insufficient opportunities for management. A study is currently being conducted to provide a broader definition of traffic which makes management easier at lower levels.

As can be seen from the above data, the increase in productivity at the mail interchange centres is much larger than in the management areas. This reflects the degree of automation in sorting the mail.

Posten Brev

Traditionally, Posten Brev used a productivity measurement system based on number of mail items produced at different steps in the production chain, divided by the number of hours. Production volume was calculated as a weighted average of mail volume in different production steps. The weights were the estimated costs for producing one item at the specific step. This method, called the Staff Productivity System (Model 1) worked fairly well at national and regional level until the late 1980s. At lower levels, however, structural differences, plus lack of valid and reliable statistics made managerial use of the system difficult and dubious.

Within the overall budgeting system, one part covers the task of managing the 13 regions and one part covers the task of establishing financial targets for the budget year. The most important feature of the target is the internal earnings, where the income is based on produced volumes at standard prices (covering manpower and other inputs). The costs consist of the actual regional cost. By expressing income as well as costs in current prices, a measure of the overall productivity change is calculated at regional and national level. This method – Regional Productivity Based on Internal Earnings (Model 2) – can also be developed even for lower managerial levels.

At the highest level another productivity measurement has been introduced recently. It covers all of Posten Brev, including its headquarters with its production and development functions. The income measure consists of revenue from external customers and from other business areas within Sweden Post for produced services. As in the regional model (Model 2) income and costs are expressed at fixed prices. The forecast calculations for 1993 show a productivity increase of 2.6 per cent.

Table 4.17 Productivity figures: Posten Brev

Productivity figures: Posten Brev

Productivity figures	1990	1991	1992 (estimate)
Staff productivity system (Model 1) In %	+ 2.1	–0.69	Not available
Regional internal report (Model 2) In %	+ 1.0 (estimate)	–1.8	+ 0.5

Both organisations measure productivity but use different yardsticks, precluding a direct comparison. The variations, however, are very small in percentage terms (but high in absolute sums), due to the relationship between volume and cost per item shown in Figure 4.2 above. Dramatic productivity increases can therefore only be achieved through structural changes.

As can be seen from the figures from PTT Post there is a big increase in productivity in the Mail Interchange Centres when an increasing volume of the mail is sorted by machines. In the Management Areas, where the collection and distribution is done mainly by hand, productivity increases are hard to achieve.

BARRIERS TO PRODUCTIVITY

The most important barriers to increased productivity within PTT Post and Posten Brev appear to be the same. The companies' operations are virtually identical, with a similar management heritage as national monopolies, ruled by the government. The staff's cultural heritage is also the same, with an obvious pride as former civil servants, responsible for an infrastructure of national importance. Their future direction is also identical, with similar problems in transforming big operations from monopolies into profitable companies. As a result, there are no existing differences that are so important that it is possible to say that either one of the companies will face bigger difficulties in raising productivity than the other.

A monopoly business

Their heritage as monopoly businesses is the most important barrier to increased productivity. There will, for a long time, be a widespread opinion among the staff that the profession of postman is best performed by civil servants, maintaining a national distributional network for trade and industry as well as for the public sector. It will be a difficult task to transform this opinion to one which recognises that the company must not only distribute the post, but it must also do so profitably. This must be recognised as a central task for top management in both companies, as there is an obvious risk that the transformation from civil servants to businesspeople may otherwise put professional pride at stake.

Superordinate goals

This problem is connected to another heritage. Both companies have similar superordinate goals, expressing an ideology based on the monopoly era. The feeling is that the mail must be delivered, almost at any cost. It carries a dynamic and customer-orientated message, that would be difficult to replace even if the top management wanted to do so. Furthermore, it would be a mistake to try to replace it with a new slogan. Top management could instead use such attitudes as tools to focus employees' attention on achieving productivity and quality goals.

Geography

Sweden's geography has, until recently, been a possible barrier to increased efficiency in the letter business, as it has forced Posten Brev to focus on the transport aspects of letter distribution. Night air carriers have reduced infrastructural barriers, however.

The significant reduction in the number of sorting centres has generated much criticism from thinly populated areas with the result that it is possible that a further fall in sorting staff will be a more difficult task in Sweden than in The Netherlands, as the goodwill of the Swedish company may be put at stake. It is important that top management do not get a reputation for not listening to their customers in thinly populated areas.

Similar measures, when undertaken by big industrial companies, are not as difficult to present. The message, that certain reductions are important if the entire company will survive, is often understood as unpleasant but necessary. But when an old, established letter monopoly, recently transformed into a business, takes the same steps for the same purpose (to reduce total costs of the value chain and to increase the profit of the entire letter business) there is an obvious risk that the decision will be seen as simply to increase its profit in the big cities.

Quality approach

Quality is not an obvious barrier to increased productivity, but it may become one. Productivity aims at decreasing costs per item, but in a service business this does not necessarily imply more investment. The message must be that quality drives productivity and that it is cheaper to produce quality from the start.

Economies of scale

Economies of scale have both a positive and negative influence on PTT Post's and Posten Brev's attempts to increase productivity and quality. On the negative side, relying too much on synergies may result in an organisational behemoth.

Organisational structure

Posten Brev and PTT Post are both big companies, with a central headquarters and offices at both a regional and local level, each with their own managers, markets and traditions. The most important management task is therefore to hold the company together, with a common shared vision, monitoring operational performance and product development throughout. If the structure is too rigid and functionally based, there is a tendency to avoid cross-functional contacts. The functional units strive at perfecting their speciality, blocking attempts to increase productivity based on the flow of the value chain. At the same time, if the structure is highly product orientated, units tend to become increasingly independent, lacking any functional depth. Any attempt to unite the company and direct its efforts towards increased productivity and quality would be understood as unimportant messages with no value or content.

It is therefore of great importance that the connections between different levels are always open, reducing the risk of functional ignorance. Staff as well as managers at the central level should have experience from both the regional and the local level, while local managers should have experience from the regional and central level.

Organisational culture

Organisational culture may be a barrier to increased productivity for two main reasons, both caused by the fact that service production is dependent mainly on personnel. The first reason is that the necessary drive to create a unique organisational culture can backfire. A very strong corporate culture can be very parochial: staff may develop an attitude that everything invented somewhere else other than inside their own company is not good enough and therefore not worth any attention. If this happens, there is a big risk that the company will not pay enough attention to the needs of the market and therefore develop into an easy target for competitors; that risk is particularly acute in companies with a monopoly heritage.

Another kind of culture that might oppose change is an 'authority culture'. In times of significant change, as in the present situation at both PTT Post and Posten Brev, staff may feel insecure. The only remedy is to take the necessary measures and establish the new direction as quickly as possible. Belief in the new direction must be established throughout the company.

Leadership

As the attitude among personnel is a crucial factor, it is logical that leadership is a possible barrier to increased productivity. As changes in the market may cause changes in strategy, there is always a risk that some managers will not approve of the new strategy. A certain strategic rigidity may therefore occur, reflecting uncertainty towards new ideas. It is therefore crucial that the new strategy be properly established and enforced over the old one.

Lack of focus

Another problem in times of large-scale change can be lack of focus of top management towards the demands of a new business situation. Focus is shown by management through strategic decision making and interaction with staff. Both companies studied have, since the late 1980s, focused on development of quality in the sorting and distribution processes and on the reduction of costs.

When changing an organisational culture, from a former national monopoly into a business-orientated company, there is always a risk of focusing on the market, but forgetting to conclude the business in a profitable manner. Such a market focus, versus a business focus, may be a barrier to increased productivity. The necessity of customer profitability must be emphasised; the goal is to make a profit by satisfying customers. For instance, not to generate a loss by giving big customers large discounts.

Monitoring system

Monitoring systems are, naturally, of crucial importance for increasing productivity and quality: what gets measured is what gets done. Both PTT Post and Posten Brev have paid a lot of attention to this problem, and appear to have been successful regarding the stated focus, to increase quality in the sorting and distribution processes, and to lower costs. The next step should be to develop systems for benchmarking between business units, as well as that already done between production departments of the business units.

Skills

Another possible barrier to increased productivity, is the level of skill that exists among the different trade representatives within the letter business. The letter business is developing into an automated business, with big changes for employees; sorting personnel, for example, will in many cases be replaced by machines. Other examples are the development of electronic post and hybrid letters. With the possibility that their jobs may be replaced by machines, it is natural that many employees will not want to co-operate in the necessary efforts to fulfil this development.

Competition

As former monopolists, both PTT Post and Posten Brev have little experience of competition. This is another possible barrier to increased productivity. A successful player today may be a loser tomorrow. The desire for renewal must also include successful products, and neither company has the experience of product failures, particularly since in these situations competition may be too small to notice.

Product hubris

What has been said above regarding competition is connected to another risk, namely the possibility of product hubris. With a heritage as monopolists, both PTT Post and Posten Brev are market leaders with their main products. With such a position, there is an obvious risk that both companies may feel that the risk and cost of developing new products, is not worth the effort and therefore not necessary. With such an attitude, it is only a question of time until their position as market leaders is challenged.

5

POSTAL GIRO SERVICES

Authors: Michael Grindfors, Dan Johnson, Mikael Lövgren, Andreas Regnell

POSTGIRO, Norway
POSTGIROT, Sweden

The postal giro services in Norway and Sweden are among the world's most efficient payment transaction systems. Efficiency can be measured in terms of how quickly, reliably and at what cost a sum of money can be transferred from one account holder to another. Historically, companies providing payment services have derived most of their income from the interest earned on the 'float', i.e. the money in the payment system. Faster payment flows reduce interest income and make it necessary to put a price on services.

About half the increased productivity of the postal giro systems can be explained by new technology. The primary factor driving this trend both in Norway and Sweden is that the government, mainly in its role as a major customer, has demanded that transactions must become faster and cheaper. Secondly, in both companies there is a competitor in the form of a giro company jointly owned by the banks. The bank giro and postal giro services in both countries have competed to be the first to launch technological improvements.

Most of the remaining increases in productivity – between 25 and 50 per cent – are due to improvements in the service production process. Previously, the postal giro services used to organise their work on a functional basis, with employees being responsible for only a certain type of task. But today both companies use work teams that handle all the tasks during the entire process. As a result, there are fewer errors to correct, faster flows through the postal giro system and smaller office space requirements.

The pricing of postal giro services still does not reflect the company's costs, Large customers subsidise small customers *de facto*. If pricing corresponded better to the costs of payment services, the trend towards more efficient payments would have moved faster.

Depending on the transaction type, 50–95 per cent of the total cost of a transaction occurs outside the giro system. Services that have reduced costs outside the giro's value chain, or at the interface between the customer and the giro, include direct debits, electronic postal services and electronic account statements.

THE POSTAL GIRO SECTOR

In both Sweden and Norway postal giros are separate business units within the post organisation. Each has a strong market share of the government, public and mass payment sectors, but weaker positions in the private sector. The giro business is labour intensive, but both companies have managed to reach and maintain high levels of service and quality, in turn resulting in strong customer satisfaction.

To derive factors that play a major part in explaining how a company succeeds in becoming more efficient and continuously improves its productivity, the study has been conducted in the following way:

- flows have been analysed from a customer perspective;
- all major processes and areas have been studied;
- each giro has been benchmarked according to a number of criteria;
- focus has been placed on the key factors explaining efficiency and success in the industry.

Postal giros have larger market shares than bank giros in both Sweden and Norway. In 1990 postal giros accounted for approximately 67 per cent of the payment flow and 75 per cent of the transactions in Sweden, and 50 per cent of the flow and 67 per cent of the transactions in Norway.

The Swedish Postal Giro handles more than three times as many transactions as its Norwegian counterpart, performing 407 million transactions in 1991, compared to 143 million in Norway. The transactions enter the system through five channels.

- Brown (Sweden) and blue (Norway) envelopes. Customers with postal giro (PG) accounts may send payment orders in special envelopes free of charge resulting in a movement of funds within the postal giro system.
- Electronic transfer. Customers with PG accounts send transaction data

122 Achieving Service Productivity

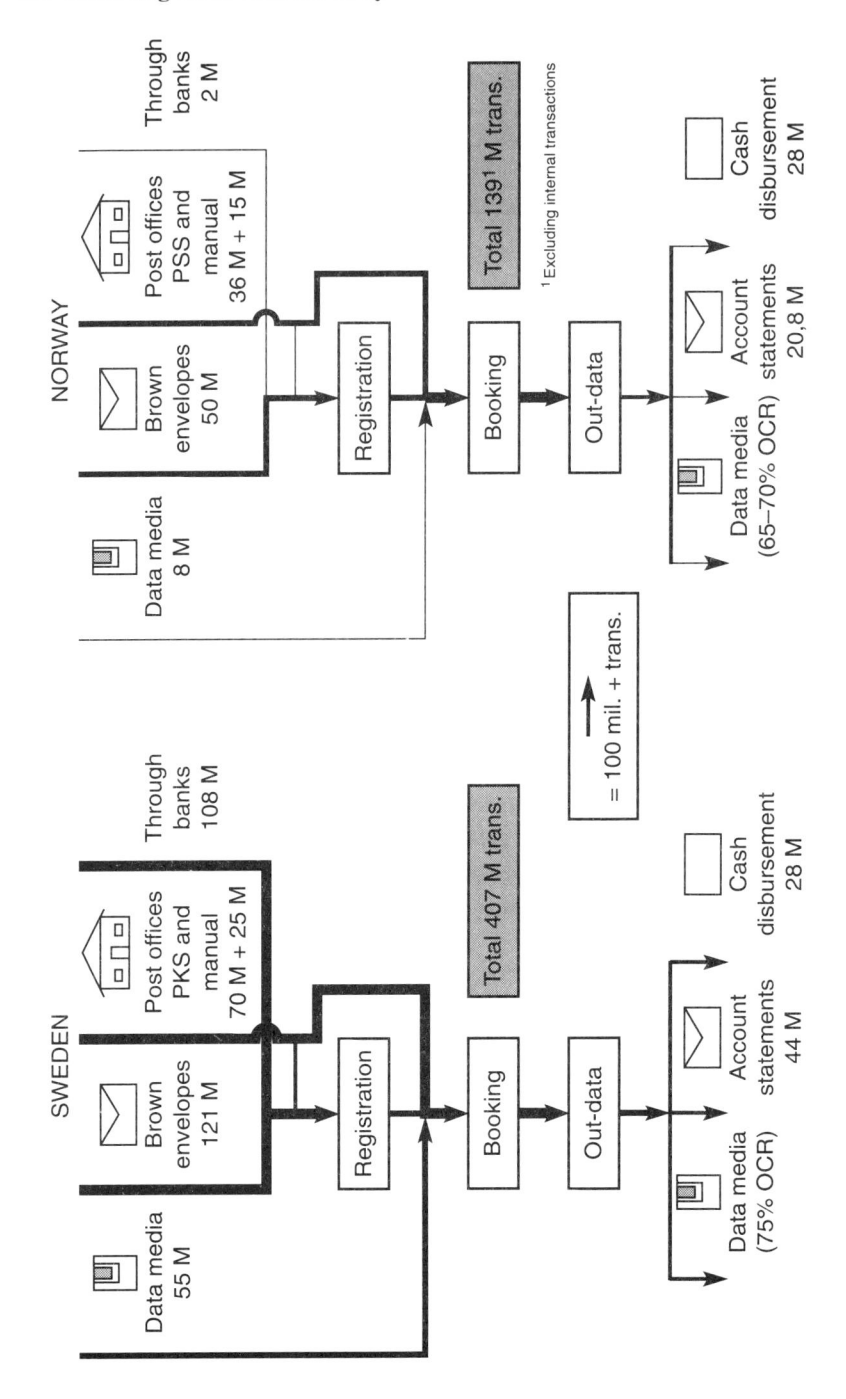

Figure 5.1 Comparative transaction volume

Source: PG Sweden and Norway: BCG estimates

electronically, either by magnetic media or via a terminal. As with the brown and blue envelopes, this is typically a transaction within the system. This type of transaction accounts for 5–10 per cent of all incoming transactions, but the share is continually rising.

- Payment orders sent to banks where the data or actual payment card is subsequently distributed to the postal giros. This is an important channel in Sweden, where Nordbanken, the savings banks, and the private giro service receive large volumes of PG payment orders. This transaction leads to the movement of funds from a bank account to a PG account.

- Over-the-counter cash transactions. Customers can go to a post office or bank and make a cash payment: this is the traditional way of making a PG payment. This channel is still used frequently, but is declining because of increased use of PG accounts and its comparatively high cost.

- Direct debits. After an initial agreement between the creditor and the debtor, the postal giro automatically transfers money from the customer's account to a creditor when an invoice is due. This type of transaction still accounts for a small portion of the total flow in both Sweden and Norway.

Figure 5.2 shows a clear increase in electronic payments and a decreasing trend in paper-based payments. In addition, it illustrates the decreasing importance of cheques as a means of payment. Cheques are not issued by

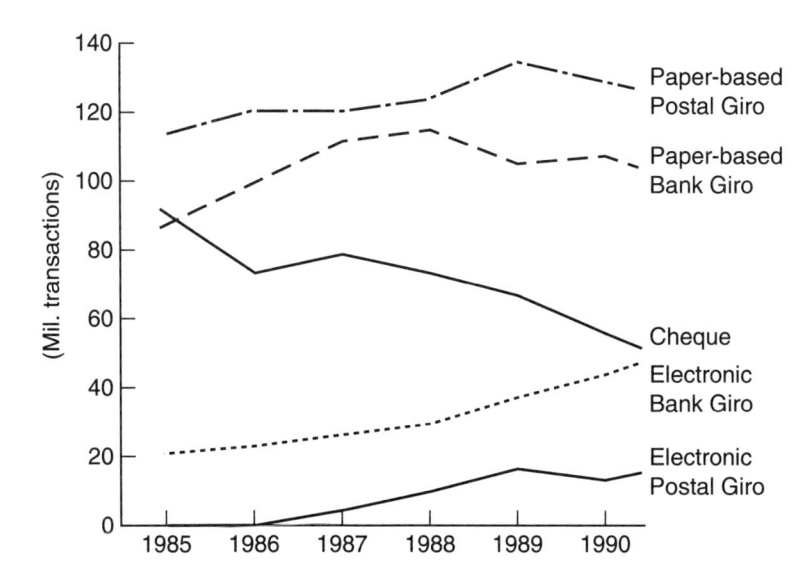

Figure 5.2 Development of different types of transactions in Norway
Source: Norges Bank

the postal giros, but are a common way of moving funds from a bank account to a PG account.

Profitability and market position

Both the Swedish and the Norwegian Postal Giros have historically profited from high income on government cash flows. However, as a result of drastically altered terms for interest compensation on government tax funds, the situation has changed in Norway and the Norwegian organisation experienced a loss in the range of US$15 M in 1991. By contrast, the Swedish Postal Giro earned a US$120 M profit in 1991.

Both giros have strong market shares in the government, public sectors and mass payment (many payments from/to one customer, e.g. telecoms, insurance companies), but weaker positions in the private sector. The Swedish Giro has been more successful in its efforts to reduce its reliance on monopoly payments and has a 30 per cent market share of the private sector, compared to Norwegian Giro's ratio of 10–15 per cent.

Personnel

As has already been stated, the Giro business has been, and still is, labour intensive. The Swedish Postal Giro employs approximately 3,800 and the Norwegian 1,700 people. Both organisations have traditionally been very personnel focused and before 1992 layoffs had never occurred. During the economic boom of the 1980s, the giros had trouble attracting registration personnel and turnover was high, reducing productivity and raising quality control costs. In the current environment, however, recruitment is not a problem. In 1991 absenteeism was 11.5 per cent in Sweden and 8.7 per cent in Norway, while personnel turnover had fallen to 4.8 per cent and 7.5 per cent respectively.

Service level

The Swedish and Norwegian Postal Giros have both managed to reach and maintain high levels of service and quality. In both countries 100 per cent of all incoming transaction requests are booked immediately and funds are available the following day. This is a central quality assurance measure, as certainty about the time required to perform a transaction is critical to an efficient payment system. Sweden sends out 96 per cent of all account statements the same day, Norway 40 per cent. The ratio is lower in Norway partly because the production process is still being adapted to a new computer system.

The giros regularly conduct customer satisfaction surveys and enjoy high ratings. In 1991, 85–89 per cent of the Swedish Postal Giro's customers were satisfied or very satisfied with the services: satisfaction levels were even higher in Norway, exceeding 90 per cent. None the less, both organisations are currently focusing on further improving the quality of their services and have made significant progress. The Swedish Postal Giro has, for example, increased the share of enquiry calls answered within 20 seconds from 57 per cent to 72 per cent: the target is 90 per cent.

FACTORS AFFECTING PRODUCTIVITY

Analysis of the postal giros, in particular, and the payment service sector in general, highlights some particularly critical factors affecting productivity. These factors are interesting, not only because they explain efficiency, but since they also illustrate dynamic development from a period when efficiency was related primarily to position (e.g. to critical mass and scale), to a new situation in which the organisations' productivity is based on superior processes. The experience of the postal giros also shows how change in the business environment can lead to a redefinition of the basis for the traditional positional advantages of critical mass and scale.

External factors

The external factors promoting productivity and efficiency are essentially positional.

Critical mass and scale

The Swedish Postal Giro was formed in 1925 and the Norwegian in 1942. Their main task was to process the increasing number of government transactions that accompanied the creation of the welfare state.

Traditionally there have been significant economies of scale in giro services. The Swedish Postal Giro has estimated economies in different cost elements that resulted in an aggregated scale curve in the 75–80 per cent range.[1] This means that the cost per transaction should decrease by 20–25 per cent with a doubling of volume. The postal giros benefited from scale economies through their monopolies on the processing of government cash

---

[1] Estimates by PG Sweden. Scale effects by cost element: letter distribution – no scale; personnel – 75 per cent scale; rents – 70 per cent scale; other (marketing, systems etc.) – 83 per cent scale.

flows, which have been substantial in Sweden and Norway. When each company was formed, the public sector accounted for approximately 15 per cent of gross domestic product (GDP) in each country. The relative importance of the public sector in the economy also had implications for the build-up of a significant account base.

Many companies chose to open PG accounts, since that simplified the management of tax payments. In 1930, five years after the formation of the Swedish Postal Giro, most large domestic companies had an account with it. A basic characteristic of payment systems is that a large account base is key, since that creates the possibility of transfers within one account system. These types of transactions are more cost-effective and convenient from a customer perspective. In its first year, the Swedish Postal Giro achieved a level of internal transfers (i.e. inter-account transactions) of 38 per cent.

Sweden and Norway have comparatively efficient payment systems from a macro economic perspective. This is largely a result of the relative strength of their giro systems, whereas in many other countries the use of cheques is more widespread. Different countries have been more or less successful in building efficient routines around various types of payments, but a median cost of a specific type of transaction can be estimated. By weighting the relative efficiency of each payment instrument by the share of total cashless transactions, the overall efficiency of a country's payment system may be estimated. On this basis, Germany and Switzerland, with a very large proportion of direct debits and few paper-based credit transfers or cheques, are very efficient. Sweden, Japan, The Netherlands, and Norway follow closely behind, with a high proportion of effective paperless credit transfers and/or direct debits.

Comparative levels of efficiency are shown in Figure 5.3, which also shows that there are large differences in cost between various types of transactions. This often makes productivity in performing a certain type of transaction less important than the transaction type when determining efficiency. As an example, the cost of a direct debit transaction is estimated to be one-third the cost of a paper-based credit transaction, while a paperless transaction could be as little as one-fifth of the cost of a cheque transaction. The early creation of nationwide structures able to handle more efficient transfer types has consequently been a fundamental driver of the relatively efficient payment systems in Norway and Sweden. At the same time, the postal giros still have very low shares of direct debits, compared to Germany, for example, where the share is more than 35 per cent. This means that while the Swedish and Norwegian giros may be highly productive in executing paper-based credit transfers, their share of the more efficient direct debits remains low.

Postal Giro Services 127

Country	Weighted average
Germany	39
Switzerland	45
Sweden	48
Japan	50
Netherlands	51
Norway	58
Belgium	61
France	63
U.K.	70
Italy	76
Canada	92
USA	95

Transaction efficiency: High ← → Low

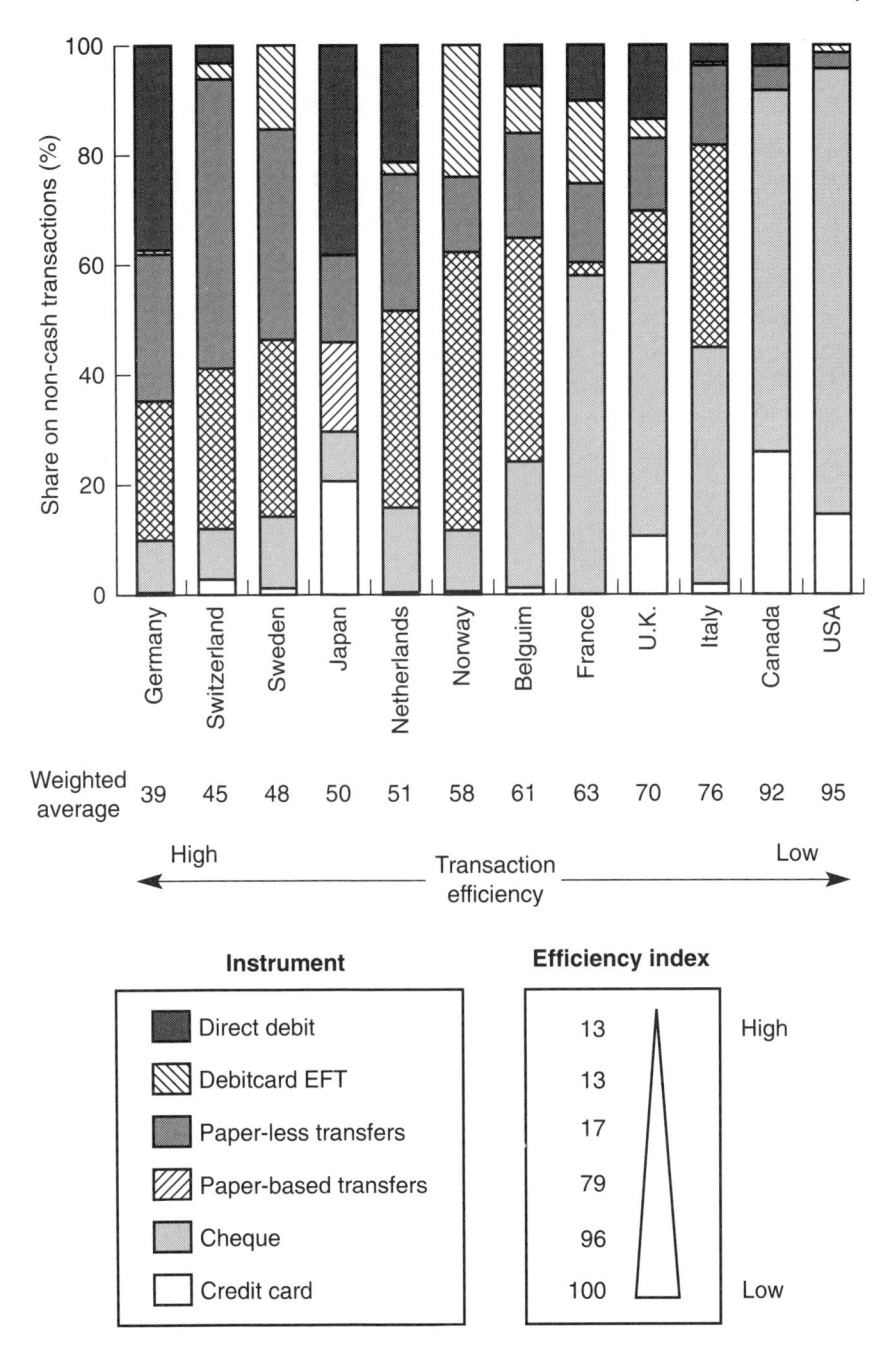

Instrument — **Efficiency index**

- Direct debit — 13 — High
- Debitcard EFT — 13
- Paper-less transfers — 17
- Paper-based transfers — 79
- Cheque — 96
- Credit card — 100 — Low

Figure 5.3 The efficient payment systems of Sweden and Norway put in an international perspective – a high degree of paper-less credit tranfers

Source: payment systems in 11 developed countries; Bank of Intl. Settlements 1989; Norska PG-kostnadsberegninger; Finska Riksbanken; BCG analysis.

128 Achieving Service Productivity

The giro systems' strong positions are, as discussed above, closely related to the importance of the public sector and the fact that each organisation achieved critical mass early. Thus, there is a potential relationship between the size of the government sector (public-sector spending as a percentage of GDP) and the efficiency of payment systems. In Sweden and Norway, concentrated mass payment markets with large customers may also contribute to efficiency.

This correlation is illustrated in Figure 5.4. It is apparent that exceptions to the pattern are Switzerland, Germany and Japan. A common factor linking these countries is that they have very strong ties between their corporate and banking sectors, which may exert the same kind of pressure on development as the government does in other countries. The widespread acceptance of direct debits in these countries may be explained by a high level of public confidence in the banking system.

However, the seemingly stable competitive advantage inherent in critical mass and scale has turned out to be less permanent than some may have expected. The environment for the giro business has not remained stable. On the contrary, several discontinuities have occurred, resulting in new challenges. These discontinuities have, as will be discussed later, forced organisations to focus on developing several capabilities that complement the initial positional efficiency factors.

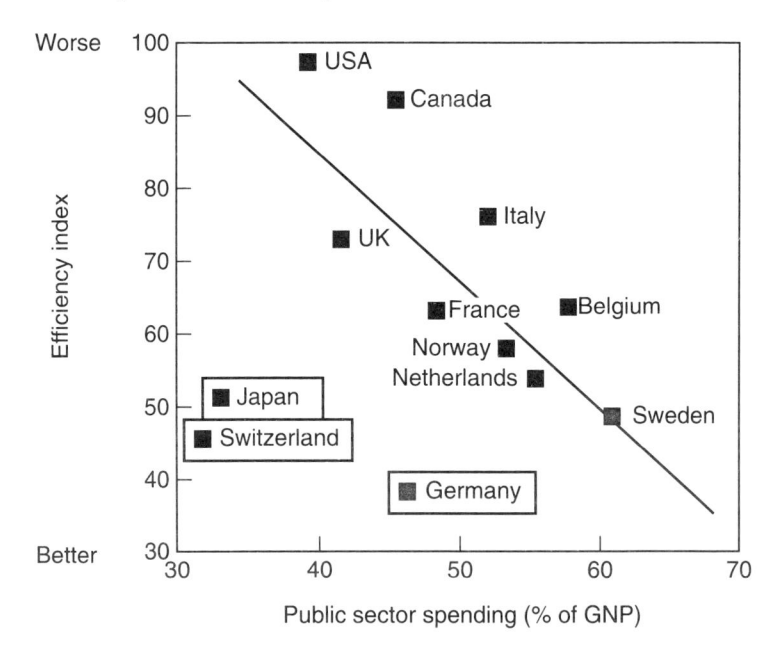

Figure 5.4 Critical mass through the public sector?

Source: 'Payment systems in 10 countries', BIS 1990; SCB 1991; BCG analysis.

New technology and political decisions are two important causes of discontinuity and, as such, reinforce the need to develop flexible capabilities to achieve greater efficiency.

New technology

Technological changes have resulted in quantum leaps in productivity. Productivity has almost tripled since the early 1970s and conservative estimates show that technology accounts for at least 50 per cent of this improvement. The giro systems have benefited from general technological advances, especially in information technology and automation, but in the case of OCR,[2] it has been the banks and giro systems themselves that have been the main forces driving development. Some of the major technological changes are:

- EDP[3] in accounting (1968–1969 in the Swedish Postal Giro, 1976 in the Norwegian Postal Giro);
- OCR (1964–1970 and onward in Sweden, 1968 in Norway);
- automated sorting systems (from 1970 in Sweden);
- image processing (first generation 1988 in the Swedish Postal Giro and second generation 1989 in the Norwegian bank giro and 1992 in the Swedish bank giro).

Image processing allows a reduction of physical flows in the central processing of paper-based credit transfers. It also allows decentralised, complementary registration and checking, which in turn can result in lower rents and personnel costs, since part of production can be moved from central cities. For BBS in Norway, the cost per transaction has fallen by 25–30 per cent (deflated) since the introduction of image processing in 1989, while labour productivity has risen by 44 per cent[4].

The general trend is towards fewer physical flows as more transactions are processed electronically and systems become more integrated. An EDI order-invoicing-payment system, which allows all transactions between suppliers and producers to be processed electronically, has been developed and is currently being used by, among others, some of the large car manufacturers, such as General Motors.

Political decisions

In addition to the discontinuities caused by technology, the postal giros, being government owned, have repeatedly been exposed to dramatic changes

---

[2] Optical character recognition; a techique by which documents are read by machines for electronic processing.
[3] Electronic data processing
[4] Source ELBET – Report from Norges Bank, May 1992.

130 Achieving Service Productivity

in business conditions brought about by far-reaching political decisions. Examples include variations in the interest paid on state accounts in Norway and the reduction of float days on state payments in Sweden. Both have substantial bottom-line consequences for the postal giros as seen in Figures 5.5 and 5.6.

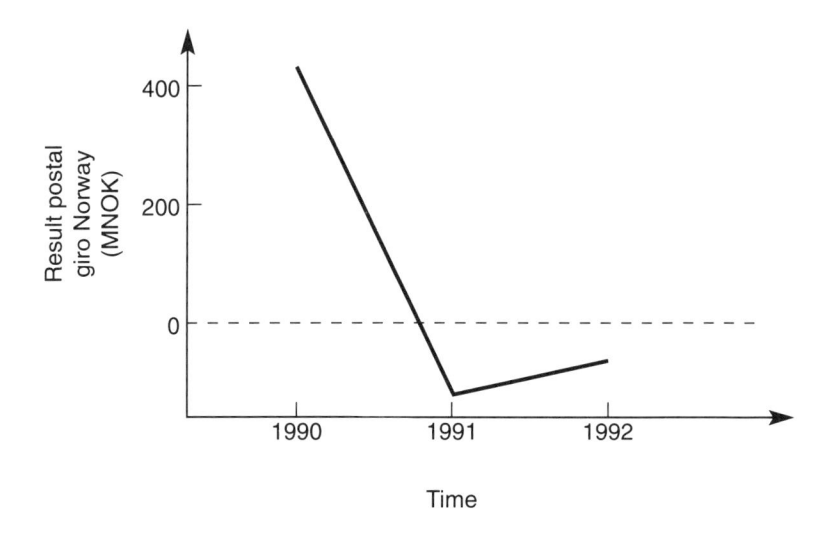

Figure 5.5 Changed interest on government accounts in Norway

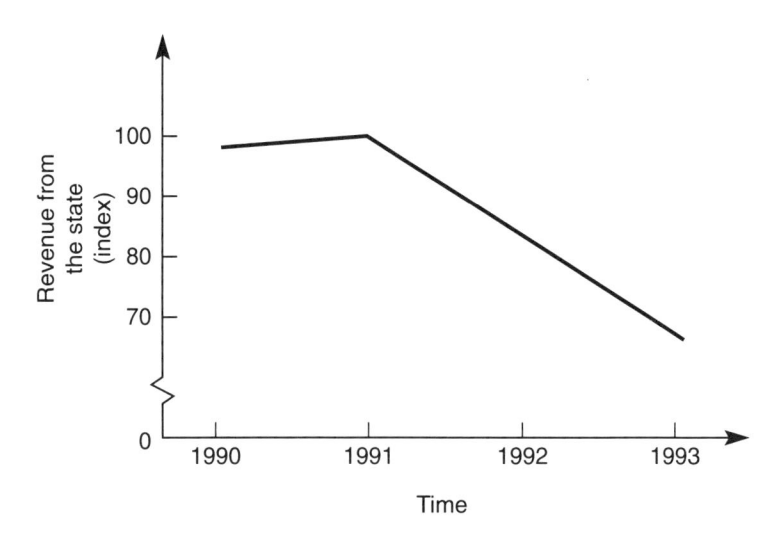

Figure 5.6 Government payments in Sweden (from 2–4 to 1 float day)

The postal giros are likely to face similar changes in their business environment in future, with the result that a critical success factor will be the flexibility to adapt the organisation and its business methods to new conditions.

Market incentives

The need to respond swiftly to changing business conditions has been reinforced by competition, owners and customers. These market forces have provided important incentives for the postal giros to exploit the opportunities created by new technology and improved business processes, and have been identified as a second positional factor explaining a high level of efficiency.

Competition

Since the formation of the bank giros in Sweden (1959) and in Norway (1971-1972), the postal giros have been exposed to direct competitive pressure, resulting in a rapid improvement in productivity. A number of products or new techniques that have reduced costs and/or improved service have been developed by each player. This has forced the other to act and thus has helped speed the overall process of efficiency improvement. In addition, customers have benefited from the improvement through better service, lower cost, or higher interest. The effect of competition is summarised graphically in Figure 5.7.

When the Swedish Bank Giro started operations in 1959, a simplified payment card which created less work for the payer was introduced. This was soon followed by a similar card from the postal giro. Other examples of competitive innovations are:

- interest-bearing giro accounts;
- an invoicing service, whereby the paying institutions manage all payments to suppliers;
- ability to transmit transactions and receive account statements electronically;
- image processing, which reduces costs and improves service significantly.

Some of these changes have had more impact on overall efficiency than others, but the important thing is that competitive pressure has forced the two players to think about, and respond to, customer demands more rapidly.

This pressure is summarised in the following quote from the Swedish post giro marketing department: 'Only the fact that there exists another alternative for the customer has put pressure on us during all these years.'

132 Achieving Service Productivity

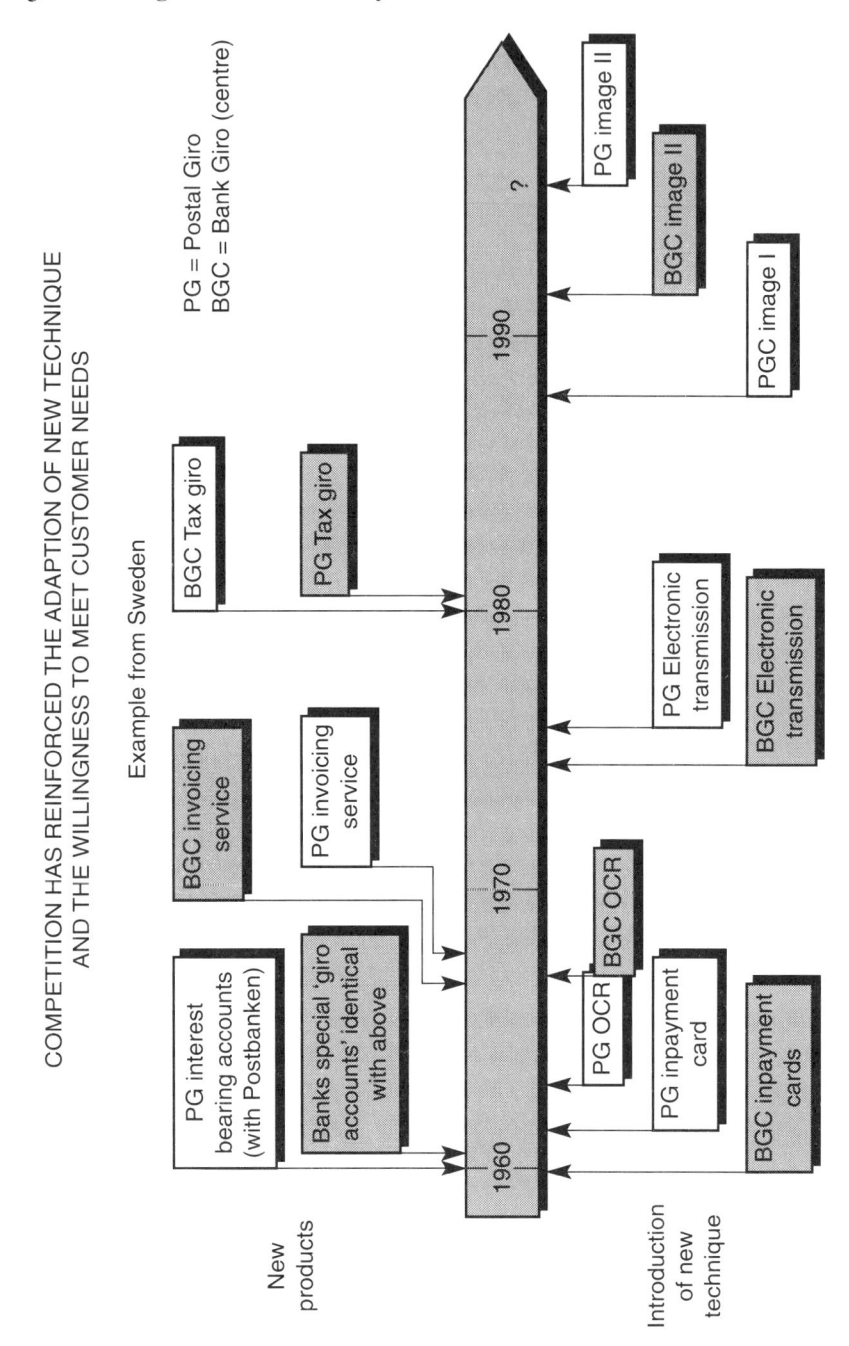

Figure 5.7 Effect of competition

Source: BCG interviews; 'Postbanken – Postsparbank and Postal Giro 1884–1974', Kjell Samuelsson, 'ELBET Norway', Norges Bank.

Owners

From the beginning, the owner of the postal giros – the government – has emphasised cost-effectiveness, accessibility and security in payment transfers. These criteria have become even more important in recent years as society has re-evaluated the role of the public sector.

Customer demand

Increased awareness of cash management, further strengthened by high interest rates, has led to strong customer demand for more efficient payment systems. In Sweden the stronger focus on cash management is reflected in shorter turnaround times for funds entering the PG system with the result that the average turnaround time has fallen from 2.3 days in 1989 to an estimated 1.7 days in 1992. The government in particular has tightened its cash management in both countries. As an example, in July 1992, the Swedish government changed the number of float days from two to four to one, resulting in a yearly income reduction to the Swedish Postal Giro of approximately US$85 M. The demand for better cash management focuses on three main areas.

- Transaction speed/Response: on-line customer systems, improved systems for transfering funds to interest-bearing bank accounts, and a maximum one-day float.
- Quality of information/Response: image processing and terminals (also improves accessibility to information).
- Pricing of transaction services/Response: competitive interest on PG deposits and receivers' fees.

A provider of cash services is also often required to offer short-term credit to balance out temporary shortfalls in cash flow. The postal giros were previously not allowed by law to provide credit, which they argued put them at a major disadvantage to the banks. This has, however, changed and today both giros can provide limited short-term credits.

In considering the increased focus on cash management, it is interesting to note that the current pricing structure may reduce the incentives for the postal giros to improve efficiency. The prime source of their income is still the float on the transaction, i.e. the interest between the time an account is debited and another credited. A quicker and more efficient payment system reduces the float income and should thus not be in the interest of the postal giros from a strict business point of view. However, a pricing structure based on transaction fees avoids this problem and is increasingly being implemented (led by US banks) throughout the industry.

Internal factors

The discontinuities in the business environment discussed above weaken the structural advantages of the giros based on critical mass and scale. This shifts the focus of efficiency improvement towards internal capabilities.

Internal process efficiency

To gain maximum benefit from new technology it is important also to improve the processes surrounding it. It has been estimated that up to half the increased productivity achieved is explained by improvements in the production process and does not relate to any technological breakthroughs.

When determining the net effect of technology-driven efficiency, a word of caution is appropriate. Two different productivity measures may be employed: labour and total productivity. Labour productivity depends on the efficiency of a given process, but also to a high degree on the type of process performed. A highly automated process and a high share of electronic transactions, however, require significantly more capital, which can lead to high costs. Total productivity provides a picture of the overall efficiency of the organisation, including all cost elements, such as the capital cost of technology.

Figure 5.8 shows how labour productivity has improved substantially in both countries over the last few years, while total productivity has remained flat. The difference can be explained by the fact that the potential to reduce personnel has been realised only to a limited extent. The staff reductions that have taken place have also been made on favourable and, accordingly, fairly costly terms. Furthermore, other large cost items, such as mail distribution, have increased significantly over the period (by over 25 per cent in Sweden for example).

It should be noted that total productivity levels in Sweden and Norway are not fully comparable because of differences in the cost of inputs, economies of scale and in transaction mix.

Process improvements

Several examples of non-technical process improvements can be found. For example, in Norway production personnel used to be organised in different functions such as registration and control. This resulted in a number of bottle necks as most people were specialists, while only the very end of the chain (control) saw the result of its work, especially errors and other quality problems. This resulted in an overload of correction work at the last minute,

Postal Giro Services 135

Labour productivity | **Total productivity**

● ———— ● Sweden
■ ———— ■ Norway

¹ Excluding cost of distribution network and operations not related to postal giro transactions.

Figure 5.8 Comparative productivity

Source: Production reports Swedish and Norwegian Postal Giro; Annual reports; BCG analysis and interviews

which in most cases led to expensive overtime and failure to achieve the service goals. A few years ago, production work was reorganised so that people worked in teams responsible for a larger part of the value chain. Everyone worked on only a few activities at one time, but because all tasks were rotated, everyone learnt to do them all. This resulted in higher quality, as people more easily understood the implications of their work, with the result that overtime for correction dropped by 80–90 per cent and the proportion of account statements delivered on time rose considerably. Although some of this improvement was offset when a new on-line bookkeeping system was introduced in 1991, overall, individuals became more motivated as their responsibility and ability to influence their work increased. The organisation became less dependent on a few specialists and more flexible. The process improvements implemented in Norway are summarised in Figure 5.9.

In Sweden the postal giro is working hard to create an 'entrepreneurship mentality'. Production is organised in work groups rather than by directives. The groups are evaluated and rewarded on the basis of these goals, and competition among the groups is encouraged. Individuals or groups are welcome to try new routines as long as their goals are met and productivity improved.

136 Achieving Service Productivity

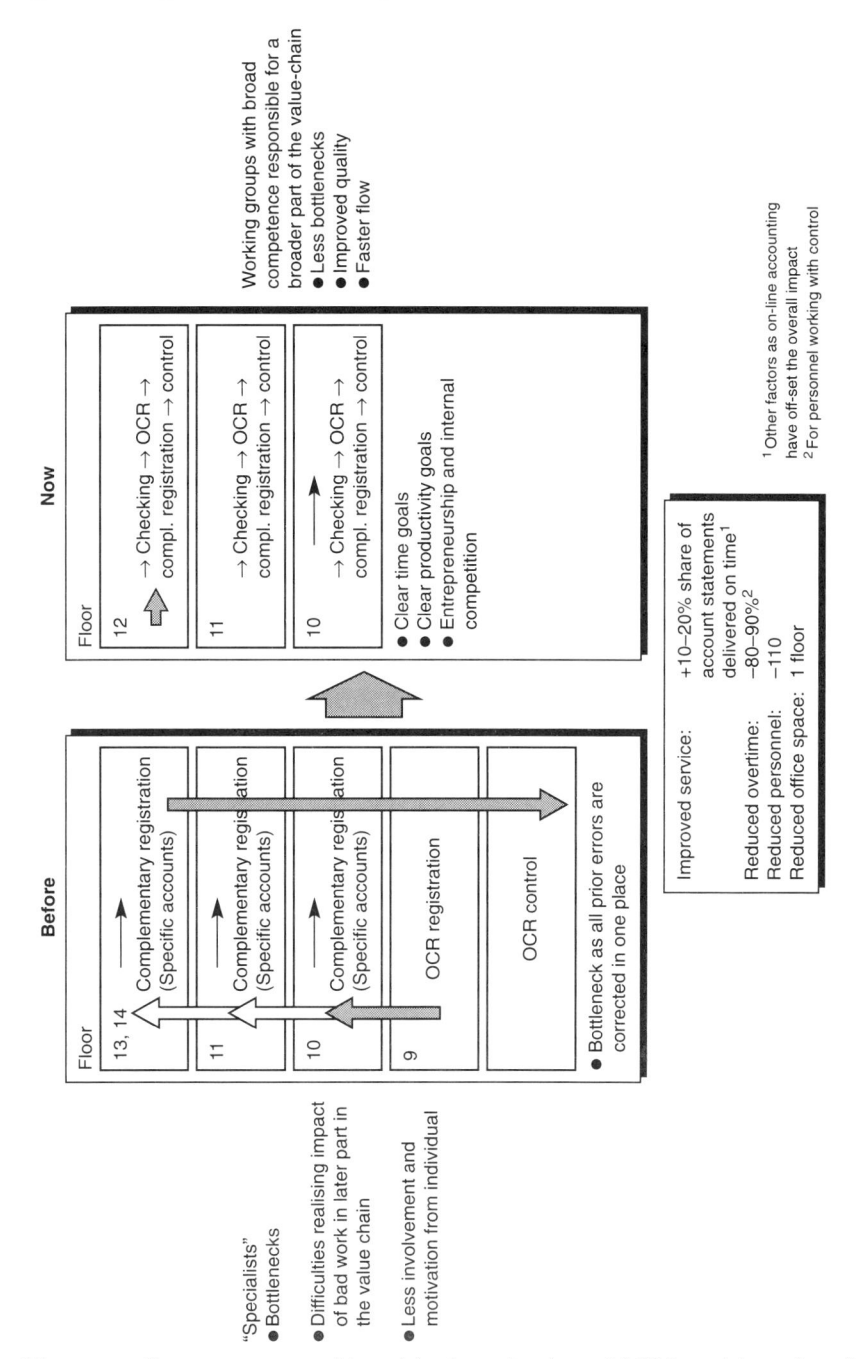

Figure 5.9 Improvements achieved by introduction of MBO and broadened areas of responsibility. Example from the Norwegian Postal Giro

Source: BCG interviews

There is also significant potential to reduce quality-related costs. Both organisations have recognised this opportunity and devoted significant efforts to it. In 1989, the Swedish Postal Giro performed a quality study, indicating that up to 25 per cent of production costs were related to quality issues. The bulk of the quality cost was caused by faulty instructions or information from the customer, and only a small part could be attributed directly to errors in the postal giro. The most important problem areas were paper-based disbursements, and illegible (for the computer) deposit slips and data media. The problems were related to substandard control systems and costly routines to protect against the risk of fraud.

In 1993, the post offices will receive on-line connections with the database controlling the paper-based disbursements. This is expected to reduce disbursement-related quality costs by 75 per cent. The problems with illegible deposit slips and data media were addressed through quicker and more focused feedback to the customer, while the company has appointed a head of quality.

During 1992, the Norwegian Postal Giro also performed a company-wide quality process survey. This focused on internal quality and traced the views of the organisation's personnel on quality-related issues based on results.

Process re-engineering

The postal giros have direct control over only 35 per cent of total giro costs in Norway and 44 per cent in Sweden: counter services and mail distribution that are bought from the post offices account for the balance as shown in Figure 5.10. Accordingly, the efficiency of external service providers is of great importance. Ongoing restructuring efforts within the Swedish post office counter services aim at reducing costs by 30 per cent, while improving the overall service should significantly improve the giro's position. Swedish mail distribution is also expected to improve significantly as a result of automation. Similar efforts are under way in Norway, but have not yet materialised in concrete plans or goals.

Sweden Post (the Swedish post office) is aggressively addressing cost problems in the branch network through a time-based management (TBM) project which includes a radical re-engineering of day-to-day operations. TBM measures include more active marketing of postal services, a focus on productivity and the adaptation of resources to customer flows. When these measures are fully implemented, costs are expected to decrease by 30 per cent (see Figure 5.11) and revenues to increase by 5-10 per cent.

138 Achieving Service Productivity

External service providers' share of total cost

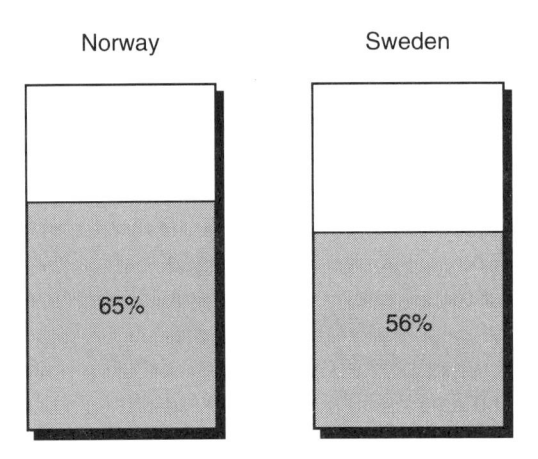

Norway: 65%

Sweden: 56%

Figure 5.10 Comparative internal efficiency

Understanding individual customers

Depending on transaction type, 50–95 per cent of the total cost of a transaction accrues outside the giro systems and there exists significant potential to reduce these costs with existing technology. The postal giros work hard to help customers transfer money by more efficient methods. One example of an incentive that is more convenient and less costly for both the giro and the customer is the use of free brown and blue envelopes in contrast to an inpayment over the counter which costs US$2.90.

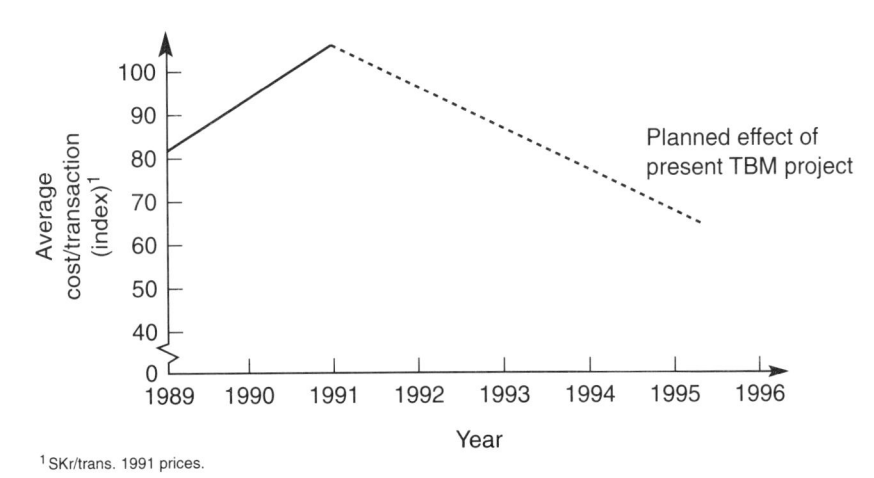

Average cost/transaction (index)[1], 1989–1996, with planned effect of present TBM project shown as dashed line declining from peak near 100 in 1991 to about 65 in 1996.

[1] SKr/trans. 1991 prices.

Figure 5.11 TBM in branch network targeting 30 per cent cost reduction

Source: The post office counter services internal accounts; BCG analysis

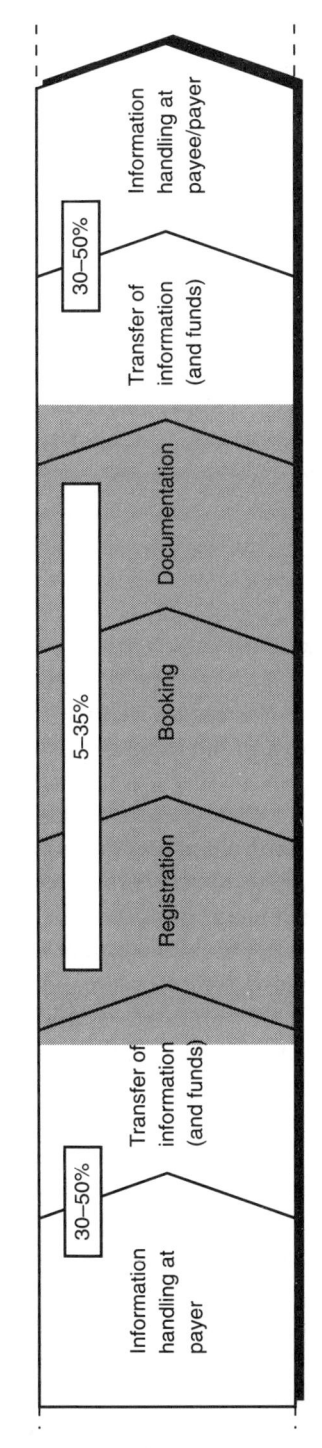

Postal Giro Services 139

Figure 5.12 Extended integration in the value chain

140 Achieving Service Productivity

Other examples of services that have been developed to reduce costs outside the giro's own value chain or at the interface between the customer and the post giro are:

- direct debits which eliminate the need for the payee to be involved in the transaction;
- electronic postal service (EPS) which allows the customer to let the PG print out invoices;
- electronic account statements – the postal giro feeds the payment data directly into the customers' receivables system.

Segmentation

The business rationale for the postal giros was originally based on the management of government cash flows. The income from this segment made it possible for the giros to provide services to other segments without applying a strict cost-based pricing and service strategy. Specifically, this made it possible for the giros to provide mass payment services through the post office network at a price below actual cost. Today the situation has changed significantly, and the owners and major customers (the governments) are exerting strong pressure on the organisations to adopt a strict, businesslike strategy.

Thus the building blocks of the PG business concept – government cash flows and the mass payment market – are under siege. Increased cash management consciousness and continuing deregulation will significantly reduce the importance of the public sector, while the giro's position in the mass payment market is threatened by pressure for a pricing structure reflecting actual costs. The latter will inevitably lead to an increase in the use of alternative, more efficient payment methods such as direct debits, where the postal giros do not have a strong competitive advantage. Their position in the corporate segment largely relies on secondary effects, i.e. companies need to be PG customers because certain flows (e.g. VAT) always go through the system. If the flows from the government and mass payment companies are reduced, there is a significant risk that the giro's position in the corporate segment will also be weakened. Furthermore, this segment typically needs banking services that the postal giros are largely prohibited from providing.

These circumstances require the postal giros to make a realistic evaluation of the attractiveness of different segments and their ability to compete. Segment profitability varies widely and is largely driven by the size of flows, and the type and number of transactions. With the current pricing structure, the cost of most transactions is not covered by the float and fees, unless the transaction is very large. This is particularly true for transactions received through the post office network. However, governments in both Sweden and

Norway recognise that certain PG services (primarily counter service transactions) could hardly be maintained if strict business considerations were applied. Therefore, both organisations have been compensated (for example through long float periods) for the payments services provided to the government to cover these costs. As of July 1992, the Swedish Postal Giro receives US$40 M per year, which corresponds to the estimated cost of providing postal giros in areas where they are not otherwise economically viable. The Norwegian Giro will receive a lump sum of US$95 M as compensation for counter service costs and costs related to the management of government payments.

The income/cost relationship means that mass payment customers, who are extensive users of counter services and have many small transactions, tend to be highly unprofitable. The government segment, however, is sufficiently profitable fully to cover the shortfall in income. The corporate sector (non-mass payment customers) on average provides adequate returns, while local communities often generate losses due to high volumes of small and expensive transactions. Private individual customers are rarely profitable.

Customer orientation

As market conditions change radically it will become even more important to understand and fulfil customers' different needs. From having focused on semi-captive customers the postal giros will now have to evaluate which customer segments are most attractive, where it can achieve real competitive advantage and how to differentiate the marketing mix specifically for each segment.

The Swedish Postal Giro has come furthest in this regard. The sales organisation, which is key for reaching corporate customers, has been significantly strengthened and currently comprises 165 full-time employees. An extensive customer profitability model was implemented in 1990 and the incentive structures have been adjusted to better reflect overall goals by focusing on customer profitability and marketing efficiency (hit rate, number of customer visits etc.). Other measures have been the development of detailed market plans, plus estimates of the total potential of different segments. The importance of increased cross-functional communication has also been recognised and customer focus teams, comprising marketing, sales and production personnel, have been formed to serve the 750 largest clients.

The Norwegian Postal Giro is currently testing a customer profitability model that is scheduled to be on-line in 1993. Its sales force, however, only comprises 22 full-time employees and these comparatively limited resources are reflected in a significantly lower market share of the corporate segment – estimated to be 10–12 per cent, compared to a Swedish ratio of 30 per cent.

142 Achieving Service Productivity

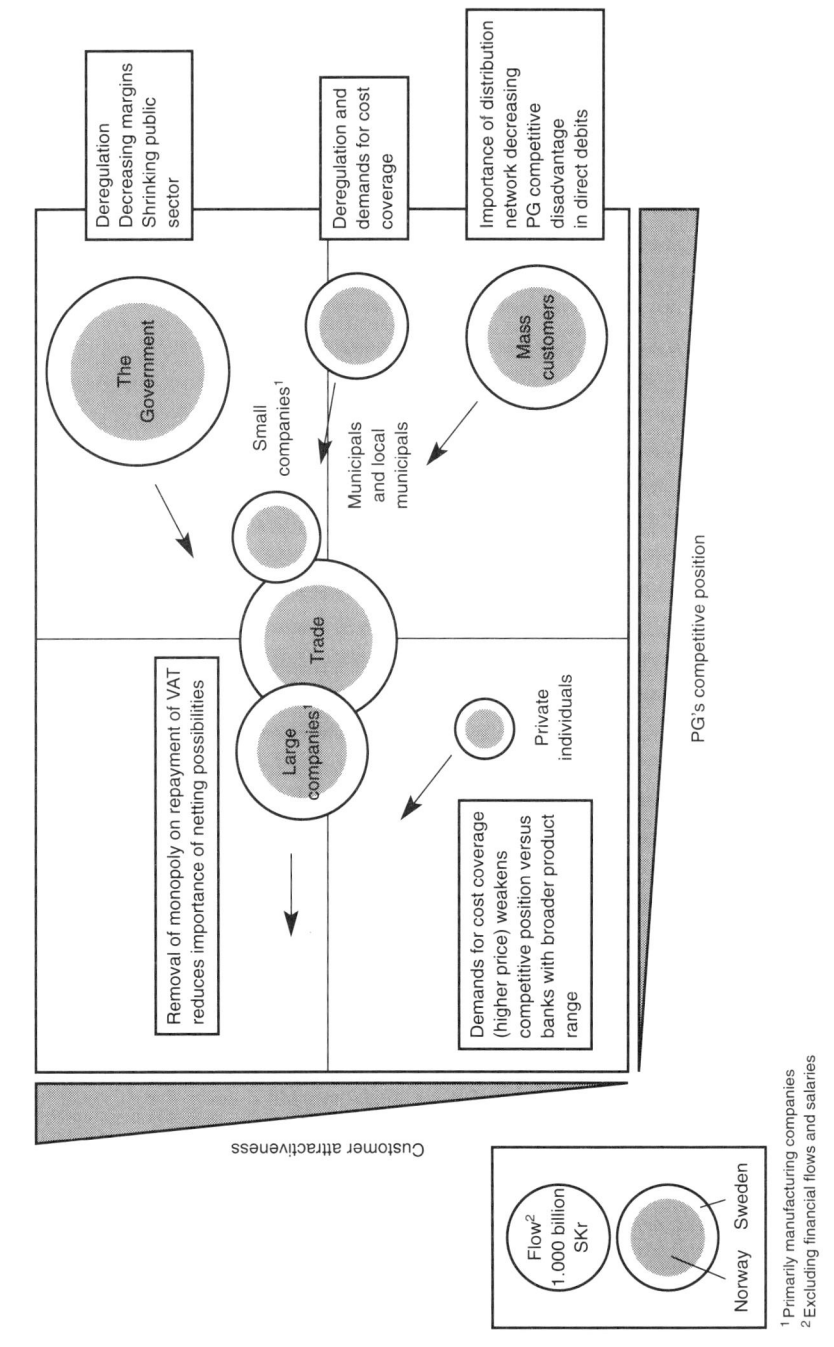

Figure 5.13 Prices reflecting cost and deregulation call for re-evaluation of segment flows and strategy (some segments are more affected than others)

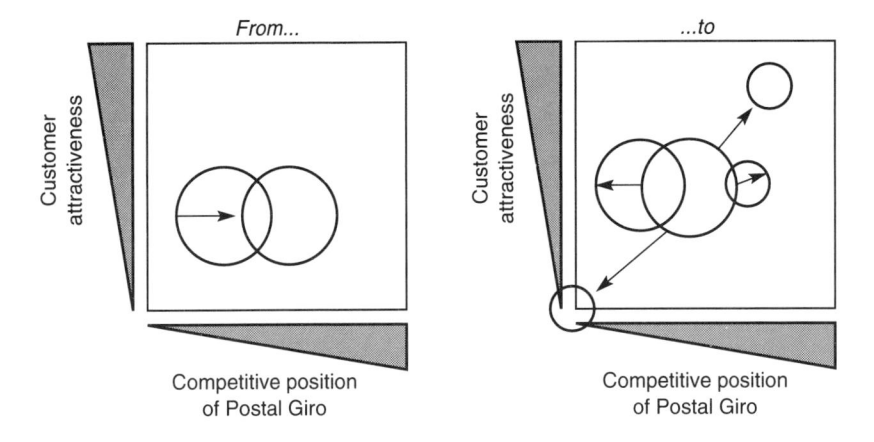

Figure 5.14 Towards individual customer orientation

To restore profitability to the mass customer segments, the Swedish Postal Giro introduced fees to be paid by the receiving company in 1991. Market reaction was initially very negative but the banks soon followed and criticism died down. Norway plans to introduce similar fees in 1993. In spite of the introduction of such changes, however, both postal giros have a long way to go before today's loss-making market segments are profitable.

A stronger focus on solving customer needs rather than selling a predefined product will lower the barrier between payment services and more traditional bank services in several customer segments. Thus, not surprisingly, there have recently been discussions in both Norway and Sweden about the possibility of integrating the postal giro into a banking group. In turn this has raised questions such as: What is the best structure for a Postal Giro in future? Are there better solutions than today's freestanding structure? What are the pros and cons of closer co-operation with a banking group?

Other influencing factors

To maintain their leading position among the world's payment systems, the postal giros will need to rapidly strengthen their internal capabilities as discussed above. This process requires starting off with an open mind about how business is conducted. Some of the approaches to developing the necessary capabilities could include:

- a strong emphasis on cross-functional teams working on process re-engineering from the perspective of individual customer segments;
- a very strong proactive search for, as opposed to reaction to, new technology opportunities;

- management of and/or co-operation with distributors and business partners as integral parts of the value chain;
- control and measuring systems focused primarily on creating customer value.

Not only, as discussed above, are the positional advantages of size and critical mass being redefined, but the battlefield is also being reshaped by the shift from physical distribution points to private account bases and from the national to the international market.

Private account base

In both Sweden and Norway, the income from government cash flows has subsidised losses in the mass payment market, which accounts for approximately 50 per cent of the postal giros' transactions. This subsidisation, however, may have reduced the pressure to develop even more effective payment methods. Had consumers been faced with the actual cost of a payment through a post office, or the less expensive brown or blue envelope, the move toward direct debits, or other more efficient payment methods, might have proceeded further. In Germany and Japan, both known for efficiency, direct debits account for 30–40 per cent of all current transactions, compared to a ratio of less than 3 per cent in Sweden and Norway.

A factor contributing to the slow shift toward direct debits may be that the postal giros have competitive disadvantages in this area. A successful autogiro service requires very high coverage of private accounts. If the service provider can offer 100 per cent coverage, the customer can send all debit instructions to one source, reducing cost and complexity. The bank giros have 100 per cent coverage, whereas the figure for the Swedish Postal Giro is 70 per cent and for Norway only 28 per cent. These ratios are illustrated in Figure 5.15

The international market

In contrast to their possible disadvantage in direct debits, it appears that the postal giro would have an advantage based on the availability of an internationally co-ordinated network. In both Norway and Sweden international flows have increased over the past two decades as shown in Figure 5.16.

The postal giros in Norway and Sweden, with 12 other international giros, have now taken the initiative to introduce Eurogiro. The plan is to take advantage of the well-established channels of communication between several postal giros, and to offer a European partner system with superior

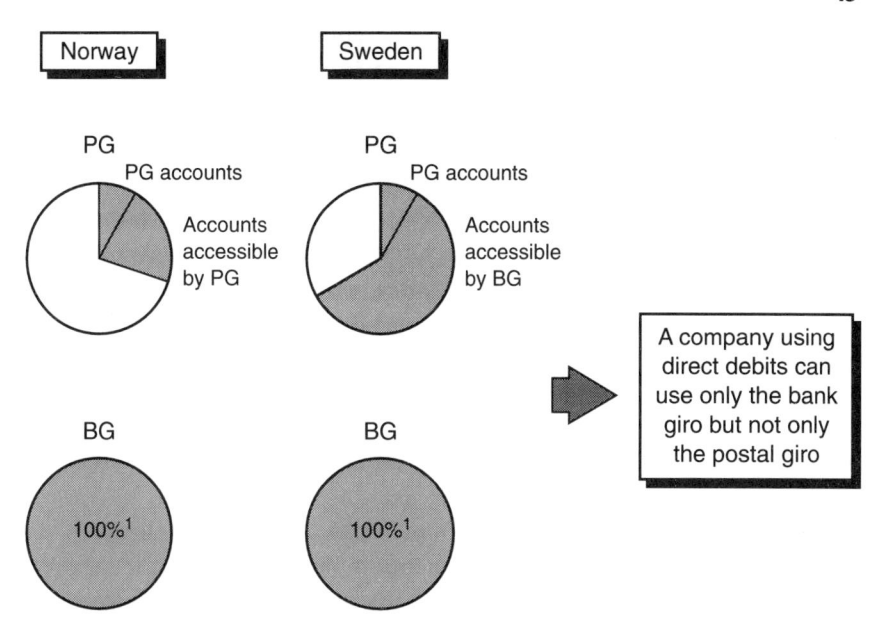

Postal Giro Services 145

Figure 5.15 Relative importance of direct debits (postal giros have competitive disadvantages versus the banks)

Source: PG Sweden and Norway; BCG analysis

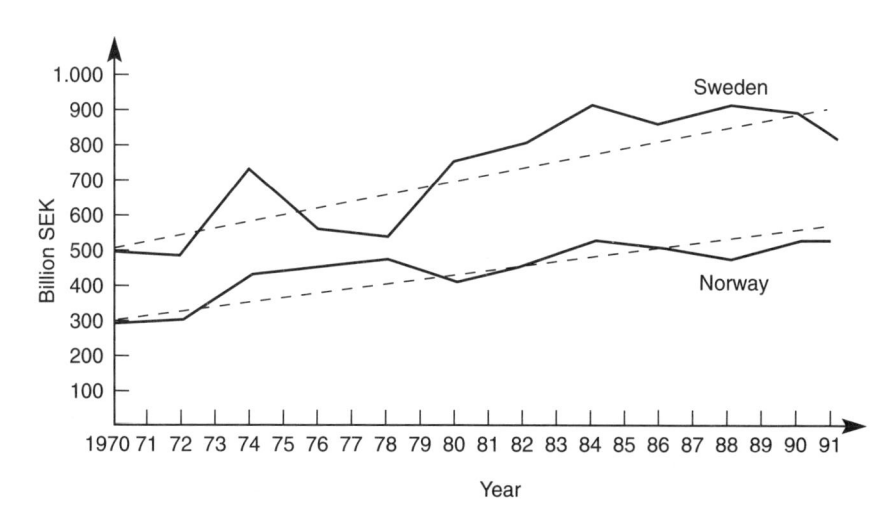

Figure 5.16 Long term trend of increasing international flows

Source: IMF and BCG analysis

service and quality. As in the early days of national payment systems, postal giros may be able to exploit the potential positional advantage of a relatively larger and more co-ordinated distribution and systems network. The features of Eurogiro seem at least to offer substantially better customer service and efficiency than most existing alternatives.

CHALLENGES FOR THE FUTURE

Change management

As discussed above, the postal giros have already had to adapt to many dramatic changes in their operating environment. In future, the most critical fundamental question may be the issue of business definition and structure in relation to the banking industry.

In addition, all the indications are that further technological advances, the opening up of new segments to competition, new government legislation, internationalisation, together with other forces, will further accelerate the pace of change. This puts a premium on the ability to adapt and respond. The increasing importance of organisational capabilities such as responsiveness, quality and understanding of individual customers, at the expense of traditional positional advantages, will make efficient change management not only an important success factor, but a prerequisite for survival.

The magnitude of this challenge cannot be stressed enough. Like any other large organisations (52,000 people in Sweden and 28,000 in Norway, including counter services and mail distribution), both giros face a formidable task of broad-based change management. Furthermore these state-owned organisations must balance the goals of increased cost efficiency, nationwide availability, excellent customer service and motivated personnel in the glare of public attention.

This complex management challenge is in sharp contrast to the giros' original task of managing government payments, mostly paper-based, at satisfactory cost levels. But the objective of meeting the challenge and maintaining a strong position has been clearly set.

Large-scale change programmes have already been initiated. An example is time-based management process re-engineering work now being carried out in the Swedish counter services. In line with the simultaneous requirements of cost efficiency, customer service and staff motivation, two key objectives have been defined: at least 25 per cent cost reduction within three years, and further improvements in customer service and employee motivation. To involve employees nationwide, the change has a grass-roots orientation, focusing on re-engineering the processes from the perspective of the local post offices and the consumer.

Strategy and planning

When managing complex organisations through change it is important to have planning, control and measurement systems that ensure a good understanding and acceptance of the corporate objectives, and help everyone to strive towards the same goal. The Swedish Postal Giro has come a long way in this regard. The company has a combined, top-down and bottom-up planning and budgeting process. A three-year plan is produced each year, based on overall goals from the post office and detailed plans from each business unit (employing 150–200 people) within the organisation. Each step in the process includes a consistency check to ensure that the objectives and activities are in line with the company's overall strategy. Three main objectives, namely profitability, satisfied customers and motivated personnel are eventually broken down to clear, tangible and measurable goals. This is a fairly extensive process but it adds, according to personnel involved, significant value to the strategic planning and gives the whole organisation a strong sense of future direction. In an internal survey, more than 80 per cent of employees felt they had a good understanding of corporate and departmental strategy.

As a complement to financial goals, the Swedish Postal Giro uses a set of physical goals, which are itemised and communicated down to unit level. This allows the organisation to set up meaningful and understandable targets at all levels; while it may be difficult to give a registration clerk a cost-reduction goal, setting a target to reduce errors by 10 per cent is possible.

External hires

Organisations challenged by a need for significant and rapid change often choose to bring in outsiders to give the process momentum. This approach seems to have been adopted by the Swedish Postal Giro, where a major proportion of senior management are employed from the private sector. Even though it is difficult to assess the direct effects of such personnel on market orientation, many argue that this is a major factor explaining the rapid progress of postal giro in Sweden.

6

SECONDARY SCHOOLS

Author: Jan Löwstedt[1]

WILLIAM H. CROCKER MIDDLE SCHOOL, Hillsborough, CA, USA
SKOLEN VID RØNNEBÆR ALLÉ, Helsingør, Denmark
BRÄCKESKOLAN, Bräcke, Sweden
RÖDEBYSKOLAN, Karlskrona, Sweden

The Crocker Middle School has been chosen three times as one of the best schools in the United States. The school is located in an area where families have very high average incomes. Nearly all its students eventually go on to college. Parents each devote an average of 40 hours of voluntary work per year to the school. The Crocker Middle School serves as something of a driving force in a regional network of middle schools.

Skolen vid Rønnebær Allé in Denmark was a problem school, with aggressive students and strained working relationships among faculty members. After a new principal took over the school and implemented a reorganisation, there was a turnaround.

Rödebyskolan in Sweden was also a problem school ten years ago. A new principal with a clear leadership style initiated the change. The school is now distinguished by a very outgoing image. The main factor behind the success of the second Swedish school, Bräckeskolan, is that it focuses on the professional development of its teachers.

Schools in the US, Denmark and Sweden that are considered especially good are distinguished by the fact that they create market pressure by subjecting themselves to the scrutiny of those around them. In the US, for instance, they do so by getting the students' parents involved in their operations. In Karlskrona, they do so by seeking regular contacts with local organisations, companies and newspapers.

[1] This paper is an analysis of four case-studies done by Rogberg & Shani, Stymne & Ryberg and Rogberg & Löwstedt. This summary is written in collaboration with Martin Rogberg. Valuable comments from Rami Shani, Bengt Stymne, Lennart Grosin, Ingrid Lindskog, Torsten Lundgren, Sven-Erik Servais, Erik Hörnell and Bo Sellstedt are greatly acknowledged.

Good schools also have head teachers who formulate visions for their schools to make up for the absence of clear goals for schools in general. The important thing is apparently not the contents of the head teacher's vision, but the fact that the vision exists. Enthusiasm for such a vision is contagious and also has an effect on areas of school operations not directly connected to this vision. Good schools also apply a process management system that provides clear instructions on what should be done in problem situations.

Good schools have organised the work of teachers into team systems. In this way, they achieve flexibility, the dissemination of good examples and built-in quality control. Contacts and co-operation with teachers outside their own school puts their own work in perspective and provides professional feedback.

THE EDUCATION SECTOR

Dual goals

Schools take on a different role as society changes. For example, mass education began in Sweden 150 years ago when compulsory schooling for all was introduced. Since then many new responsibilities have been incorporated into the school system. The students' smooth adjustment into social and work life has assumed greater importance, while urbanisation and the development of previously isolated housing mean that schools have adopted the role of surrogate parent by caring for local children while their parents are working. In addition, schools are becoming a political instrument with the expressed goal of creating a 'better' society.

The years that a child spends in school are of enormous importance, in terms of their personal, cognitive and social development. Traditionally a school has been evaluated purely in terms of student knowledge and proficiency. Standardised tests have been developed to assess the students' level of knowledge, while the resulting marks can also be used to judge quality. Such evaluations, however, clearly only reflect part of a school's goals.

Educational research, however, shows ambiguous results on the importance of the school *per se* in relation to the students' level of knowledge and proficiency. Studies in the 1970s indicated that the students' social background and natural ability had the greatest influence on academic performance (Jenck *et al.* 1972). Other research highlights the significant importance of a student's home environment in knowledge absorption (Coleman *et al.* 1966), although the individual's school situation also plays a key role.

There is, however, tangible competition between the goals of knowledge and proficiency on one hand, and the goals of socialisation on the other. A school's long-term goals are complex, if not confusing, and are therefore difficult to evaluate when the school's function is no longer simply to teach, but also to be responsible for students' social development. Schools must therefore have dual goals to develop a child's social and cognitive skills.

Organisation

The Swedish school system provides an example of how organisational changes can help in the attainment of these dual goals.

Class structure

Students aged between 7 and 12 are taught by a single 'class teacher'; between the ages of 13 and 16 they are taught by teachers specialised in particular subjects and their week is divided into blocks of time, corresponding to these subjects (language, science or practical). Until the beginning of the 1970s, however, students were grouped into classes or divided according to interests. This is no longer the case. Students now remain in their original classes throughout their schooling.

Product organisation

In secondary schools the organisational framework can be said to facilitate both a 'functional organisation' (the subject areas) and a 'product organisation' (the students and class groupings). Teachers are grouped according to different subjects such as languages, science and practical disciplines, but stress is placed on the class groupings or working units, each of which is led by a co-ordinator who has specific responsibilities for co-ordinating the curriculum. Within these groups, one teacher is normally responsible for maintaining an overview of the development of each subject.

Teamwork

Instructors work in teaching teams, called working units, in order to better follow the students' development, organise class instruction plans and co-ordinate the teaching of different subjects. The creation of teaching teams is part of the overall decentralisation process, but it also helps to balance the workload for each individual instructor. Teachers within a team are responsible for carrying out their colleagues' work if necessary. Team work also facilitates local development of the institution while reducing the need for outside control. This type of organisation makes it easier for each teacher's specific knowledge to be utilised and properly communicated to others. Equally, less experienced teachers can absorb the knowledge and practical experience of colleagues. However, although the advantages of teamwork have been recognised in other sectors for some time, the system has met some resistance in Swedish schools.

The dominance of this kind of 'product organisation' is in line with the techniques employed in goods and service production, where the smooth flow of the product through the process is the main priority. Emphasis is placed on keeping costs and quality predictable rather than creating the best possible product or service. This makes schools different from businesses. If it was just a matter of getting students through nine years of schooling with a certain basic knowledge and no 'drop outs', the task at hand would be considerably simpler and comparisons easier.

THE SCHOOLS STUDIED

A number of considerations were taken into account when selecting schools for this analysis. Should each be the best their country had to offer or should they be more representative? Should they be of similiar size, location or socio-economic background?

Selecting a school which can be said to be truly representative of each respective country would only be feasible by studying many more schools than was possible for this study. Instead, different examples have been taken to focus interest on certain aspects shared by each organisation. The schools chosen were considered 'good' within the educational community and had something interesting to present. The key question thus became: How does one manage a school so it is regarded as a model school?

Skolverket (the Swedish National Agency for Education), and its equivalents in Denmark and California, were asked to suggest some appropriate schools to study. After contacting the suggested institutions, speaking to some of their employees and appropriate local authorities, the following were chosen:

Rödeby School near Karlskrona, Sweden

Bräcke School, Bräcke, Sweden

Rønnebær Allé School, Helsingør, Denmark.

William H. Crocker School, Hillsborough, California, USA

These schools have succeeded better than others in emphasising the social rather than purely educational goals of the school. Each provides interesting examples of successful work achieved through inspired and visionary management. Some of the issues in question are:

- the parents' role in the educational process;
- the development of a positive image of the school – for both the students and the general community;
- reorganisation and development of staff;
- achieving compromises among opposing interests within an organisation.

In Sweden, an important factor influencing the choice was each school's recent participation in a comprehensive national evaluation of schools led by the National Agency for Education. In the US, the Crocker School is one of the most highly rated schools at both state and federal level, while the Danish school chosen is involved in interesting organisational and management developments.

It is also worth mentioning that the Swedish and Danish authorities chose schools whose students came out as average on a national scale. However, due to extra efforts on the part of the school administration these schools have enjoyed remarkable improvements during recent years. The students at the Crocker School have very high marks and the school is located in a financially affluent suburb. Thus by choosing these schools it is possible to compare and evaluate Scandinavian schools where social goals are prioritised with an American school where more emphasis is placed on knowledge.

Rödeby School

Rödeby is a community with just over 3,000 residents. It is located 20 kilometres from Karlskrona, a town in south-eastern Sweden known for its harbour industry and military associations. The town is the administrative centre for the neighbouring forestry and agricultural industries.

Rödeby School had significant problems during the early 1980s. The general atmosphere was uneasy and typical grades were below the national average. The school had a reputation for disorder and the physical environment was poor: the oldest parts of the school were built in 1948 but most sections date from the early 1970s. Mould and damp created problems and the entire building was in need of renovation. An overall renovation was undertaken between 1985 and 1987, which proved the signal for a broad review of the organisation of the school as a whole.

Rödeby School and its 925 students 89 teachers and 20 additional staff members, constitute one of Sweden's largest compulsory schools, with students at both primary and secondary levels. This study focuses on the secondary level, comprising 497 students in six classes.

The secondary level is located in some of the more recently built sections of the school although overcrowding has resulted in classes being held in various nearby buildings. A community library, gym, recreation centre, indoor and outdoor swimming pool, ski slope, and access to track and field activities are all available in the immediate environment.

Today, the management team take great pride in the fact that there is virtually no vandalism in the school and average grades now slightly exceed the national figure. The social climate has been deemed exceptionally good by national experts, and local articles about the school are frequent and positive. The school has also enjoyed great success in athletic competitions.

Bräcke School

Bräcke is a community of 8,000 residents in the south-eastern portion of Jämtland County, close to the geographical midpoint of Sweden. Since the mid-1980s Bräcke has participated in a 'free municipality' project – a recent experiment in deregulation of municipal tasks mandated by national legislation – which was a contributing factor in choosing the school for analysis. The free municipality project gives local authorities more influence, providing an opportunity to manage schools in a less regulated manner than is usual in educational institutions. For example, rather than having one committee which oversees all formal educational activities in the municipality, Bräcke's three municipal divisions each have their own educational committee and principal.

A lack of formal routines is readily apparent at Bräcke School. The school's motto, 'More people – less paper', illustrates the desire to emphasise the human element rather than traditional approaches and expectations of how things should be run. The teachers' expectations and developmental needs are considered very important by the head teacher, not for their own sake but, as a means of meeting the long and short-term planning requirements of the school.

The school is highly integrated with other community functions. A day care centre, recreation centre and gym facilities border the school grounds. Instead of preparing food at the school, the school's cafeteria purchases the students' meals from Folkets Hus (the Labour Movement Community Centre), which is open to the public and provides various services.

Today the school has 263 students, 84 of whom are at secondary level. The number of students has recently fallen, but is expected to increase in the near future. There are 58 employees, 35 of whom are teachers. The student population includes children who are mentally and physically handicapped. Children from families seeking political asylum in Sweden periodically attend Bräcke School as the community contains a refugee camp. The school also works co-operatively with the *fritids* or recreation centre in that all students begin and end their day at the same time. *Fritids* are an organisation funded by tax money; children who attend regular school use the *fritids* as an after-school club until their parents arrive or until they can go home. Having the *fritids* within the school grounds is an enormous convenience to parents as they do not have to worry about children commuting from one location to the other.

The school has been able to develop quite independently as a result of being a free municipality project. The school's personnel consists of five teaching teams organised around groups of students from different grades, one cafeteria team and one housekeeping team. Each team is co-ordinated by a person who, together with the head teacher and an administrative assistant or local official, is part of the school's management group. The school has chosen not to have a special director of studies. The financial and accounting function has recently moved from the local council to the school, and is now looked after by the administrative assistant.

The educational programme is divided into forms according to age, not into classes. The lower and upper primary levels are handled by two specific work units. Department heads are the 'administrators' of these units, and are also responsible for certain subjects such as languages, social studies, natural sciences and the more practical disciplines. This kind of structure makes it possible for fewer employees to co-ordinate the teaching teams and subject-specific course planning.

The school's teachers have worked at the school for many years and obviously enjoy their jobs. Their satisfaction is certainly due to the high degree of decision making and independence they enjoy, and the head teacher's very personal approach as the leader of the school. Opportunities for personal development also play an important role and the staff absentee rate is quite low – between 1.9 per cent and 2.4 per cent. Part of the individual's responsibility of working as a team member is to cover for other members, whether this is necessary because of short-term illness or other job-related obligations: in this way the teaching team is able to operate without having to employ substitute teachers. The majority of the teachers responsible for the older students have a reduced amount of teaching time as a result of their other duties at the school; for instance, maintenance of the school's computers or audio-visual equipment, student counselling activities, project development or research etc.

Rønnebær Allé School

Rønnebær Allé School is in the Danish town of Helsingør, a community of 52,000 residents which has developed around its shipyard. Helsingør is similiar in size, geographic location and type of local industry to Karlskrona and Rödeby, although it is a more working-class area than Karlskrona.

The school is also similar to the two Swedish schools studied, in that academic performance is at the national average. However, the school is involved in new and interesting organisational and management developments. It has adopted a corporate approach in its reorganisation and by introducing a matrix structure, financial department functions are accorded more emphasis, working relationships among members of the teaching staff have improved and the overall organisation of the school has generally profited.

Six hundred and twenty-five children attend Rønnebær Allé School, approximately a third of whom come from an area with many neglected social groups. The balance of the pupils is almost equally divided between the working and middle classes. The school has 67 employees: 50 teachers and 17 staff members filling a variety of positions ranging from school psychologist to custodian. The recreation centre has six employees and the school health clinic, 12. Many of the school's students suffer from social problems and, as a result, approximately 20 per cent of the resources and 30 per cent of the teachers' time is dedicated to providing support for those students.

Danish schools have been decentralised for some years. The schools are run by committees, most of whose members are parents and the principal's authority has been broadened to embrace a number of assignments from the municipal administration. The difference between Swedish and Danish decentralisation is that the position of the Swedish local council has strengthened in comparison to the state, while the authority of Danish schools and involved parents has increased at the cost of the local council.

The school's administrative structure has changed significantly, but this has occurred without a rise in the number of administrators. Instead, it is the teachers who have increased their administrative responsibilities. In order to improve both the school's financial situation and the ability of different departments to work in harmony, a matrix organisation has been developed where forms and subjects are integrated. This precludes negotiations and compromises, resulting in the decentralisation of economic prioritisation and decision-making. Decentralisation is responsible for a 10 per cent saving in the cost of the school system, largely as a result of reducing the need for substitute teachers. At the same time, teaching quality has improved due to better co-ordination of subjects and superior course material. Like Rödeby, Rønnebær Allé School has taken a bad situation and made it better. In this case, however, the improvement can be directly traced to a fresh management attitude and a new organisation rather than to changes in the physical environment.

William H. Crocker Middle School

William H. Crocker Middle School is located in Hillsborough, a wealthy San Francisco suburb; it is a school which lives up to its motto, 'The best, and getting better'. Academic performance exceeds the average both at state and national level. Crocker has received awards for educational programmes and has been chosen as one of the best schools in the US three times (1983, 1989, 1993). Nearly all (99.8 per cent) of Crocker students later begin a university education and 98 per cent of them complete an undergraduate degree. The school management fosters active parent involvement and participates in several educational networks whose goal it is to reform teaching while encouraging comprehensive co-ordination of subjects and classes.

Hillsborough's school district contains three elementary schools and one middle school, Crocker, which has 394 students, covering the 6th, 7th and 8th grades. Teachers are organised in an overlapping team structure. Students are organised in six groups of 6th graders, four groups of 7th graders and six groups of 8th graders. Students attend high school after they complete middle school; high school consists of grades 9 to 12.

More and more schools across the US are being transformed into middle schools. This change is largely a result of a comprehensive investigation, 'Caught in the Middle' (1987). This study established that grades 6 to 8 should be regarded as more than a simple preparation for continued scholastic efforts. Pupils in these grades need a school organised in such a way as to balance the interest between scholastic matters and the psychological development of the child.

Crocker School was chosen for this study largely because the degree of parental involvement is significantly different from the other three schools. Parents are involved in managing the library, cafeteria, task forces, and joint committees with teachers and in teaching electives. Whereas over the last three years the school's teachers taught a total of 20,000 hours, volunteer hours 'given' by parents totalled 11,000 hours. Crocker employs 24 teachers, one remedial teacher, two school administrators and ten additional members of staff.

Each year the Hillsborough school district engages in various types of fund-raising activities with the help of 100 volunteers: over US$400,000 was collected in 1991. The state of California is ranked thirty-first in the US when it comes to the amount of federal and state funds spent on education and the students' parents raise approximately 10 per cent of the district's annual budget. Seeking funds, awards or recognition for special projects and otherwise improving the institution's financial situation is an important activity for the school administration.

COMPARATIVE PRODUCTIVITY

Productivity is not a frequently used concept in the evaluation of schools. Table 6.1, however, provides some idea of relative productivity by comparison of student/staff ratios.

Table 6.1 Comparative productivity

	Rödeby	Bräcke	Rønnebær	Crocker
Students per teacher	13.1	7.8	12.5	15.8
National average	10	10	11	n.a.
Students per school leader	368	263	312	197
Students per non-teaching staff	51	19	30	39*
Students per total staff	8.8	5.6	8.6	10.6†
Number of students in secondary level	497	84	137	394
Total number of students in the school	925	263	625	394
Total number of school administrators	2.5	1	2	2

*If the total parent contribution were included the figure would be 21.
†If the total parent contribution were included the figure would be 8.8.

The student to teacher ratio in Swedish schools averages 10:1. This is a comparatively low ratio and is explained by the fact that considering it includes many teachers involved in native language training for immigrants, special education instructors and the low student/teacher ratio in the extensive, less populated areas of Sweden. Denmark has 11 students to one teacher, but comparable figures are not available for the US.

Crocker School enjoys a student to teacher ratio markedly higher than the other schools. At the same time, Rödeby and Rønnebær Allé schools both exhibit higher productivity than other schools in their respective countries.

Can one therefore conclude that Crocker school is more productive? If the definition of productivity hinges on the student to teacher ratio then the answer is yes. However, further analysis is needed. It has previously been shown that there is a strong connection between a student's socio-economic background and academic performance. A school which is located in an affluent district such as Crocker School has less need for special teachers. By contrast, Rønnebær Allé School's students come from difficult backgrounds and, as a result, one-quarter of the teaching staff is occupied with providing services for these students.

Furthermore, when making such comparisons it must be remembered that teachers have different schedules and class times in different countries. For example:

- at Crocker, teachers have 23, 60-minute lessons/week;
- at Rödeby and Bräcke, teachers have 24, 40-minute lessons/week;
- at Rønnebær, teachers have 25, 45-minute lessons/week.

None the less it is apparent that although the work year is approximately the same (180 days), Crocker enjoys higher productivity partially because its teachers spend more time actually teaching in the classroom.

However, looking at non-teaching staff, including those who work in the library, cafeteria and housekeeping department, Rödeby School emerges as the most productive. Parents undertake much of this work at the Crocker School; when their contribution is included the school's productivity is reduced to one member of staff per 21 students – approximately the same as at Bräcke, the smallest school in the study. Total productivity, taking into account the parents' time contribution, also becomes more comparable with that at Rödeby and Rønnebær. The number of people in the management team (school administrators) varies from 2.5 in Rödeby to one in Bräcke.

Overall, however, Crocker School does appear more productive. One possible explanation for this is the relatively greater amount of resources spent on school management and the extra support the school receives from parents. This allows the teachers to concentrate on teaching and therefore be more productive. Whether this method is superior or more effective can only be determined by examining the goals the school has set.

However, a simple productivity comparison is not the sole basis for evaluating the schools in question, although such an analysis, which focuses on an institution's unit costs, is in line with a budget-linked system's evaluation of resource needs. Increasing productivity by focusing on unit costs is, analytically speaking, very simple: to raise productivity in schools is more a matter of increasing class size or the student to teacher ratio. Whether or not that type of action is desirable is much more debatable.

FACTORS INFLUENCING PRODUCTIVITY

A number of external and internal factors help explain why these four schools are indeed 'good schools'.

External factors

Local environment

Every organisation is influenced by, and is dependent on, its environment. Due to the complexity of a school's goals and responsibilities, evaluation is made by those who have the most at stake: parents, students, teachers and the administration. It is important that the schools' personnel judge the institution in relation to its environment, an environment which can be influenced in many ways. What these four schools have in common is just that – the interested parties are actively involved in influencing the environment.

Rödeby School's attitude toward the local environment can be regarded as an attempt to change the school from the outside. The school's contacts with the local press and business world are a further attempt at positively marketing the school. The broad range of contacts that the Crocker School possesses due to parents' activities is also another form of marketing and customer relations. Parents quickly discover both defects and improvements at the school, as well as providing constant feedback regarding the latest developments.

Fund raising

Fund raising should not be restricted to special projects, but should be an active commitment involving parents and the community in the school's organisation.

Relationship with the community

A school is an important member of the surrounding society. While, unlike a company, it cannot react strategically and choose a market, it can have a co-operative relationship with the local community.

Decentralisation

Decentralisation and fewer regulations increase opportunities for a competent school to change and grow. Strong leadership within the school can achieve the same goals despite regulations, by seeking to influence local politicians.

Networking

Participation in a greater network of schools is a way of supporting developing ideas, projects and experimentation. Active participation by management in a network is essential for the continuous input of new thoughts and resources.

Image

A school's image is important. What opinions do students, parents, personnel, politicians and the public have of the school? A positive image perpetuates its success.

Rödeby School

Every possible opportunity is taken at Rödeby to positively influence the public's image of the school. It is in regular contact with the local papers and aims to have at least one positive article per month published about the school. This has been school policy for the last five or six years – since the buildings were renovated. The majority of the articles report on sports events, student participation in competitions, special activities etc. Rödeby's sister-school programme with schools in the Baltic states, including exchange of teachers and students, has also been of interest to the newspapers. The school also undertakes other imaginative projects such as a co-operative work project with local companies. As part of the Vocational Guidance System, the project aims to improve students' attitudes to industrial work. In addition, the school publishes an annual catalogue of various activities and opportunities available to students in the local community (sports and social clubs etc.). Parents and students are kept actively informed on relevant information such as the teachers' weekly and yearly teaching schedule.

Bräcke School

Bräcke School's involvement with the free municipality project has resulted in greatly increased independence for the school and its management. Today the school's relationship with the local council is largely a matter of determining how large the school's financial resources will be. The school has been quite successful in attracting funds, not only because it is located in a sparsely populated area, but also because it has integrated handicapped children into the student body. In addition, Bräcke has long worked with the public recreation centres, *fritids*, and various other groups in developing an integrated schoolday whereby secondary school students begin and end their day at the same time without any inactive gaps in their schedule.

Another factor contributing to the school's quality is the principal's active participation in a much-appreciated network for the continued education of teachers. As the school is located in a fairly small community, it is natural that the head teacher and teachers play an important role in the community as a whole – not just the school.

Rønnebær Allé School

Although the disadvantaged community surrounding Rønnebær School exerts a significant influence on it, the energies of a new management team have enabled the students to receive a worthwhile education. While the reasons for these improvements are largely internal, the key external factor influencing productivity has been decentralisation. Since 1990 the school has been directed by a board consisting largely of parents. Immigrant parents are also represented, giving them an unusual chance to be involved with, and influence, the Danish school system. Although it is too early to say what power shifts may occur due to the composition of the school board, it does seem that the power of the local council and politicians has diminished, whereas that of the school's head teacher and personnel has increased. The school has, however, an important resource in the learning centre run by the local council from which teachers can borrow material and participate in various kinds of educational programmes.

The Crocker School

The children's family background plays an important role at the Crocker School as it does at Rønnebær, although in quite a different way. Most of the students have parents who are well educated and earn high incomes. The parents dedicate a good deal of time to their children's school and this is certainly a contributing factor to its quality. Parents spend an average of four work days per year at the school and their activities range from helping in the library or the cafeteria to sitting on committees and fund raising.

The school has developed an ability to secure a variety of resources, including scholarships, prizes, contributions and awards from foundations, institutions, state and federal organisations. It belongs to a network of 100 middle schools in California which is used as a partner in development projects and for the continued education of school personnel.

The framework of the Crocker School's curriculum is provided by the California Department of Education. However, considerable freedom is given for local development at the school level. The work that the school personnel undertake in organising the curriculum is developmentally stimulating and contributes to higher competence among the teachers. Innovative experimentation in collaboration with university researchers results in conference presentations and visits from teachers from other schools, all of which promote a teacher's continuous skills development.

INTERNAL FACTORS

Three internal factors emerge as being most critical to the success of the four schools.

- Leadership: The effect of the four head teachers' ideas and values on the work of the schools is striking. Leadership is development and action orientated, but differs between each institution. It may be directed towards activities, finance and administration, the development of human resources and towards the development of staff competence.
- Work organisation: The way in which teachers are organised in teams, working units, subject groups or a matrix structure is important. Organising teachers into units increases opportunities for development and discourages professional isolation. The organisation provides a framework for co-ordination and co-operation, facilitates a decision-making process that is in touch with activities and gives teachers responsibilities other than direct teaching.
- Evaluation: Students in the Swedish schools work actively in evaluating teaching. They are also given information about, and some influence over, the content and form of their education. The evaluations carried out in Rödeby School can be compared with how other businesses investigate customer attitudes towards their services. At Crocker School, on the other hand, students are evaluated, as are teachers, by the management of the school, an evaluation that is used as a basis for development and modification of work routines. This is essentially a form of production control.

Rödeby School

Rödeby School is known for its pleasant and courteous student atmosphere. The teachers seem to be able to spend the majority of their time on classroom teaching, while the school took advantage of its physical renovation also to improve the general working environment.

The students are involved, as part of their art and workshop classes, in the interior design of the school and thus the design process is constantly changing as one class graduates and a new group takes over the classrooms.

The increased influence of students on their surroundings is also manifest in a number of other projects, both practical and academic: exhibitions may display the results of the latest evaluation of the school, while formal teaching may occasionally be adjourned to allow for discussion and written documentation of students' opinions and suggestions.

The school has a very active sports club which also arranges theatrical events and an annual Christmas party which is open to students' families.

The school's general policy is to create a positive working atmosphere for all concerned by dedicating time for discussion of problems, questions or new ideas. Problems or dissatisfaction that occur between parent/student and teacher are handled systematically. The situation is first discussed between student and teacher in the classroom. If a solution cannot be found at that stage then the class teacher is called in as a negotiator: the next stage is to involve the principal and the parents.

Bräcke School

Bräcke School's motto 'More people, less paper,' exemplifies the head teacher's personal approach to management rather than Bräcke's plan to diminish bureaucracy via its free municipality project. The principal's approach allows great independence; each work group is headed by a project manager (a teacher) who also participates in the school administration. Each project manager therefore spends less time in classroom teaching and has an office for administrative work. The head teacher plays an important part in this process by supporting these individuals in their new roles.

Nearly all the teachers at Bräcke School have a work assignment in addition to their teaching responsibilities. Some are project managers, others may be accountable for the school's computers or student counselling. Due to the organisation of the teaching team (members 'cover' for each other's classes, rather than employing substitutes), individual members are able to participate in important conferences and projects which are developed for a network of schools in the local area.

Projects within certain areas can be regarded as work leading to increased personal development. This belief is perhaps the most distinctive characteristic of the school. The time teachers dedicate to extra projects, conferences, courses etc. is detailed in a long-term plan. The aim of this investment is to increase teachers' competence, enabling them to cover both a broader range of subjects and to teach in greater depth.

Rønnebær Allé School

Rønnebær's strength, as is the case with the two Swedish schools, lies with its head teacher. He arrived in the late 1980s to find a school plagued with problems not just among the students. The teachers were entrenched in a hierarchical system of their own making, and inter-group tension hindered effective work. The head teacher was able to turn the situation around so that today the school is an efficient and optimistic workplace. The changed emphasis in the areas of financial planning and organisational problem solving have been essential factors in this transformation. These changes have brought about a renewed interest and dedication among school personnel.

The teachers are organised in a matrix system; they are connected to both a form, and to a specific subject and decisions concerning the allocation of funds are made according to the 'rules' of the system. The principal has also invested energy in numerous projects in the hope of not only attracting interest and new funding to the school, but also of providing inspiration to its teachers.

The Crocker School

The Crocker School belongs to a network of approximately 100 schools that has been established to further the development of middle schools in California. Membership of this network provides a stimulus for both head teachers and teachers, while also serving as an impetus for continuous improvement. Teachers and head teachers are also members of professional networks. Combined with Crocker's ambition to be one of the outstanding schools in the state, the school's policy is proactive; for example, staff do not attend conferences purely to listen to other speakers but to make presentations themselves. The teachers' participation in conferences and other networks encourages a kind of 'product development', since teaching methods and pedagogical techniques are developed, discussed and evaluated by colleagues.

Teachers are principally responsible for a group of students, but there is no specific subject responsibility. Teachers are considered primarily to be educators and are expected to cover for each other, teaching different subjects. They are organised in overlapping teams (with the head teacher as the 'coach') and have a heavier teaching load than in Sweden (23, 60-minute lessons per week). Furthermore they are expected to involve themselves in development work within the school, without a reduction in teaching hours in compensation.

Teachers are assessed after two years' employment to decide whether or not they should be offered permanent employment: subsequent assessments are on an annual basis. While it cannot be said that the teachers' work at the school is characterised by heavy input from parents, their contribution does create both a natural link between the home and school environments, and focuses on the teachers' role as educators. The teachers take care of the teaching, while other functions are not only the responsibility of the school, but are also shared with students and parents.

COSTS AND QUALITY

It would clearly be interesting to compare the quality of each school's product and services, but also to relate quality to the cost of production. However, previous comments on the duality of school goals have served to highlight the complexity of this type of comparison and, as a consequence, cost and quality are considered separately.

Comparative costs

In general, financial data on each school proved both difficult to obtain and patchy. For example, the school buildings are not listed as an asset in Crocker's accounts nor are they regarded as an expense. Despite this lack of information, however, it is possible to make some comparisons on relative costs.

Total costs per student vary greatly between different schools in Sweden – from US$5,000 to 9,600. Such significant cost differences can be explained by variations in the size of the school and its teaching staff since the two main components of a school budget are teachers' salaries and the cost of premises. Average costs and the student/teacher ratio are generally higher in smaller towns and in rural areas, while the most cost-effective schools have large classes and utilise the building space as efficiently as possible.

Modern business management, however, is less concerned with narrow cost-per-unit comparisons and is more interested in broader dynamic analysis and the discussion of an organisation's cost drivers. This is achieved by evaluating factors such as product range, variety, capacity utilisation, maintenance and quality. How, therefore, can this approach be taken into account when discussing education?

The dynamic approach states that the cost drivers in a school are connected to decisions about form divisions, age divisions and the number of optional subjects or 'lines' (study programmes) from which a student may choose. Add to that the degrees of variation among the students and, according to this line of reasoning, a quite homogeneous group of students requires fewer resources to obtain a certain goal than a heterogeneous group. There are, however, no simple linear connections between resources and effect when it concerns these cost drivers.

Parental participation in school activities is also important, particularly at Crocker School. It increases the desire for quality but probably has less of an effect on cost consciousness. Increased parental participation, unconnected to economic decision-making, runs the risk of becoming cost determining. It can be assumed, however, that parents at the Crocker School can accept the limited resources since they are heavily involved in fund raising.

The budget process which decides the distribution of a school's resources, dictates the financial allocation of teaching services. This process, therefore, does not contain any incentive to increase efficiency by replacing teachers with work-saving methods. The structure of the teachers' work, which is mainly quantified in lesson hours, can be made more effective by reducing the lesson time, and replacing it with managerial and developmental contributions. An example of this is Bräcke School, where several teachers spend less time actually teaching and more time with other work assignments. This approach can have quite an influence on a school since it raises overall quality, but it can also be counterproductive in certain specific areas. Similarly, the availability of many optional subjects or courses increases costs but can, at the same time, reduce internal differences between students in the classroom.

Quality

Unlike other institutions or businesses, schools make their own decisions about the quality of their product – students' knowledge. Although there are national tests in Sweden which facilitate the comparison of students' achievements from school to school and with the national average, schools do not seem to actively use grade averages during an evaluation process. Variations among students can usually be explained by the disparity of their qualifications. One possible exception to this is the rise in grade averages at Rödeby School which can be used to 'prove' that recent policy changes are producing positive results.

When business economists discuss quality in terms of the production of goods, they use the term to mean a number of things: the product's life expectancy, reliability, and the company's ability to produce and deliver the goods to customer satisfaction. The key factor influencing the customer-related end of the quality issue is therefore flexibility, that is, how much variation the company is capable of, and how quickly it can adapt and innovate.

Adapting the language of quality analysis to the education process is not without problems. For instance, the grades of a school's graduating class cannot be the standard measure by which the goals of the entire school should be judged. With a wider understanding of quality, however, it becomes possible to evaluate other aspects of the school's performance. For example, how many students graduate from secondary school? How many continue on to college, university or professional schools? What are the positive and negative aspects of students continuing their studies and how much time is spent learning a profession?

One of the important goals for a business is to constantly improve; it needs to develop and adapt the goods or services it offers in order to meet consumer demand. The organisation thus undergoes continuous rationalisation in order to keep production costs at a level that is acceptable to the consumer. Companies producing goods react to a number of complex market signals and thus know how low or how high to set their prices. A company's 'quality' therefore can be judged on how effectively they respond to these signals, and one must evaluate the continuous changes occurring in the company and its eventual potential. An in-depth analysis can take into account the organisation's ideas, management and personnel competence, and the functioning of certain key processes within the firm.

In contrast, quality assessment in schools is a less direct, more subjective judgement by parents. That judgement is made on the basis of the information and impressions they receive from their children, factors which, in comparison with other organisations, result in reduced requirements for cost efficiency but at the same time improved quality. There are, however, possible objective measurements also in a school. Factors analysed in such an evaluation could, for example, include: absentee rate due to illness, turnover rate of staff and students, late arrivals, no-shows and participation in the meal programme.

BARRIERS TO INCREASED PRODUCTIVITY

The foregoing sections review those factors or circumstances which are of importance to successful schools. It is equally important to consider those factors constituting obstacles to improvement.

Decentralisation by policy

The decentralisation process in Sweden means that the municipalities are taking on a greater part of the state's previous role.

As a part of the decentralisation process, a decision has been taken in Karlskrona to divide the various local school districts into smaller units. This means that a well-functioning area with strong and successful leadership will be divided into smaller units, one for each level of education. Since one of the possible reasons why Rödeby and other Swedish schools have been successful may well be that well-qualified administrators have had a large enough unit and sufficient staff to work with, this decision raises the question as to whether leadership objectives have been placed too low.

This example shows that, compared to both Denmark and California, Swedish schools will, in future, still be subject to more political control. By contrast, parents and head teachers in Denmark and California have a greater influence than they do in Sweden.

Leadership

Leadership in a school has been suggested as one of the most important factors in its success. The differences in relative authority between a school head teacher and a company executive are however great, both when it comes to the content and organisation of activities, and to the recruited personnel. The head teacher acts within a relatively structured field of activity and up to now, generally speaking, only ex-teachers have been appointed as head. (Typical career progression is from teacher to deputy head and later to head.) Is this the best way to satisfy a school's legitimate need for good leadership?

The words leadership and boss are hardly ever mentioned in schools. Traditionally, teachers are not led – they work independently, although the work can be co-operative, organised in working units. When asked who their boss is, teachers answer unwillingly, 'If it's anyone, it's the head teacher.' Few teaching staff realise that leadership in general is not necessarily restricted to management and control, but also embraces co-ordination, development and change.

Tradition

Tradition can be another obstacle to improvement. One factor in the high cost of running schools, particularly in sparsely populated areas, is the division of students into classes according to their age. Although with traditional divisions, costs can be reduced by amalgamating schools to form larger units, one alternative to exploiting economies of scale in this way, would be a more or less classless school, with a freer use of premises, teachers and other resources.

Another example of a traditional barrier is that it is rarely necessary to justify a school's existence. Schools just exist. In interviews with teachers and head teachers in the four schools, issues such as the identity of the school's customer are not discussed specifically, rather the discussions are typically of a general nature.

Conflicting goals

The unclear objectives that govern schools mean that any evaluation of service efficiency or quality is difficult to interpret. This difficulty can be explained to a large extent by the complexity of school activities in that they simultaneously offer education, social training and care of children so that their parents can work. There are therefore several goals to be considered which may sometimes be incompatible. Increased clarity and priorities about goals should facilitate evaluation of the efficiency of the activities.

Organisation

Many assumptions taken for granted within the context of the school mean that discussions about different forms of organisation do not take place and relatively little is said about the significance of how groups, working units, work or project groups are organised. None the less it is valid to question whether the school as the institution we know it today is primarily a convenient way of collecting together children in a building, divided up according to age. If we instead simply accept that schools should educate and develop children so that by the age of 16 they have achieved certain levels of knowledge, skill and maturity, there will be a considerable degree of freedom as to how these goals are achieved.

Today's school system is steered by a number of more or less hidden institutional factors which explain why schools are the way they are. A first step, if we wish to improve our schools and prepare the way for development, is to try to show and clarify the central assumptions that are taken for granted. Given this background, an organisational perspective is probably of greatest value.

7

HEALTH CARE

Authors: Bengt Jönsson, Clas Rehnberg

HENRY FORD HEALTH SYSTEM, Detroit, MI, USA
PRINCESS ROYAL HOSPITAL, Telford, England, UK
UDDEVALLA HOSPITAL, Uddevalla, Sweden

A hospital is an organisation where specialists have great influence on *what* services should be provided and *how* they should be provided. Customers – that is, patients – often do not pay directly for these services and also have limited opportunities to evaluate their quality. Instead, these services are paid for by a third party, which may be a public agency or an insurance company. The crucial factors behind increased productivity are how the ground rules of this system are formulated and especially how the third party determines its rules for compensation to hospitals.

The Henry Ford Health System – a health maintenance organisation (HMO) centred at the Henry Ford Hospital – has high labour productivity but also, like most American hospitals, very high costs in international terms. One reason why the system has performed so well is that the Henry Ford Hospital, located in the inner city of Detroit, suffered a resource scarcity during the 1970s because many people moved into the suburbs. The hospital responded to this challenge by expanding its operations, establishing suburban ambulatory care centres. Unlike most American hospitals, the hospital uses only physicians employed on a salary basis. Its physicians thus have a greater incentive to improve medical services. The Henry Ford Health System also taught us that it is possible to have rapid, detailed financial reporting in a hospital.

The Princess Royal Hospital is a cost-effective hospital. A large part of its efficiency is explained by the fact that the goals of its senior physicians and the hospital coincide. Senior physicians are expected to perform a certain number of operations per week and may also treat a certain number of private patients. Senior physicians function as a kind of entrepreneur in the hospital and it is in their interest to put pressure on their staff physicians to perform well.

Sweden's Uddevalla Hospital does not require its physicians to perform a given quantity of services. Instead its owner, the county council, has begun to manage productivity by penalising the hospital if waiting times for certain elective *surgeries* become too long. After a certain waiting period, the patient is entitled to seek care elsewhere, at the expense of the original hospital.

THE HEALTH CARE SECTOR

During the past three decades health care has been one of the most rapidly expanding sectors among industrialised nations. Regardless of the measure used – total expenditure, employment, or percentage of gross domestic product (GDP) health care emerges as one of the dominant 'businesses' in the industrialised world. During the early 1960s, the sector's share of GDP was approximately 4 per cent in the Organisation for Economic Co-operation and Development (OECD) nations: today that figure has doubled. Figures 7.1 and 7.2 illustrate the increase in health care expenditure and employment in Sweden, the UK and the US during the period 1960-1990.

Sweden and the US (in particular) devote substantially more resources to health care than does the UK. The difference between Sweden and the US largely reflects differences in absolute and relative prices (wages). Sweden, for example, has a higher share of health care employment and more doctors per capita than the US but a significantly lower share of the GDP devoted to health care. However, trends over time in all three countries are similar, i.e. an increase in resources and costs. International comparisons indicate that high expenditures in health care correlate mainly to a high GDP per capita. As health care costs have increased, public financing has covered a greater share of health services.

Is this expansion reflected in terms of improved health status, better accessibility and higher quality? One problem with productivity analysis at the macro level is to specifically identify the contribution which health services make towards improvements in health status. Many factors such as education, housing standards and social services contribute to the population's health, while health care also comprises a complex production chain in which hospitals, nursing homes and primary care each contribute various services that together influence health status. Identifying the contribution which each sub-sector makes to the health status of the population is even more difficult. Therefore, it is more practical to focus on the productivity of health care services (Table 7.1).

172 Achieving Service Productivity

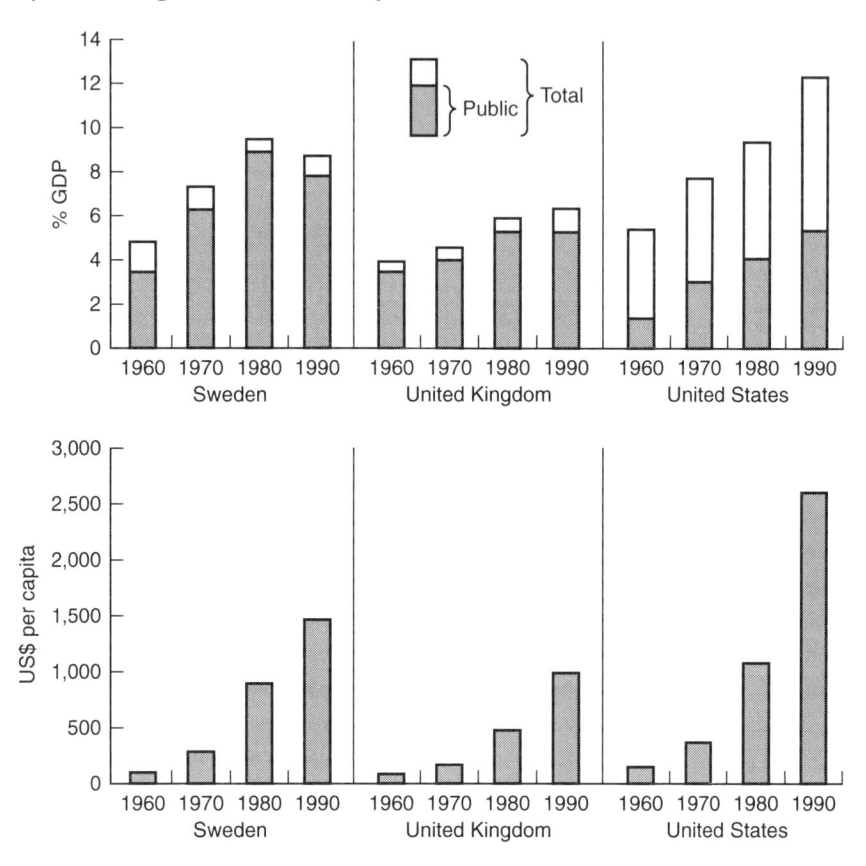

Figure 7.1 Total health expenditures as a percentage of gross domestic product and per capita spending (in US dollars[1]) for Sweden, the United Kingdom and the United States

[1] Measured in GDP purchasing power parities.

Source: OECD 1992

Table 7.1. Annual number of visits per physician in Sweden, the UK and the US, 1970–1985

	1970	1975	1980	1985
Sweden	1,447	1,516	1,181	1,044
United Kingdom	3,645	3,158	3,442	3,023
United States	3,026	2,978	2,467	2,450

Source: OECD 1992

Health care employees as a percentage of employment

Physicians per 10,000 inhabitants

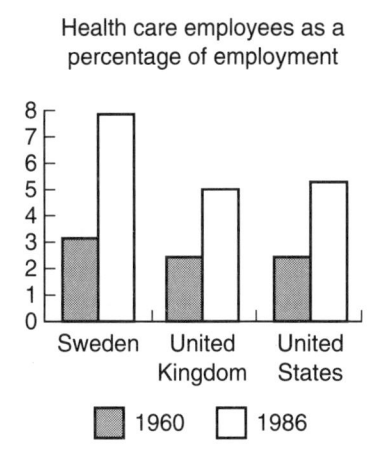

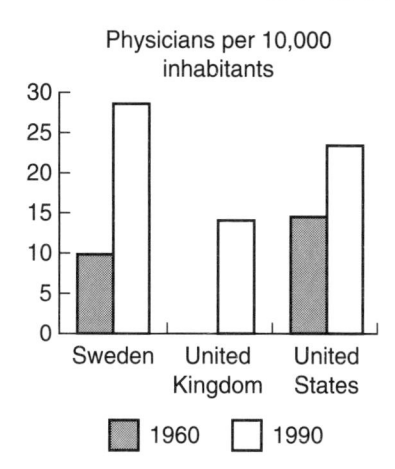

Figure 7.2 Health care employment and physicians per capita 1960 and 1986/90

Source: OECD 1992

The data in Table 7.1 show that all three countries are facing a decrease in productivity measured as visits per physician: a similar trend is shown if productivity is measured as cost per bed-day or cost per admission. This development is usually attributed to changes in technology and case mix demanding more intensive use of resources and improvements in quality. The more intensive use of new technology during a visit or an admission and the ability to treat more severe illnesses have increased costs per treatment. Thus, a proper analysis of productivity in the health care sector must take the benefits of these changes into consideration.

Hospital services

During the twentieth century, hospitals have emerged as the central production unit for health care. Hospital care accounts for about 40 per cent of total health care costs in the US and 60 per cent and 70 per cent in the UK and Sweden respectively. This difference is partly explained by the fact that physicians in the US are not generally employed by hospitals, i.e. their costs are not included in this ratio.

Major differences exist in the services provided by hospitals in the three countries. The general trend in each is a sharp reduction in the number of bed-days per capita. This trend is explained by a shift from in-patient care to out-patient care (day surgery), particularly in the US. Hospitals play a dominant role in the Swedish health system as reflected in the high figures for

174 Achieving Service Productivity

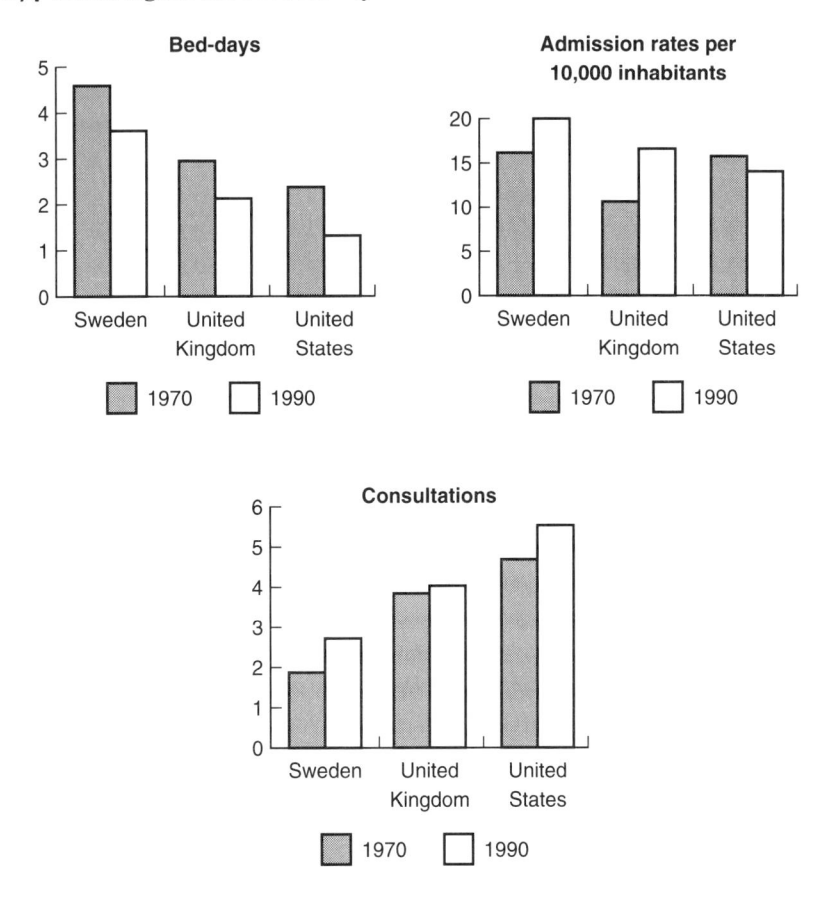

Figure 7.3 Bed-days, admission rates and consultations per capita

hospital days and hospital admissions while, in addition, hospitals account for half of all physician visits. By contrast, patients in the UK and the US receive much of their health care outside the hospital, via British family physicians and US private practitioners, who are often specialists.

The structure of the hospital sector also differs between countries. The UK and Sweden have a long tradition of publicly owned and controlled hospitals. In the US, however, private interests dominate although it is important to note that most private hospitals are voluntary, non-profit making organisations (Figure 7.4).

Although the hospital sector varies in control and ownership, it is the most regulated part of health care provision in all three countries. In the UK and Sweden the expansion and investment in hospitals is controlled by public authorities through ownership. Competition between hospitals in the US is limited by regulation of prices, expansion and entry into the market.

Productivity studies in the hospital sector indicate a downward trend. In Sweden, studies of the public health services by the Ministry of Finance (ESO) showed that the productivity of acute short-term care in hospitals declined by an average 5.7 per cent per year between 1960–1980. However, it should be noted that some reservations exist concerning both the methodology and the interpretation of the results of this study, particularly the very definition of hospital services. Productivity studies have used non-homogeneous production measures such as hospital days, admissions and physician visits. A modern acute care hospital today deals with approximately 4,000 diagnoses and provides approximately 2,000 different surgical procedures. The *per diem* cost of a hospital day thus varies substantially according to the type of operation.

Furthermore, hospital productivity studies are often aimed at studying cost-effectiveness in a strictly technical sense. Quality aspects of a purely medical nature, as well as 'service quality', such as adapting services to patient preferences, tend not to be addressed. The emergence of new treatment methods means, for example, that patients today may be treated for a shorter period which results in a more intensive (and expensive) hospital stay. The trend towards treating patients on an ambulatory basis instead of admitting them has the same effect. Several examples exist where pharmaceutical and ambulatory treatments can replace in-patient care at a considerably lower cost per treatment. These examples show that technological innovation can also improve productivity in the service sector.

Health insurance and productivity management

In a competitive market, the consumer judges the price of goods and services in relation to their quality (doing things right) and according to preference (doing the right things). However, one essential characteristic separates health care from other markets – the existence of a third party in addition to the consumer and the producer (provider). Since illness is unpredictable and can result in serious economic consequences for the individual, various insurance arrangements have emerged. The insurer may be a public authority as in the UK and Sweden, or multiple private insurance firms as in the US. This third party provides insurance protection to patients for reimbursement in the form of taxes or actuarial-based premiums. This economic relationship is summarised graphically in Figure 7.5.

176 Achieving Service Productivity

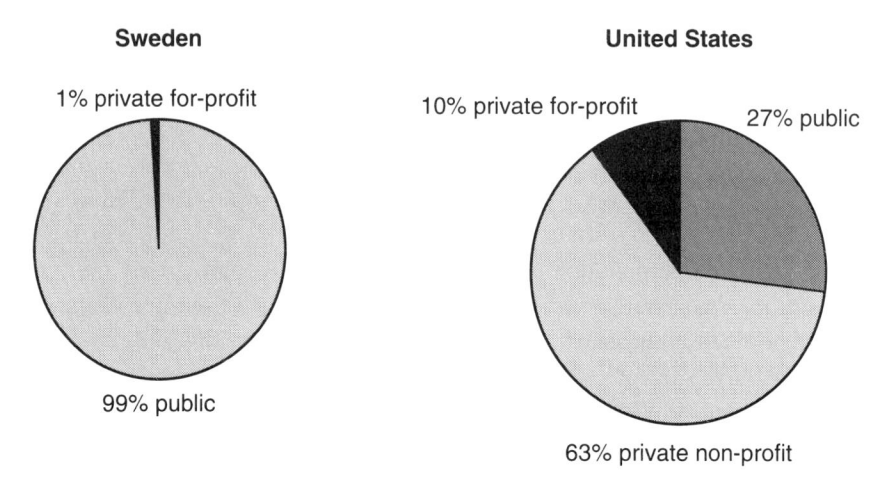

Sweden

1% private for-profit

99% public

United States

10% private for-profit

27% public

63% private non-profit

United Kingdom

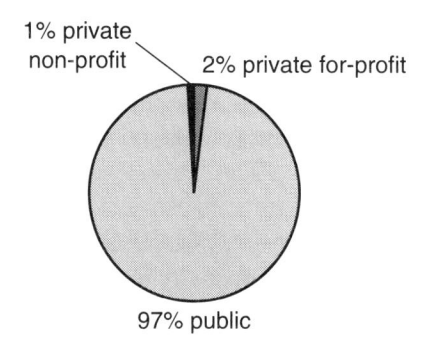

1% private non-profit

2% private for-profit

97% public

Figure 7.4 Ownership status in the hospital sector

Source: The directory of independent hospitals and health services 1988/1989, Raffel & Raffel 1989

Many of the productivity problems in health care may be traced back to this triangular relationship. The patient and the provider exchange little money directly. The patient pays a fee for health care which covers only a small portion of the total cost of the service. Insurance protection is managed by one or more insurers from whom the providers of care receive most of their revenue. This means that neither the patient nor the provider is particularly interested in costs or cost-effectiveness when choosing treatment alternatives. That responsibility falls on the third party, which is directly responsible for payment. Consequently, the productivity of the various health services depends to a great extent on how successfully the insurer can

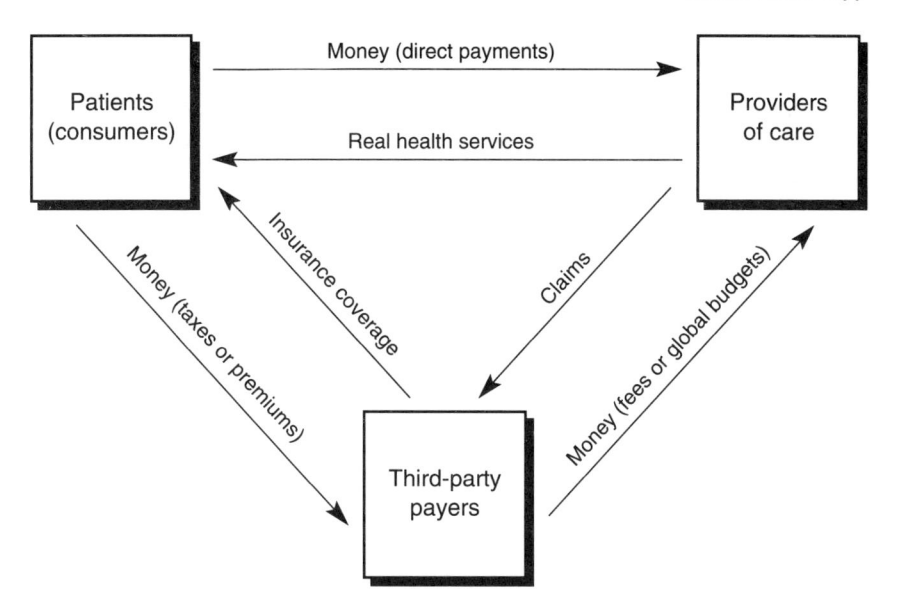

Figure 7.5 Economic relationships in the delivery of health care

influence the provider. Both incentives and administrative processes may be used to reduce costs and achieve cost-effectiveness.

Insurers may also contain costs through, for example, patient charges and deductibles. However, patient-directed measures such as these often conflict with political goals of resource distribution in society and sometimes have little effect. The information advantage which the provider has over the patient is one reason why direct fees etc. might have little effect. Patients evaluate only the qualitative aspects of the service since the price they pay is low.

The influence of a strong profession is another key factor which impacts on productivity in health care. The information advantage of the provider also affects the relationship with the insurer. Because the medical profession has superior information concerning the need for various treatments, insurers have had considerable difficulty in managing productivity and the quality of services provided. The objectives of the medical profession have therefore played a central role in the configuration of health care services. One consequence, besides a limited interest in productivity, is the dissemination of increasingly advanced technologies, the effects of which have not been assessed either by well-informed consumers in the marketplace or by payers through health insurance.

THE HOSPITALS STUDIED

The task of choosing successful and productive hospitals is difficult; hospitals serve different local markets to which their productivity is adapted, in turn making comparison of different systems difficult. The choice of hospitals was therefore initially based on which health care systems would be interesting to compare. Thereafter, a successful hospital was selected. An important reason for choosing a British hospital was, as discussed earlier, the low cost of the British health care system by international standards. British hospitals are also considered to be efficient by researchers who have studied their internal efficiency. The Princess Royal Hospital in Telford was selected following discussions with consultants, researchers and personnel in the Swedish health services who are familiar with British health care.

The US spends more on health care than any other nation and its health care system is the most dynamic. Indeed, many organisational reforms which are being introduced in Europe originated in the US. Selecting the Henry Ford Hospital in Detroit, Michigan, was easier than selecting the other two hospitals. It is widely regarded as among the leading hospitals in the country and a health care management journal has identified it as 'One of the best hospitals in America' (Holt 1987). The Henry Ford Hospital is also part of a Health Maintenance Organisation (HMO), which is a type of health care organisation that has a particular relevance for comparison with Sweden and UK.

Selecting a Swedish hospital presented similar problems as in the British case. The choice of Uddevalla Hospital in Bohus County was based on productivity measures traditionally used in health care: contact with researchers who had studied productivity in the public health sector revealed that the hospital has demonstrated good productivity in various ways. Also, Bohus County has been a leader in developing and implementing new financial systems to manage productivity in health services. The County has also shown lower health care costs per inhabitant than the national average for several years.

But uniform productivity measures do not exist within health care. The Princess Royal and Uddevalla Hospitals should be viewed primarily as 'good representatives' of their respective health care systems. Another criterion in the selection was to avoid university hospitals where research and education may influence productivity and provision of health care.

Conditions such as ownership, market structure and size vary between the three hospitals as summarised in Table 7.2.

Table 7.2 Varying conditions at Princess Royal Hospital (PRH), Henry Ford Hospital (HFH) and Uddevalla Hospital

	PRH	HFH	Uddevalla
Ownership	Public	Private (non-profit)	Public
Market structure	Monopoly	Competition	Monopoly
Beds	300	740	569
Employees	794	4,000	2,700
Medical staff	432	1,600	2,100
Population served	200,000	400,000*	160,000
Admissions	13,900	35,400	23,800

*Refers to the insured who are served by the HFH. In addition the hospital serves citizens with other insurances.

The major difference is that the Henry Ford Hospital competes with other providers and thus has a market share of about 10–15 per cent, while the other two hospitals have a monopoly within geographically defined catchment areas. Henry Ford is also a more specialised hospital, primarily responsible for more advanced care. Also noteworthy, when comparing capacity in terms of beds and employees, is the fact that the Princess Royal Hospital serves its catchment with relatively few beds and employees.

Princess Royal Hospital

The Princess Royal Hospital in Telford (near Birmingham, England) opened in September 1989. Its catchment area includes mainly the new city of Telford and older small villages in East Shropshire. The total population of the area is approximately 200,000. The hospital provides services which are normal for a modern district general hospital, i.e. in-patient and out-patient services within the broader areas of general surgery and medicine, emergency and intensive care and rehabilitation.

Until 1990 the hospital was directly managed by the West Midlands Regional Health Authority and the Shropshire District Health Authority, which determined the hospital's budget and mix of services. With the introduction of the Community Care Act of 1990, the British health care districts have become purchasers of hospital services. Thus, from April 1991, the Shropshire District Health Authority has been the largest buyer of hospital services so that today, the hospital's revenue is based on negotiations with the district. The hospital has applied to become an NHS (National Health

Service) Trust hospital, which means that it would be governed as a public institution with greater freedom to make operational decisions. The hospital expects the application to be approved during 1993.

Henry Ford Hospital

The Henry Ford Hospital was founded in 1915 by Henry Ford and other leading businesspeople in Detroit. From the outset, the hospital has operated as a non-profit organisation and employed its own physicians contrary to the general practice in the US. The Detroit region and particularly the automobile industry expanded rapidly during the first 30 years of the hospital's history, contributing to its growth. During the 1960s, it became recognised for its pioneering work in such areas as open heart surgery.

The economic and social changes during the late 1960s had drastic consequences for Detroit and also impacted on activity at the hospital. The riots and social unrest of 1967 brought many people to its emergency facility but many blue and white-collar workers moved to the suburbs. As a result, the Detroit inner city population declined while the percentage of poor increased. While other hospitals in the city moved to the suburbs, the management of the Henry Ford Hospital decided to remain in central Detroit. At the same time, the hospitals in the suburbs, because of their geographic location, became highly competitive in recruiting both physicians and patients. However, public legislation regulating hospital beds during the 1970s prevented Henry Ford Hospital from moving its activities to the suburbs, providing it with a new strategy – to establish large ambulatory care centres in the suburbs.

In 1978 the Ford Motor Company and the United Auto Workers, together with Henry Ford Hospital, created a health maintenance organisation which was named the Health Alliance Plan (HAP). The strategy of offering customers comprehensive health care services – everything from primary care to highly specialised hospital care – guided the organisation during the latter part of the 1980s when it took its present name, the Henry Ford Health System (HFHS).

Uddevalla Hospital

The hospital, which dates back to the late 1700s, has a catchment population of approximately 160,000 in north Bohus County. The hospital is a county district hospital with 26 departments and 13 clinics offering several medical and surgical specialities. It enjoys a leading position in some treatment areas related to new medical technology; for example, it was one of the first county district hospitals in the 1990s to install an extra-corporeal shock wave lithotripsy (ESWL) unit.

When the so-called 'Bohus Organisational Model' is implemented in 1993, the hospital will sell its services to district units within the county. For several years the hospital has been preparing for this new system of internal markets. An important component in this work has been to install information systems which integrate medical and financial information to create a better base for setting prices and managing productivity.

COMPARATIVE PRODUCTIVITY

The comparative performance measures presented in Table 7.3 should be interpreted in light of the comments about the difficulties in defining productivity in hospital care. For example, a hospital with a larger share of severe cases would show higher costs per admission or bed-days and a longer average length of stay.

Table 7.3 Comparative performance: 1991/1992

	PRH	HFH	Uddevalla
Length of stay	6.6 days	7.4 days	6.3 days
(hip replacement)	16.0 days	6.8 days	10.0 days
Occupancy rate	80%	85%	91%
Cost per admission	US$2,650	US$6,400	US$4,060
Cost per bed-day	US$345	US$1,000	US$520
Medical staff/bed	1.4	2.2	3.7
Nurses, nurse assts./bed	0.9	1.8	2.5
'Surgery hours'/surgeon per month (orthopaedics)	60 hours	40 hours	20 hours

The Henry Ford Hospital is a more specialised hospital, which may partly explain the higher cost per admission and hospital day. Since the hospital treats many severely ill patients and offers services such as transplantation, average stays tend to be longer, more intensive and thus more costly. However, the case of hip replacement shows that when a specific treatment is compared, stays are shortest at the Henry Ford Hospital. The hospital also operates at a much higher cost level than the other two, where cost per case differences are smaller. In terms of labour productivity, the Princess Royal

Hospital shows higher performance in nursing care and surgeries, well above the low figure for Uddevalla which may partly be explained by more out-patient visits at surgery clinics.

It should be noted that the above comparisons of performance and productivity are actually of little interest to the hospitals themselves, since they are each active in different geographic markets. What *is* of interest to them is their productivity in relation to other producers in the same local market. As the external factors differ in each of these local markets it provides the opportunity to analyse how hospitals react to different environmental factors.

FACTORS INFLUENCING PRODUCTIVITY

External factors

All three hospitals analysed are similar in that only a small percentage of revenue comes directly from patients. The Henry Ford Hospital receives revenue from multiple insurers, public and private. For the public-owned hospitals, Princess Royal Hospital and Uddevalla Hospital, the public authority also serves as the insurer. All three institutions are part of a system which integrates production and insurance. This arrangement has been motivated by improved opportunities for monitoring and management control by the insurer. However, it also obscures the boundary between the 'firm' and the external factors since the hospital has the same owner as the insurance provider.

For each establishment there are several options for defining what the 'hospital' really is, and thereby defining the external and internal factors. Since each hospital is relatively independent, and because British and Swedish public health systems are increasingly separating financing and production, this analysis considers the hospitals as 'the firms'. External factors, via insurers with the same owners as the hospitals, are exercised through both administrative processes and economic incentives, including prices and contracts.

The importance of these factors varies among the three hospitals studied but those with the greatest influence on hospital productivity are the regulatory framework, the actions of the insurer, the demands from the referring physician, and patient demands for responsiveness and accessibility.

Regulatory framework

Public regulation can influence hospital productivity both positively and negatively, and its effects are not always as intended. When the white

Health Care 183

middle class in Detroit moved to the suburbs in the 1960s, the Henry Ford Hospital was not permitted to move because of a State Certificate of Need (CON) programme regulating hospital beds. The programme permitted the State of Michigan to regulate the number of hospitals and hospital beds, major capital investments in medical technology and changes in service. The objective was cost containment. It was effective since hospitals were required to have a Certificate of Need before they could be reimbursed from the Medicare (the elderly) and Medicaid (the poor) public health insurance programmes.

As Detroit's inner city population declined during the 1970s, the percentage of poor increased, reducing the hospital's revenue and putting it under strong external pressure. Under the direction of the board chairman at that time, Benson Ford (brother of Henry) and subsequently the hospital's CEO during the 1970s, Stanley Nelson, the hospital decided to remain in the inner city but to establish larger ambulatory care units in the suburbs. In 1975 the hospital opened two larger centres for advanced ambulatory care, including day surgery, emergency care and dialysis in which patients were permitted to stay for 23 hours before being discharged. This shows how regulation can have an innovative effect on a hospital's strategy to attract new patients. The introduction of day surgery and ambulatory treatment has clearly proved to be cost-effective, while treatment in ambulatory care settings has demonstrated a lower cost per procedure and a reduced risk of infection. Another positive factor is a lower time cost for patients. Today, Henry Ford Health System owns 35 ambulatory care centres.

Insurers

A key external factor common to all three hospitals is their financial dependency on insurers. Their relationship with these institutions, however, differs both in terms of the number of insurers and in the principles by which costs are reimbursed.

The Henry Ford Hospital receives its revenue in part from the HMO (included in the Henry Ford Health System) and from external public and private insurers. As Figure 7.6 indicates, the public Medicare (elderly) and Medicaid (poor) programmes account for approximately 36 per cent of hospital revenue. Blue Cross/Blue Shield (private, non-profit insurer) and commercial insurers account for approximately 23 per cent and various HMOs account for approximately 40 per cent of revenues.

The public hospitals, Princess Royal Hospital and Uddevalla Hospital, have basically one source of financing, their regional health authority. The move towards separating production from financing in the NHS and the

Bohus County means that the number of buyers of health services will increase. Hospitals can now sell services to regional health authorities outside their own geographic areas.

The GP fundholding reform in the NHS, which gives general practitioners (GPs) some responsibility for hospital budgets, means that the Princess Royal Hospital now has several other payers beside the regional authority. This reform gives GPs the responsibility to purchase elective surgery and all ambulatory care for their patients. The Princess Royal Hospital estimates that GPs will provide approximately 10 per cent of hospital revenues within a few years.

Even at Uddevalla Hospital the importance of payers other than the county council has increased. The so-called 'freedom of choice' agreement among county councils in western Sweden gives patients an opportunity to freely choose their hospital. This has provided the hospital with new patients who are reimbursed by other county councils. It also reduces the hospital's monopoly power, since the patients in the catchment area can choose another hospital.

The effect which the number of financing sources has on hospital productivity is not easy to determine. Pluralism and competition in the insurance system should mean that insurers place greater demands on hospital producers in comparison to insurers with one public monopoly. Insurers in the US health care system have discovered that comprehensive coverage is a more important means of competition than the cost of the premium. Health insurance for the working population is usually paid by the employer as an employee benefit, which further releases the individual from cost considerations. Also, because of their superior information, the providers can play different insurers off against each other through, for example, price discrimination.

Patients with generous insurance plans are treated at a considerably higher price than the average patient at the Princess Royal and Henry Ford hospitals. At the former, private patients provide the hospital with profits to invest in new facilities.

In addition, control of total costs for a defined population is influenced by the number of financing sources. It has been noted on several occasions that health care systems with public financing find cost containment easier. Cost restraints imposed by the Princess Royal Hospital and the Uddevalla Hospital are primarily caused by problems with their public financing.

This economic pressure has made it easier to implement changes in the hospitals' internal management control systems.

Insurance control over care may take many forms. Contracts are used to manage financial relations between care providers and insurance institutions

Health Care 185

Uddevalla Hospital

☐ Bohus County Council
▨ Other county councils
■ Others

Henry Ford Hospital

■ Medicare
▦ Medicaid
▨ Private insurance (non-profit)
▧ Commercial insurance
☐ External HMOs
▨ HAP
■ Others

Princess Royal Hospital

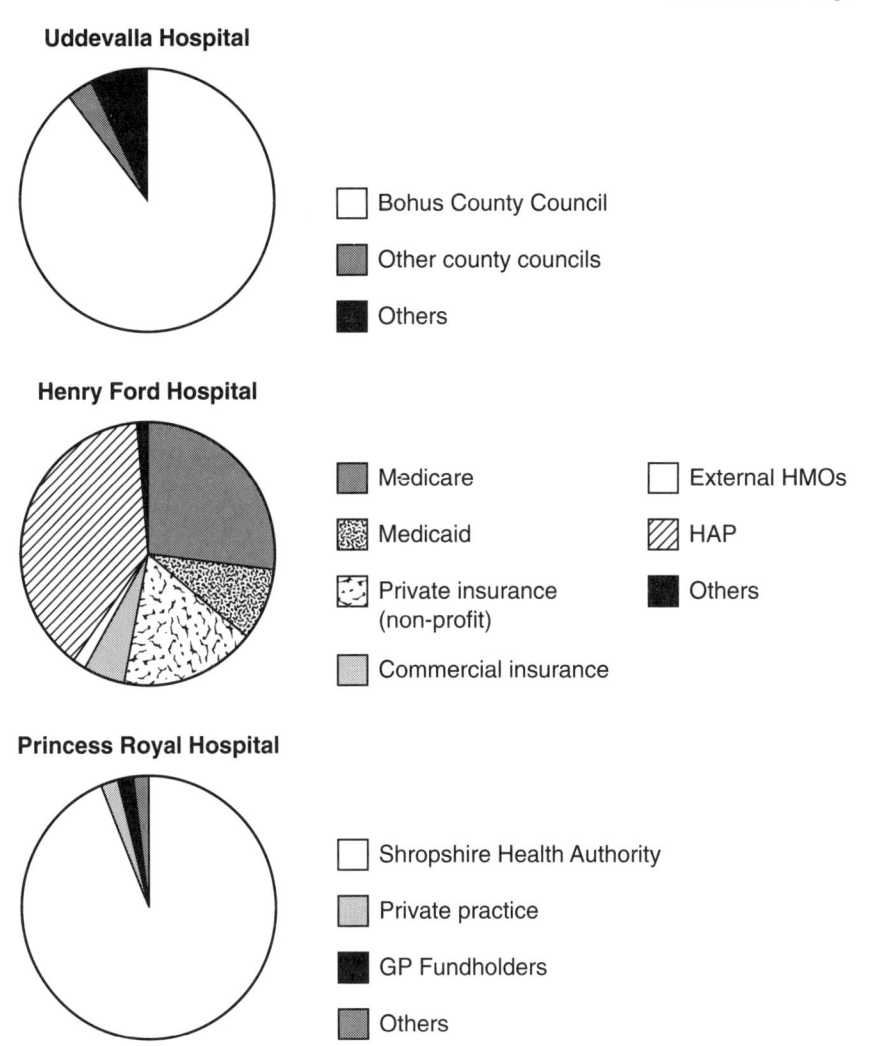

☐ Shropshire Health Authority
▨ Private practice
■ GP Fundholders
▨ Others

Figure 7.6 Sources of revenues for Uddevalla Hospital, Henry Ford Hospital and Princess Royal Hospital

which do not produce care. Another alternative is to integrate insurance and care under the same governing body. Here, administrative rules within the organisation are used to control the providers.

The reimbursement system largely determines how well the insurer controls the hospital. In health care, insurance institutions have had difficulties in determining the value of compensation, i.e. the cost per case. Hospital providers may be reimbursed in several ways including:

186 Achieving Service Productivity

- budget;
- fee-for-service (FFS);
- per care day;
- per episode or case treated (diagnostic related groups: DRG);
- capitation;
- related to outcome;
- negotiated contract.

It is well known that budgets provide little incentive for high productivity, but must be combined with administrative processes which guide the organisation. Reimbursement per unit produced provides a strong incentive to produce many units, but may also promote unnecessary care. Reimbursement per care day provides an incentive to keep the patient longer. Reimbursing the hospital per case treated provides the incentive to economise resources during the care episode and to treat many patients. The reimbursement principles which confront the different hospitals are summarised below.

Princess Royal Hospital:
Contracts with DHA (94%):	Block contracts(= budget)
Private patients (2.2%):	FFS
GPs (2.1%):	Volume and reimbursement per episode of care

Henry Ford Hospital:
Health Alliance Plan (38%):	Capitation (per member)
Medicare/Medicaid (27%):	Reimbursement per episode (DRG)
BC/BS (15%):	Reimbursement per episode (DRG)
Others (11%)	FFS

Uddevalla Hospital:
Bohus County (89%):	Budget
Other county councils (3%):	FFS
Others (8%)	

The Henry Ford Hospital received FFS reimbursement from all insurers for many years but the rapid cost increases in US health care caused public insurance programmes to review their reimbursement system. As a result, during the Reagan administration, the Medicare programme changed its system from retrospective, cost-based reimbursement to prospective reimbursement based on DRG rates. When other insurers such as Blue Cross/Blue Shield later began to use the same system, hospitals were forced to look at their cost per case, which in turn led to changes in, for example, cost accounting. The changes in reimbursement principles led to improved efficiency since hospitals were no longer motivated to overtreat patients: it also encouraged treatment by means of less expensive ambulatory care. However, reimbursement principles based on performance also lead to high administrative costs with the result that the Henry Ford Hospital has a separate billing department to deal with insurers.

The hospital reports that patients with different insurance plans cannot be treated differently simply because of the reimbursement principles. Medical ethics prohibit such behaviour. Hospital administrators observed, however, that insurers will play a more active role in the future by determining the types of service that insurance will cover.

The Princess Royal and Uddevalla Hospitals receive budgets from the health authorities, a procedure which has been effective in containing overall expenditure. In contrast to the reimbursement system at the Henry Ford Hospital, budget allocation is a closed system which limits total costs but at the same time provides little incentive for productivity and efficiency.

Insurers use various administrative processes such as goal setting and sanctions to manage production units, in systems where insurance and production are under common ownership. One directive which has had considerable effect is the goal concerning reduced waiting times within the British NHS and the Swedish county councils. As shown in Table 7.4, waiting times at each of these country's hospitals are long, in contrast to those at the Henry Ford Hospital which reports no such problems.

Table 7.4 Comparative waiting times in 1992 (weeks)

	Princess Royal Hospital	Uddevalla Hospital
General surgery	25	5–24
Orthopaedics	23	16–24
Urology	20	22

The NHS ruled in 1991 that no patient should wait longer than two years for medical treatment. Since then, the Shropshire Health Authority has lowered the maximum wait to one year. This goal has placed considerable pressure on the Princess Royal Hospital to treat patients within the specified time frame in turn, giving priority to patients approaching the one-year limit. Should they fail to meet this goal, the regional health authority has the opportunity to contract with other hospitals.

In 1990, the Swedish Ministry of Health and Social Affairs offered a so-called 'care guarantee' which meant that the waiting time for certain surgical procedures should not exceed three months. When Bohus County accepted these conditions it also received extra state funds. The care guarantee means that if Uddevalla Hospital is unable to treat a patient within the stipulated time, the patient may choose another hospital and the county must pay the bill. The effect has been to significantly improved cost-effectiveness among the surgical specialities and the number of operations has increased without additional resources.

The public insurers for the Princess Royal and Uddevalla Hospitals have thus combined expenditure limitations with demands on the hospitals' activities and performance. Although this is relatively new within the public health care sector, administrators at both hospitals report that these external requirements have increased productivity, improved awareness of the need for cost-effectiveness and facilitated necessary internal changes. For example, at the Uddevalla Hospital, physicians no longer require extra benefits to work overtime; in the past special incentives were required.

Relationship with primary care

When patients receive health care they generally do not receive a single treatment, but rather a course of treatment involving several different activities and the services of several care givers. Advancements in health care have shifted an increasing share of treatment into ambulatory care settings while hospital care has been limited to more complex and specialised cases. Such care, however, depends heavily on co-ordination with other care providers prior to, and following, the hospital stay (Figure 7.7).

The process starts with a visit to a primary health care centre, a visit that can be repeated. The decision to have an operation is made at the hospital's out-patient department before the patient is admitted to the hospital. Post-operative care, such as follow-up treatment, has been taken over by primary health care.

As hospital care has become more specialised, several health systems have consolidated into fewer and larger units. In Detroit this has intensified competition and although the Henry Ford Hospital has survived this structural change, several hospitals in the region have been closed. The increase in market share secured by the Henry Ford Hospital was achieved through its strategy of building a network of primary care settings. Similarly, while Bohus County cut down on hospital care by closing emergency services at several hospitals, the Uddevalla Hospital has been able to avoid reductions and has taken over the closed units. (This restructuring, however, does not necessarily reflect relative productivity at the different hospitals.)

```
┌─────────────────────────┐
│ Primary health care     │
│  – diagnosis            │
│  – tests                │
│  – minor treatment      │
└───────────┬─────────────┘
            ▼
┌─────────────────────────┐
│ Hospital out-patient care│
│  – diagnosis            │
│  – tests                │
└───────────┬─────────────┘
            ▼
┌─────────────────────────┐
│ Hospital in-patient care│
│  – admission            │
│  – major treatment      │
└───────────┬─────────────┘
            ▼
┌─────────────────────────────┐
│ Hospital out-patient/primary care │
│  – follow-up                │
└─────────────────────────────┘
```

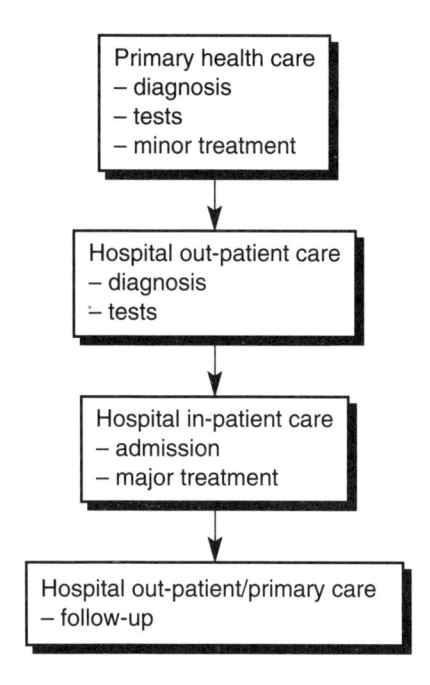

Figure 7.7 The production process for a health care episode

Primary care and free-standing ambulatory clinics have increased their share of health services. These units are generally responsible for the patient's first contact with the health system. Primary care makes an initial judgement about the need for treatment and referral to a specialist or hospital. Primary care physicians have a strong influence on the patients' choice of hospital and they have an interest in well-functioning co-operation with the hospitals, so their patients can receive quick and effective care.

The relationship between the hospital and primary care varies at the three hospitals, reflecting different national traditions. At Uddevalla the hospital's own ambulatory care clinics are responsible for a large portion of the hospital's activity, reflecting the dominance of hospitals in the Swedish health care system. At the Princess Royal Hospital only emergency cases have direct access to the hospital; patients are referred from primary care physicians. Similarly, at the Henry Ford Hospital, initial visits account for a small share of activity except in an emergency where many visits involve uninsured residents who live near the hospital.

Contact with ambulatory care is important to productivity in two respects. First, ambulatory care functions are a link between the hospital and the patient, selecting patients for hospital care. The Henry Ford Hospital in particular recognises this function. With the migration of the white middle class to the suburbs during the 1960s the hospital adopted a strategy of co-operating with the area's physicians. With the establishment of two larger ambulatory care centres in 1975 (including day surgery, emergency care and dialysis) the construction of a network of ambulatory care units was initiated. The current network includes 32 centres spread over a radius of 30 miles in the Detroit area. These satellite units mean that patients in the suburbs can be referred to Henry Ford Hospital but they also represent a move towards a comprehensive network of health care services, in turn giving the hospital a broad customer base.

Secondly, ambulatory care is an external factor which influences hospital productivity by creating demands on the organisation. The ambulatory care centres in the Henry Ford Health System co-ordinate with the hospital via administrative processes. In addition, several independent physicians' practices can choose to refer to several hospitals in the Detroit region, taking into account factors such as accessibility and quality.

The other two hospitals studied have become more dependent on primary care physicians since the introduction of the internal market in public health care systems. This applies mainly to the Princess Royal Hospital, which must adapt its services to the demands of the GPs. The hospital's marketing activities to the GPs in the region reflect this dependency; whereas previously, marketing was an unknown phenomenon for the hospital, visits by hospital managers to potential contracting GPs are now important. Uddevalla Hospital is less dependent on primary care since a relatively large percentage of patients seek care directly at the hospital; the division between hospital care and primary care is more strict and the number of contact points fewer. The patient's freedom of choice in western Sweden, however, means that it has more incentive to attract patients from other county councils. Primary care physicians therefore become an important customer for hospital services through their role as an agent for the patient.

The concentration of hospital services and the move to internal markets have made primary care and other external services more important to hospitals. It is not primarily short-term productivity or cost-effectiveness that influences the relationship with primary care, but rather that hospitals are being forced to become more innovative. This creates demands and offers opportunities for co-operation. It also concerns accessibility and the reception accorded to patients who have been referred from primary care. In the past, non-emergency patients were placed on waiting lists at public hospitals but this has become less common. Today primary care physicians are frequently engaged in a discussion over which patients should receive priority. There is a greater tendency to treat primary care as an equal partner in the production processes involving patients.

Prior to the introduction of the public health system in the UK, the revenue received by the hospitals and hospital physicians depended on referrals by primary care to hospitals. With the establishment of the NHS in 1948, however, hospitals received budget allocations changing this dependency; a good relationship with hospital physicians was necessary for GPs to provide good patient care. Since the GPs purchase services from the hospitals, primary care has gained a stronger position relative to the hospitals.

Consumer demands

Health services differ from other sectors when it comes to meeting customer preferences. The price which the patient pays directly to the provider represents only a small portion of the true cost of the service. Competition for patients is largely through 'non-price competition', which means a competitive edge is gained by offering accessibility, responsiveness and quality. As a result it is obviously impossible for health care systems to satisfy every demand when the price of a course of treatment is either zero or negligible in relationship to its cost.

Patient preferences play the greatest role at the Henry Ford Hospital. Most Americans who have health insurance have a free choice of hospital. However, patients who are insured by the Health Alliance Plan, HFH's own health insurance, do not. They can receive care only from those providers with whom the insurance plan has contracted. Consumer preference is also culturally based and it appears that American patients place greater demands on their treatment.

The Henry Ford Hospital pays serious attention to making the organisation responsive to patient needs in terms of accessibility and quality. For example, their specialists also spend time in primary care, which in turn has become more accessible by opening from 7 a.m. to 9 p.m. and at weekends. The rapid diffusion of new medical technology exemplifies the hospital's desire to satisfy all care needs as well as possible; although not a university hospital, it has invested in major equipment. The hospital also performs heart and liver transplants, operations which in the UK and Sweden are limited to university hospitals. The hospital's extreme adaptation to consumer preferences is not, however, cost-effective from a production point of view. Although services meet customer quality expectations, the bill by international standards is very high.

Public health systems have, for some time, been subjected to criticism concerning the patients' limited choice of physicians or hospitals. Limited choice meant that activities reflected a 'producer perspective' with care rationed through queues, compulsory referral and regulation of services. Initially patients in the Bohus County were assigned to a specific community health centre and hospital, but the agreement in 1991 to permit a free choice within the county councils of western Sweden means that patient preference will affect hospital revenues. While Uddevalla Hospital today has a much more positive attitude towards receiving patients from nearby county councils, patients in its own catchment area do not necessarily choose that hospital.

The Princess Royal Hospital requires a referral for access except in emergency cases. This means that patient preferences are less important since the hospital primarily depends on referrals from GPs. Nevertheless, some direct customer contact does exist through private patients. Consultants at the hospital have the right to treat a certain number of private patients who pay directly out of their own pockets or through private health insurance. These private patients may freely choose their hospital and the Princess Royal maintains a unit with more exclusive furnishings, private rooms with television, special menus etc. to care for such patients. Both the physicians and the hospital receive revenue from private patients, any profit from which is used for general investment.

Internal factors

The internal factors exerting the greatest influence on productivity are the contract with the medical profession, management's access to information and the internal organisation. The relative importance of each of these differs among the hospitals.

Contracts with the Medical Profession

The health care sector is highly labour-intensive; around 70 per cent of costs typically go to employee compensation. Staff composition, however, varies substantially (Table 7.5).

Table 7.5 Personnel breakdown

	PRH	HFH	Uddevalla Hospital
Physicians	21%	20%	20%
Nurses, nurse assts.	45%	35%	58%
Others	34%	45%	22%

The above breakdown is based on salaries for the Princess Royal and Uddevalla Hospitals, and on the number of employees at the Henry Ford

Hospital. The proportion of direct care givers is greatest at Uddevalla Hospital, while figures for the Henry Ford Hospital indicate a greater percentage of other service staff. The latter can be explained by the relatively great salary differentials between physicians and other personnel in the US. Although opportunities for rationalisation and automation are greatest among service staff, their low salary levels may delay the implementation of such measures. Furthermore, service staff at the Henry Ford Hospital perform many functions which at Uddevalla are either automated or not done at all, for example, information, valet parking and other guest services.

An important factor in health care is the influence of a strong profession – the physician community. Although physicians represent a minority of total employees they function as a 'motor' in the system.

Physicians are organised differently in the three hospitals, but at each there exists a long tradition of employing physicians at a fixed salary. This has been the case for some time in the UK and Sweden, but at the Henry Ford Hospital the system differs from the traditional American method whereby physicians often have their own practice and use hospitals only as needed.

Employment contracts with physicians are handled differently in each of the three hospitals.

- At the Henry Ford Hospital, physicians belong to a professional organisation – Henry Ford Medical Group (HFMG) – which is a sister division of the administrative and care functions of the hospital. Physicians are divided into specialities headed by a clinical chief.
- The consultants at the Princess Royal Hospital have created leadership teams for each speciality, each headed by a consultant who is chosen as chairperson for two to four years.

At both of the above hospitals senior physicians have a strong internal position and extensive freedom to organise their work themselves. It is also important to note that physicians undergoing training have an important role in keeping productivity at a high level.

- At the Uddevalla Hospital, physicians are employed by their clinics in the same manner as other staff. The clinic is run by a senior physician, who has a joint medical and administrative responsibility. This includes the administration of nurses and other staff employed at the clinic. Overall, the physicians at Uddevalla are to a larger extent dependent on administrative decisions.

The above differences are also reflected in employment contracts; the main terms of which are as follows.

Princess Royal Hospital:
- Individual salaries
- Agreement about 5–6 'sessions' a week
- Private patients

Henry Ford Hospital:
- Individual salaries
- Patient work >30 hours a week

Uddevalla Hospital:
- Agreement about working hours
- On-call compensation (time off or salaries)
- Movement towards individual salaries

The concept of 'sessions' at the Princess Royal Hospital refers to a half-day (approximately) block of work. For a surgeon, a session generally means three operations. If a physician wants to increase their percentage of private patients, this must be approved by the hospital administration. Surgeons at the Princess Royal Hospital treat approximately two private patients per week who pay a fee to the hospital and to the physicians. Patient load is a key element of the physicians' employment contracts at the Princess Royal and Henry Ford Hospitals. Administrators at both hospitals indicated that, except for the salary level and the conditions on patient load, their physicians are largely free to manage their work. Hospital administrators do not manage the medical production processes.

Uddevalla Hospital uses another management method which coincides with Swedish labour market regulation of working hours. No regulations directly address the content of physicians' work. As noted above, labour productivity among surgeons is lowest at Uddevalla, largely reflecting the agreement for on-call service which allows physicians to be compensated in vacation time. However, the external pressure to reduce waiting times has helped promote better productivity. This pressure has been directed at the clinical department heads who are responsible for implementing policy decisions.

Physicians sometimes have objectives which tend to prioritise research, education and development before patient care. Management at the Princess Royal and the Henry Ford Hospitals choose to focus on patient care as a common way to manage physicians; a strategy which works best with elective surgery. It is less effective among medical specialities which handle many emergency cases. The system also challenges physicians to be innovative in planning their work and making patient care more effective.

Physicians at these two hospitals are less tolerant than their counterparts at Uddevalla of cancelled examinations or surgeries caused by inefficient ancillary services such as anaesthetics.

For many years Uddevalla Hospital has based salaries on centrally negotiated labour agreements. The Princess Royal Hospital and, in the main, the Henry Ford Hospital use individual measures to set salaries based on education, experience and performance. The chairperson or the head of the clinic has an important role in setting salaries, although formal decisions are made by top management. Salary ranges are widest at the Henry Ford Hospital, followed by the Princess Royal and Uddevalla Hospitals. The lowest paid group are freshly recruited physicians who continue their training while serving as hospital residents; the highest paid physicians are the clinical department heads and consultants.

Managerial information systems

The ability of hospital management to communicate goals, expectations and results with the clinics or service units depends largely on information flows throughout the organisation. Traditionally, hospitals have not integrated their administrative and medical information systems. Most administrators largely rely on revenue, cost and performance data to manage their organisations. None of the three hospitals systematically monitors their quality of care. Medical information systems are controlled by the physicians, and used for research and development purposes. Medical outcome measures such as surgical mortality, infection rates and treatment complications are used internally to improve treatment. A central problem in determining cost-effectiveness, however, is that the use of resources is not correlated with medical outcomes, but only to less relevant data such as hospital days and hospital admissions.

The Henry Ford Hospital has the most advanced information system. Certain performance and revenue data are available to the hospital administration and board one day after their calculation. In comparison, the time lag at the Princess Royal and Uddevalla Hospitals is approximately seven to 14 days. The administration of the Henry Ford Hospital uses this information as a powerful management tool, particularly for relating costs to revenues for various activities. The information is also used to identify cost deviations to which administration must respond.

None the less, none of these information systems provides all the relevant data needed for decision making. One problem has been to design a system based on cost units, to which both costs and quality can be related. Measures such as cost per hospital day or cost per admission are too broad

196 Achieving Service Productivity

to be useful as a cost unit. Diagnostic related groups (DRGs), however, do provide a classification system which can be used to identify cost units. When the Medicare programme began reimbursing hospitals by DRG, the Henry Ford Hospital overhauled its accounting system. Subsequently the Medicaid and Blue Cross/Blue Shield programmes (non-profit insurers) also began reimbursing hospitals by DRGs. Table 7.6 shows DRG reimbursement by different insurers.

Table 7.6 Examples of DRGs (volume) by insurer at the Henry Ford Hospital in 1991

			INSURER		
DRG	Description	Blue Cross	Medicare	Medicaid	Costs per case
89	Simple pneumonia Age>17w/o CC	–	260	69	$6,126
127	Heart failure and shock	55	674	91	$4,786
143	Chest pain	92	255	88	$2,588
209	Major joint and limb reattachment procedures	53	231	–	$12,213
373	Vaginal delivery w/o compl. diagnosis	115	–	457	$2,188
391	Normal newborn	84	–	357	$694

The hospital can monitor the cost of various interventions by comparing the outcome with established reimbursement levels. Although it does not directly try to influence clinical practice, such information is used to eventually achieve a balance between revenue and cost per DRG. Reviews of the use of laboratory tests have also been conducted to balance costs and revenues. The information collected for claims administration is also used for internal monitoring purposes.

Comparable data are not available to administrators at the Princess Royal and Uddevalla Hospitals, although the latter has invested in a new, more accurate, system providing access to administrative information. Administrators at these hospitals use traditional measures such as cost per hospital day, which provides them with less exact information for making decisions or communicating with and managing the operative units. But these measures are not used for managing productivity, largely because of opposition from the medical profession. Their acceptance is none the less necessary if productivity measures are to be used successfully in managing hospital activity.

Organisation

Noteworthy differences exist in each hospital's organisational framework, particularly in terms of management structure and organisational principles. At Uddevalla the organisation is divided by medical speciality, a framework which has been used by Swedish hospitals for some time. Each speciality is organised as a clinic/department or medical service unit and each clinic is led by a clinical department head (physician) who is responsible for the care unit and associated staff (Figure 7.8).

A company or organisation which uses this type of functional model has the opportunity of taking advantage of the benefits of specialisation. The disadvantage of such a model is that as the organisation grows it is difficult to co-ordinate the various functions, creating inflexibility in the utilisation of medical and surgical units and different support services. This includes, for example, co-ordinating the surgical clinics, anaesthetics and the operating theatres. The problem has been solved at Uddevalla Hospital by including the 13 clinical department heads on the hospital management team which is charged with the task of co-ordination.

Another factor which creates organisational problems at Uddevalla Hospital is the extensive ambulatory care activity. This splits the work day for physicians

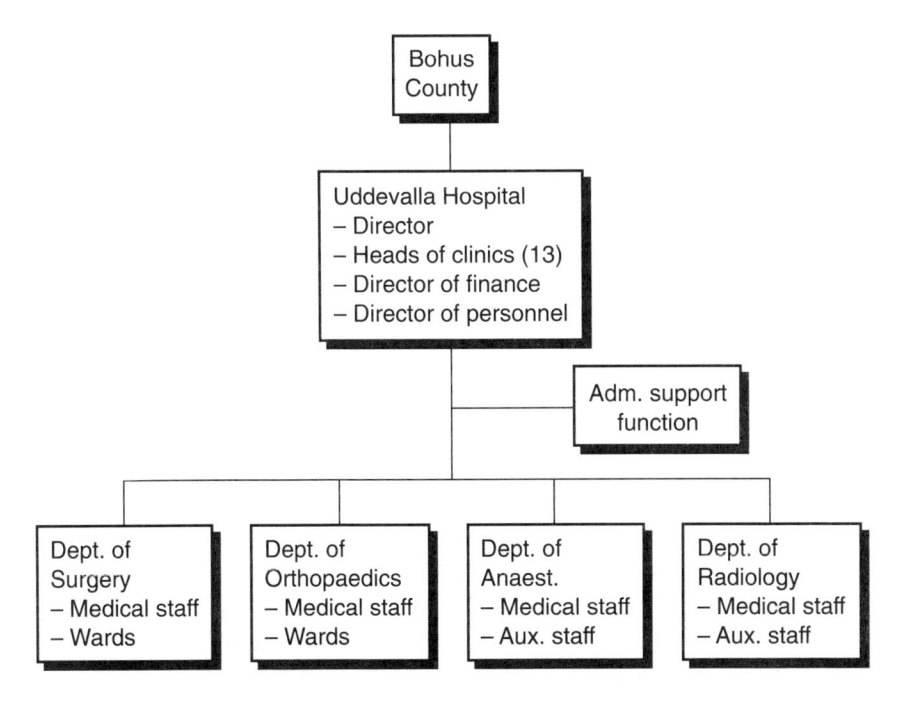

Figure 7.8 Organisational structure at Uddevalla Hospital

who must work at the ambulatory care clinic, but who are also responsible for treating and operating on patients at the hospital. Some of the patients at the ambulatory centres could be seen by a general practitioner outside the hospital.

Physicians at the Princess Royal Hospital are divided into medical specialities, but they do not have financial or administrative responsibility for other staff; activities are co-ordinated by senior physicians in an informal manner. This more flexible organisation offers physicians greater opportunities to co-ordinate activities and deal with problems without involving hospital administration. The nursing departments operate within a type of functional model, but with less distinct boundaries between specialities than at Uddevalla. For example, it is not unusual to mix patients from different clinics/departments in the same nursing unit.

At the Henry Ford Hospital all physicians belong to the Henry Ford Medical Group. Similar to the internal organisation at the Princess Royal Hospital, they co-ordinate medical activities as a group without the involvement of top management. The organisation is to some extent divided by speciality since several centres have been established which focus on particular groups of diseases – the centre for musculoskeletal diseases, for example, which includes orthopaedic surgery, rheumatology and elements of radiology. The boundaries of specialisation are not as rigid as in a functional organisation: patients with different problems are often mixed on the nursing units. In addition, nursing functions enjoy a stronger position since they are independent from the clinics. The department of nursing is not under the physician structure, but reports directly to hospital administration. Career opportunities for nurses are thus considerably greater at the Henry Ford Hospital than at the other two, and nurses hold several managerial positions requiring administrative skills and qualifications such as MBA. Figure 7.9 summarises the organisational structure at the hospital.

Differentiating activities provides an opportunity for specialisation. However, the hospitals indicate that as size increases, internal units must be co-ordinated to prevent each from defining cost-effectiveness from their own perspective. The risk of sub-optimisation becomes great when internal relationships are strong. In Uddevalla the hospital attempts to solve the co-ordination problems inherent in a functional organisation by developing a broad leadership structure and introducing internal debiting. Another method of co-ordination is to organise divisions as at the Henry Ford Hospital, by integrating the units which frequently interact with each other. It is, none the less, difficult to determine which strategy has the most positive influence on productivity, although it appears that the administrators at Uddevalla spend more time co-ordinating activities.

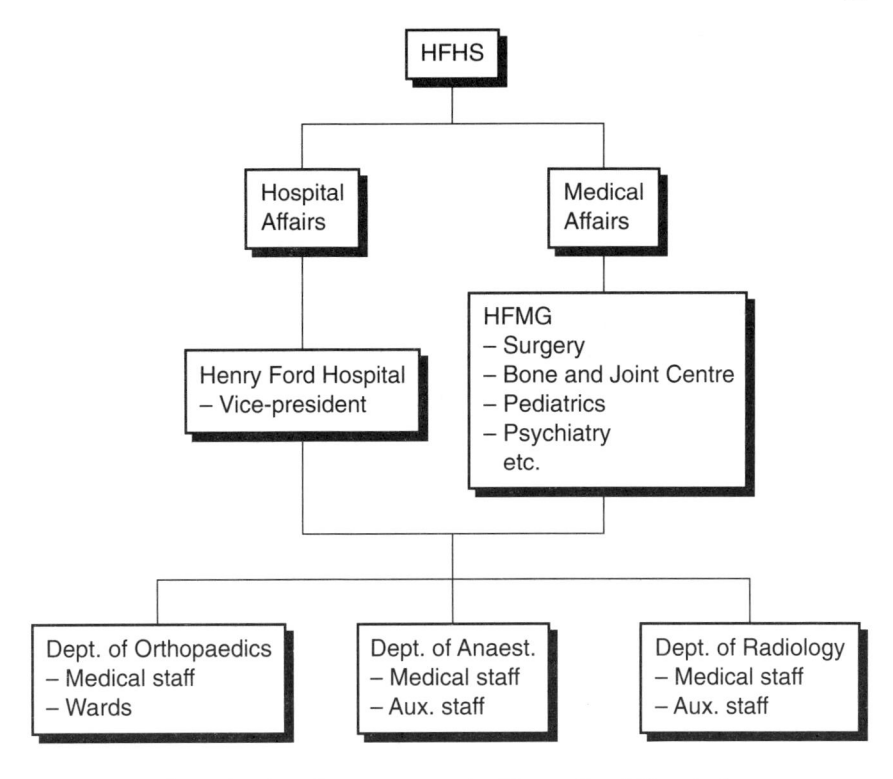

Figure 7.9 Organisational structure at the Henry Ford Hospital

BARRIERS TO PRODUCTIVITY

Generally, health care in all three countries expanded during the 1960s and 1970s. However, it is well known that during periods of expansion organisations do not use their resources optimally, while during periods of stagnation they are forced to consolidate and become more efficient. There are a number of other obstacles, however, to increased productivity:

Monopolies

Geographic monopolies are being dismantled and public hospitals are beginning to compete with each other. This means that one of the former obstacles to productivity, the public hospital monopoly, is beginning to break down. However, there is a long way to go before a real competitive situation exists in the hospital marketplace.

Information systems

Inadequate information systems on cost and performance hamper productivity improvements at the two public hospitals. Hospital administrations have insufficient data upon which to make decisions, which, combined with the strong information position of the medical profession, makes effective productivity management difficult. At all three hospitals it appears that management have little knowledge about the production process. Such processes are generally not documented, but are included in general medical education. Treatment methods are regularly changed without informing hospital management, while only those changes demanding new investment need to be sanctioned by administration.

Workload management

One factor which affects productivity in Uddevalla is the insufficient management of physicians' patient load. Since physician work is central to the performance of the total organisation, such management is a key to high productivity. Compared to the Princess Royal and Henry Ford Hospitals, there is a lack of incentives among Swedish physicians, who need to have an organisational structure which permits them to act independently, while at the same time formulating performance goals.

The health care system

Obstacles to high productivity at the Henry Ford Hospital relate to the characteristics of the American health care system. Although some competition exists between the various insurers, high productivity in terms of cost-effectiveness is not a particularly strong competitive advantage. The hospital is acting in a system which lacks incentives to contain costs. As noted above, health care consumers are more responsive to high quality and good accessibility, to be expected in a market characterised by 'non-price' competition. Thus the job of maintaining high cost-effectiveness rests with insurers who, in the US, have not succeeded in fulfilling this task.

Malpractice

The increase in malpractice claims is another factor contributing to high costs. The average premium for professional liability insurance which Henry Ford Hospital must pay per discharged patient is about US$270 out of a total cost per admission of US$6,400. In addition, the hospital and physicians may perform several diagnostic tests which may not sometimes be considered necessary from a medical point of view. The percentage of malpractice litigation is highest in gynaecology and obstetrics.

8

CONVENIENCE GOODS DISTRIBUTION AND RETAILING

Authors: Peter Blomqvist, Anders Ferntoft, Mats Graffman

WOOLWORTHS, Fairfield, New South Wales, Australia
HEMKÖP, Mora, Sweden

The Australian company Woolworths (no connection with the US-based F.W. Woolworth variety stores) is an integrated wholesaling and retailing chain that warehouses and transports convenience goods, including dry groceries, fruits and vegetables, other perishables and frozen foods. Hemköp is a successful new convenience goods chain in Sweden which buys in products from independent wholesalers.

A comparable food basket costs about twice as much in Sweden as in Australia. This is partly because margins in the various stages of distribution are somewhat higher in Sweden. The main reason, however, is that food and other convenience goods are already more expensive in the production or processing stage and that the subsequent percentage mark-up during distribution is about the same.

Woolworths' gross margins are six percentage points below the average for Sweden convenience goods distribution. In addition, Woolworths buys its goods at lower cost than Hemköp. There is stiffer competition among food processors in Austrialia. The most important external factors behind Woolworths' lower costs in the distribution chain are stiffer competition, lower barriers to market entry, tighter control by owners and far lower general cost levels.

Woolworths has measurable goals, which are broken down throughout the organisation. Feedback occurs more frequently than in Sweden. Woolworths is also ahead of Hemköp in terms of using the latest information technology.

202 Achieving Service Productivity

The company uses detailed bar-code scanner data to manage purchases, warehousing, shipments and use of shelf space in the stores. The result is better capital utilisation in both the wholesale and retail stages. In addition, goods are dispatched and received at night. The Australian company also uses information from external market surveys more than its Swedish counterpart, while the latter relies on its own surveys.

The advantages of an integrated value chain offset the disadvantages in the form of less profit-centre responsibility. Woolworths has successfully dealt with this by having a very thorough profitability monitoring system and paying performance-related bonuses to managers.

THE CONVENIENCE GOODS DISTRIBUTION/RETAILING SECTOR

Food and beverages typically account for a significant proportion of household expenditure. In the two countries highlighted in this chapter, Australia and Sweden, food and beverages account for 17 per cent and 19 per cent respectively of total private consumption.[1]

Food prices are about twice as high in Sweden as in Australia. This is illustrated in Figure 8.1 which shows that Australian prices are also lower than overall Organisation for Economic Co-operation and Development (OECD) values.[2]

[1] Private final consumption expenditure at current prices (Source: Australian Bureau of Statistics; Statistics Sweden)

A$	Australia 1990–991 (US$ million)	Sweden 1990 (SKr million)
Food and beverages	21,000	29,000
Total	108,000	176,000
Food and beverages/Total	16.7%	19.3%

[2] OECD regularly presents benchmark purchasing power parities (PPPs) and estimates of real expenditure on gross domestic product (GDP). PPPs are the rates of currency conversion that equalise the purchasing power of different countries. A given sum of money, when converted into different currencies at the PPP rates, will buy the same basket of goods and services in all countries. Comparative price levels are defined as the ratios of PPPs to exchange rates. They indicate for a given aggregate the number of units of the common currency needed to buy the same volume of the aggregate in each country. (Source: OECD 1992, Purchasing Power Parities and Real Expenditure 1990). The food price comparison is based on a sample of 254 food products purchased in 30 outlets all over the country (Source: Statistics Sweden).

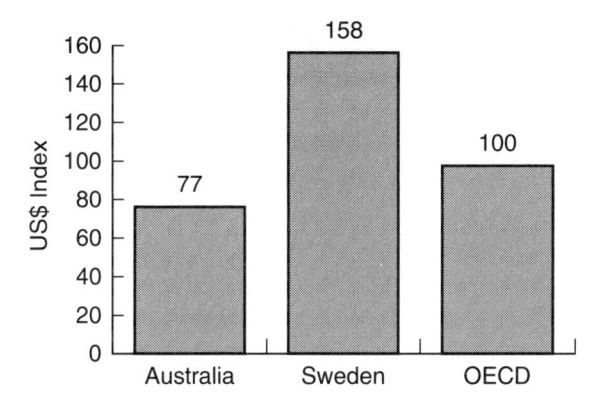

```
         158
160
140
120                      100
100
 80   77
 60
 40
 20
  0
   Australia  Sweden   OECD
```
(US$ Index)

Figure 8.1 Comparative dollar price levels for food

Source: OECD 1992, Purchasing Power Parities and Real Expenditures 1990

Similar results are indicated by two recent food basket surveys: one carried out twice yearly by the US Foreign Agricultural Service and the second by the research team in the autumn of 1992.[3,4]

Previous studies[5] show that food price variation in different countries not only depends on different macro economic variables (affecting exchange rates), but also on different income levels, VAT or other indirect taxes and the degree of protection of the agricultural sector. Although other factors may come into play (relative productivity within food distribution and retailing for example), when comparing Australia and Sweden, Sweden has higher income levels, higher indirect taxes and a higher degree of protection of the agricultural sector.

It is not unlikely that a high degree of protection of the agricultural sector leads to low productivity within the distribution channels. It seems as if the

---

[3] One of these surveys is carried out twice yearly by the US Foreign Agricultural Service. The sample is a 15-item food basket of basic commodities priced at local supermarkets in each major capital. The items are steak (sirloin, boneless), pork (roast, boneless), chicken (whole), eggs (large), butter, cheese (Cheddar/Emmenthaler), milk (whole), oil (cooking), potatoes, apples, oranges, flour, rice, sugar and coffee. Exchange rates used are those in effect when the survey was conducted (June 1992). The food basket cost US$42.34 in Canberra, Australia and US$107.80 in Stockholm, Sweden (Source: Food Marketing Institute, Food Retailing and Distribution, Pacific Rim Edition, 1992.)

[4] The other survey was carried out by the research team during the autumn of 1992. The sample is a eight-item food basket priced at the two supermarkets selected as participants in this study. The items are tomatoes, cream, frozen French fries, tea, flour, bread (white, sliced), roast beef, Coca-Cola. The food basket cost US$18 at Woolworths in Orange, Australia and US$36 at Hemköp in Mora, Sweden. Only brand products were included.

[5] Lipsey, Swedenborg, 1992, 'Why do food prices differ between countries?', SNS Occasional Paper (Source: Bolin, Swedenborg, Andersson *et al.*, 1992, Mat till EG-pris?).

204 Achieving Service Productivity

high costs, which are accepted within the agricultural sector due to the degree of protection, are also accepted throughout the whole food manufacturing and distribution sector.[6]

The purpose of this analysis is to learn about productivity within food distribution and retailing by studying some examples. The examples are not just one company, but a network of companies: Woolworths, a major food retailer in Australia; Hemköp, a food retailer with a small market share in Sweden; and the wholesaler Dagab, also in Sweden. Each are considered as being very successful in their respective markets.

It aims to answer two principal questions.

- Are there differences in productivity between the two networks and can measurable productivity indicators be found?
- What are the possible reasons (internal and external) for these differences?

The process of distribution and retailing is to make food and other convenience goods available for the end user – the consumer. This means that the process must transport the convenience goods from the producer to the consumer, combine the convenience goods and provide them to the consumer according to their preferences, for example, level of service, opening hours, parking facilities, product variety and price.

This is the core process. It is organised differently in different countries depending on history, size of the country, consumer patterns and many other factors.

In this study, the convenience goods distribution and retailing process embraces the time when the goods leave the last manufacturer until the consumer purchases the goods in the store.

To a certain extent, the process in both Australia and Sweden is organised in a similar way. Foods originate with a farmer or grower and are then normally shipped to one or several distribution centres (DCs) and subse-

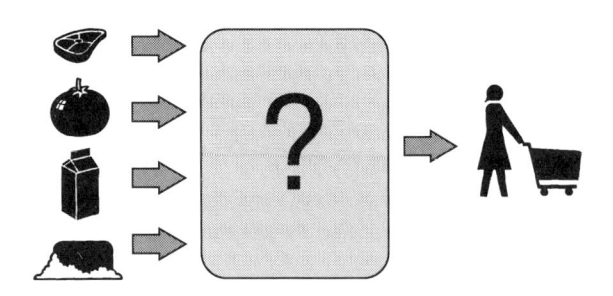

Figure 8.2 The core process

[6] The phenomenon is not unknown in protected economic sectors. It is often referred to as factor rent sharing (Source: Bolin, Swedenborg, Andersson *et al.*, 1992, Mat till EG-pris?).

quently to the stores. Some of the goods are shipped directly to the DCs and the stores, such as fresh potatoes, and some of them are first delivered to a manufacturer for processing, for example frozen French fries. At the end of the chain the consumer purchases food at the store.

COMPANIES STUDIED

In this analysis the retailers, wholesalers and hauliers are represented by a number of companies.

Retailers	Hemköp in Sweden and their supermarket in Mora
	Woolworths in Australia and their supermarket in Orange
Wholesalers	Dagab Nord, Borlänge, Sweden
	Liljas, Vansbro, Sweden
Warehouses	Woolworths dry grocery warehouse division, Yennora, Sydney, Australia
	Woolworths produce warehouse division, Homebush, Sydney, Australia
	P&O Cold Storages, Woolworths perishables warehouse, Arndell Park, Australia
Hauliers	Coldsped, Sweden
	Bilspedition in Östra Skåne, Sweden
	Refrigerated Roadways, Australia

An important difference between the two networks is that Hemköp and Dagab have a retailer/wholesaler relationship, whereas Woolworths is an integrated chain operating both supermarkets and distribution networks. Hemköp is a retail chain, i.e. the company operates several stores, but no DCs. Hemköp uses the DC of the wholesaler Dagab. Dagab, besides operating a normal DC, also purchases the goods from the producers and sells to the retailers.

Figures 8.3 and 8.4 show how the eight items in a food basket survey are distributed from the manufacturer on the right to the retailer on the left. In each, the shaded area, which shows what functions the retailer controls, highlights the difference between the integrated chain and the retailer/wholesaler solution. The integrated chain controls the whole distribution process: there is no buying/selling relationship between the DC and the retailer. Woolworths is a retailer with several stores, which also controls its warehouses and transport network. Hemköp is a retailer owning several stores, but does not have direct control over the DC or transportation. Socomins, SJ Norman and ASK are importers or other middlemen, and are not included in this study. Blacktown warehouse is also excluded.

206 Achieving Service Productivity

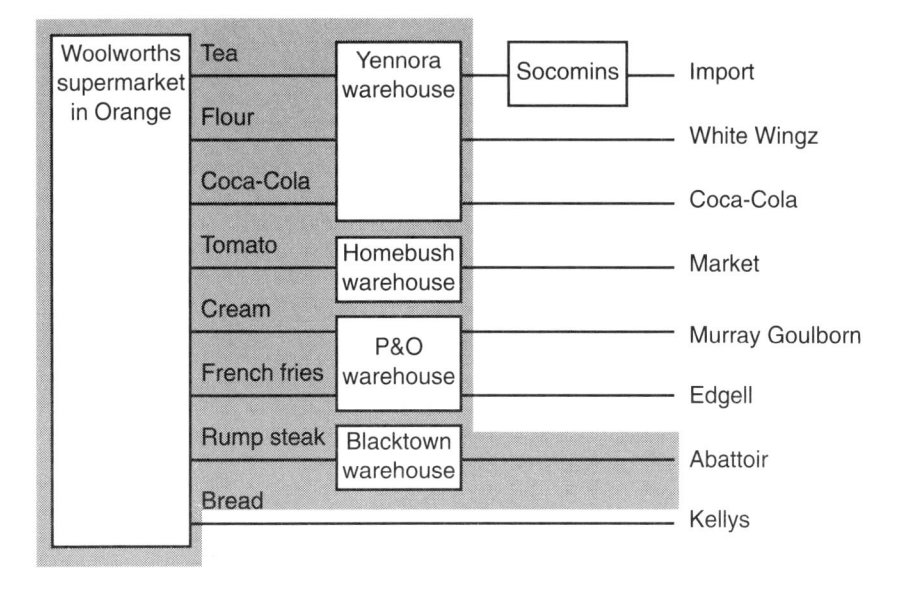

Figure 8.3 The Australian process

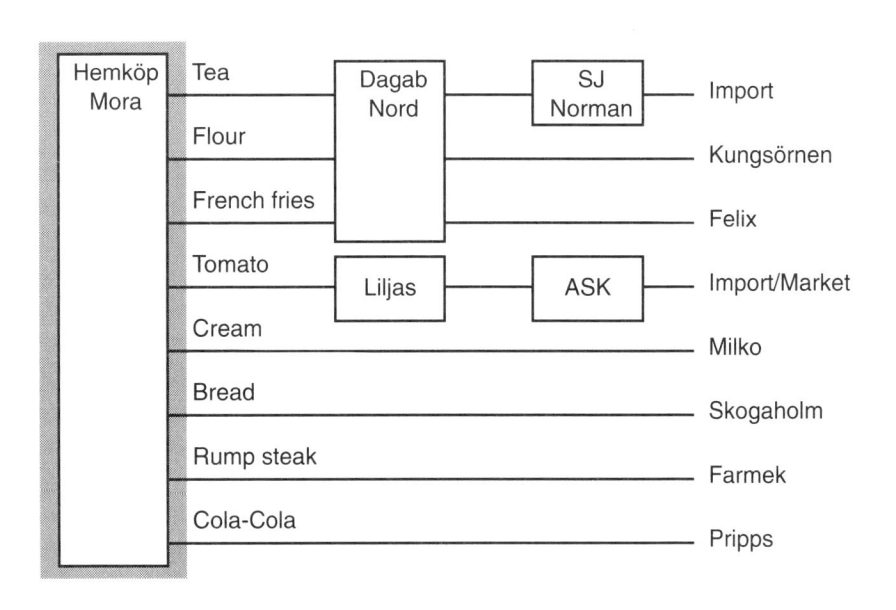

Figure 8.4 The Swedish process

PRODUCTIVITY

Theory and practice

There are several ways of assessing the performance of distribution/marketing channels: effectiveness, efficiency, productivity and profitability are examples of important performance measures.[7] In this study we concentrate on productivity. Productivity is defined as the relationship between input factors (I) such as labour or capital and the output of grocery distribution (O).

$$\text{Average productivity} = O/I$$

Actual and theoretical productivity measures may differ. If one asks a supermarket manager about the operational productivity measures employed the common answer is sales per labour hour or sometimes sales per square metre. When consulting more theoretical sources, however, output measures tend to be more difficult to define. In many studies the retailer's output is defined as bundles of services such as size, location, business hours, product variety and consumer services.[8] Because, therefore, there is no simple way of measuring these attributes and combining them, researchers often use measures such as sales, gross margin and value added as substitutes.

The output measures discussed in this study are gross margin, sales and number of cartons. The gross margin is employed to assess productivity in the distribution channel, i.e. the aggregate output of the warehouse, the transport function and the retail function. There is no available measure for labour or capital input to relate to the gross margin.

Sales and number of cartons are output measures used to try to evaluate the performance of some individual distribution channels. Corresponding input measures are labour hours and, as proxy for capital, floor area.

However, in order to compare productivity between distribution channels and individual firms it is first necessary to discuss structural differences as well as differences in the services provided by the participants.

Industry structure and services provided

Differences in industry structure or services provided have an impact on productivity. Here are some examples.

- Comparing a supermarket that has an in-house bakery with a supermarket that has none, will affect both the output and the input measure. The

---

[7] Source: Louis W. Stern, Adel I. El-Ansary, *Marketing Channels* (1992) Prentice-Hall International Editions.
[8] Source: Magnus Eliasson, Claes-Robert Julander, *Productivity in Swedeish Grocery Retailing* (1991) The Foundation for Distribution Reasearch, EFI, Stockholm School of Economics.

208 Achieving Service Productivity

services provided, i.e. the output measure, will vary but it is difficult to quantify the difference. The supermarket with the bakery will probably need more personnel and maybe some machinery, both of which will result in variances in both labour and capital input.

- The process of grocery distribution is significantly influenced by geography. There are 2.2 inhabitants per square kilometre in Australia compared to 18.9 in Sweden. However, in both countries the population is concentrated in certain areas – in the southern and eastern parts of Australia and in southern Sweden.

- Overall costs are higher in Sweden, as are the barriers to entry; competitive pressure however is lower.[9]

- Whereas Woolworths is an integrated chain, Hemköp and Dagab have a retailer/wholesaler relationship.[10] None the less, each distribution channel performs warehouse and supermarket functions and distribution from warehouses to supermarkets. Manufacturers tend to handle the distribution to the warehouses or, in case of direct supplies, to supermarkets.

- Australian stores are generally larger than Swedish stores; there are also fewer of them. In Australia each supermarket and food store serves about 2,600 persons.[11] In Sweden the corresponding figure is 1,100 persons.[12] A similar comparison of floor space shows that an average Woolworths supermarket or food store is almost 3,000 m². For Hemköp the corresponding figure is 1,900 and for ICA, the major Swedish retail chain, it is 500–600 m².[13]

- Woolworths supermarkets are more likely to have a full bakery and butcher. Hemköp have these functions but to a lesser extent. Some Woolworths supermarkets are open 24 hours per day, seven days a week, and each outlet has employees on site performing different tasks 24 hours per day. Hemköp's supermarkets are open seven days a week but they are not performing 24-hour services.

- Woolworths warehouses are generally larger and more specialised, whereas Swedish warehouses tend to be smaller, yet carry a full product range. At Woolworths, about 95 per cent of the supermarket's product range is distributed via the warehouse. At Hemköp the corresponding ratio is approximately 70 per cent; the balance is distributed directly by the manufacturer to the supermarkets.

- Trucks are contracted by Woolworths, whereas Dagab Nord mainly run their own truck fleet.

[9] See 'Factors influencing productivity', below, pages 214–232.
[10] See Figures 8.3 and 8.4.
[11] Source: *Retail World*, Australian Grocery Industry, Marketing Guide 1992.
[12] Source: *Supermarket*, no. 5–6, 1992.
[13] Source: Internal records and interviews.

Gross margin

Different gross margins in Australia and Sweden indicate that there might be differences in productivity between the distribution channels in the two countries. However, there are several problems regarding the use of this measure:

> ... the only situation in which margins should be compared in productivity analysis is that between two establishments, two firms, two areas, or two points in time in which the same marketing functions are being performed and the same inputs result in comparable productivity potentials. If market structure and inputs can be assumed to be identical, margin comparison can be meaningful.[14]

Although, as we have seen above, the industry structure and the services provided by the two distribution channels varies, the gross margins for Woolworths have been compared with the combined gross margin for a

Woolworths, Australia

22%
78%

Average Swedish wholesaler and retailer

28%
72%

■ Cost of goods

□ Gross margin

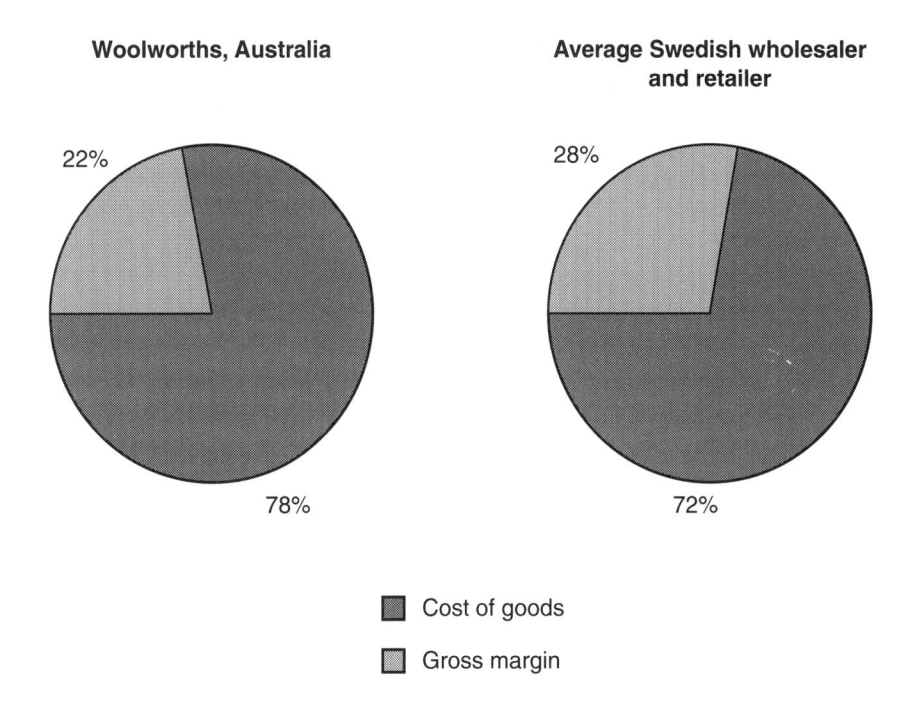

Figure 8.5 Comparative gross margins

Source: Woolworths internal records 1992; ICA-Förlaget, Butikskalender, 1992; AB Handelns Utredningsinstitut, Grossistens roll i dagligvaruhandeln, 1991.[15]

[14] Source: E. Douglas, *Economics of Marketing*, (1975), New York: Harper & Row.
[15] Swedish figures based on wholesalers average gross margin of 7.1 per cent of the retail sales excluding VAT (8.9 per cent of the wholesale sales) and retailers average gross margin of 20.5 per cent.

210 Achieving Service Productivity

typical Swedish wholesaler and an average Swedish retailer. Comparable data are unfortunately not available from Hemköp and Dagab Nord. Therefore, since actual Woolworths figures, representing 30 per cent of the Australian market, have been compared with estimated Swedish average figures, the results should be interpreted with caution.

None the less, the figures show that Woolworths can operate its business on a gross margin of approximately 22 per cent while the combined gross margin amount for an average Swedish wholesaler and retailer is 28 per cent. (Interviews with managers in Hemköp and Dagab suggest that the estimated Swedish figures correspond to the actual figures of Hemköp and Dagab Nord.)

Taking price level variations into account using the information from Figure 8.1, absolute differences between the systems can be visualised. In Figure 8.6 (which has been adjusted for differences in exchange rates), Swedish costs are higher. Comparing two identical food baskets the Swedish wholesaler/retailer would sell its basket for an indexed price of 205; an identical basket would cost an indexed price of 100 in Australia. Including the percentage figures regarding cost of goods and gross margin from Figure 8.5 the absolute cost of distribution will be 49 indexed units in Sweden and 22 indexed units in Australia.

In Figure 8.6, value added tax (VAT) of 25 per cent is included for the Swedish case;[16] in Figure 8.5, however, VAT is excluded. In Australia VAT is not applied although there is a wholesale sales tax on some supermarket items.[17] This tax is included in the cost of goods.

Comparative productivity

As discussed above it is difficult to compare productivity between companies since output and/or input measures often need to be adjusted in order to provide comparable data. In this study, figures have been adjusted for differences in exchange rates and price levels. Adjustments have not been made for structural differences. The productivity ratios below should therefore be interpreted with caution, but the findings may be summarised as follows.

- Labour productivity in Mora and Orange supermarkets is about equal. On the other hand, floor area productivity is almost three times higher in the Woolworths (Orange) store.

[16] In Sweden before July 1990 VAT of 25 per cent was applied to most sales including groceries. Today VAT on food is 21 per cent and on general merchandise 25 per cent.
[17] Basic food is exempt from wholesale sales tax. It is applied at a rate of 10, 20 or 30 per cent. The tax is levied in the sales situation between the retailer and the supplier, i.e. wholesaler, other middleman or producer. Wholesale sales tax amounts to approximately 6 per cent of the wholesaler's sales receipt. (Source: Price and Cartel Office, Inquiry in Relation to Retail Prices of Food and Groceries, 1986.)

Figure 8.6 Estimated absolute cost structures based on price level differences
Source: OECD 1992, Purchasing Power Parities and Real Expenditure 1990; Woolworths internal records 1992; ICA-Förlaget, Butikskalender, 1992; AB Handelns Utredningsinstitut, Grossistens roll i dagligvaruhandeln,1991.

- In terms of area productivity, the Australian distribution centres are more productive.
- The level of automation and use of information technology among the warehouses varies in both countries.
- The study has not resulted in any reliable measures of transport productivity.
- Comparative labour productivity is very similar between Dagab and Yennora.
- The results from the food basket survey (covering eight products) are not directly comparable. This is partly due to the fact that manufacturers undertake a variable proportion of the distribution work,[18] a proportion which is typically larger in Sweden.

Productivity measurement

Supermarkets

Labour productivity in a store has been measured as sales/labour hour. Floor area productivity has been measured as weekly sales/sales area (m^2). Sales in Sweden do not include VAT. In order to compare the outlets at Orange and Mora, the former's figures have been adjusted for the exchange rate difference[19] and the difference in comparable dollar prices.[20]

[18] See Figures 8.3 and 8.4.
[19] Average exchange rate between 1986 and 1991; A$1 = Skr4.7.
[20] Comparative dollar price levels for food result in index 100 for Australia and index 205 for Sweden (Source: Purchasing Power Parities and Real Expenditure 1990, OECD, 1992.)

Labour productivity in Hemköp, Mora is about the same as in Woolworths, Orange. The productivity figures are representative of an average Woolworths supermarket although labour productivity at Hemköp in Mora is slightly higher than both the company and national average. Area productivity is almost three times higher in Orange than at Hemköp.

Warehouses

In the warehouse, throughput rate (total cartons distributed/total warehouse hours worked) and pick rate (total cartons picked/hours worked), have been used as a measure for labour productivity. Area productivity is measured by monthly cartons handled per total warehouse square metres.

Analysis of labour productivity in the warehouses at Dagab Nord, Woolworths Yennora and P&O Cold Storage show that P&O is more productive than the others. Labour productivity at Dagab Nord and Yennora is about the same. Area productivity is higher in the Australian warehouses:

Transport

The study did not produce any clear results regarding productivity within the transport companies although two interesting findings emerged.

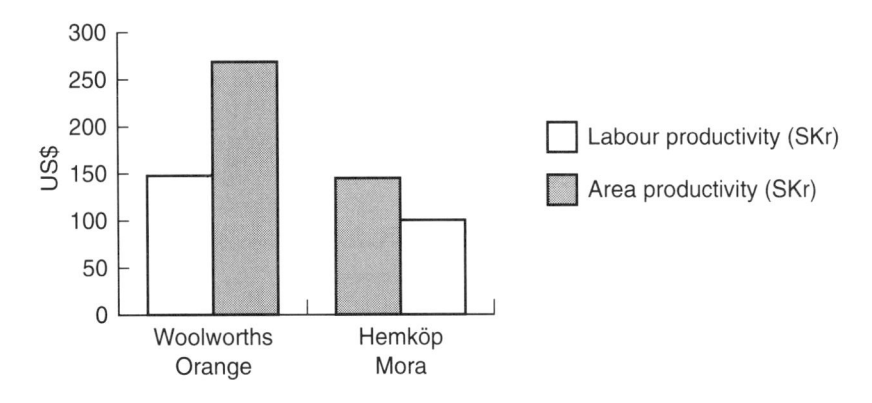

Figure 8.7 Supermarket productivity[21]

	Woolworths Orange	Hemköp More
Weekly sales adjusted for VAT, exchange rates and CDPL	US$491,000	US$157,000
Weekly labour hours	3,300	1,000
Sales square metres	1,778	1,900

[21] (Source: Internal Records)

Convenience Goods Distribution and Retailing 213

☐ Throughput rate ▨ Pick rate ■ Cartons/m²

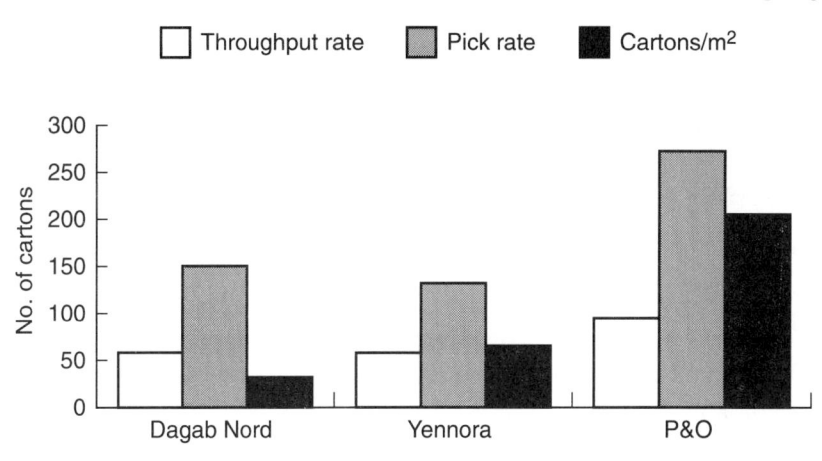

Figure 8.8 Warehouse productivity[22]

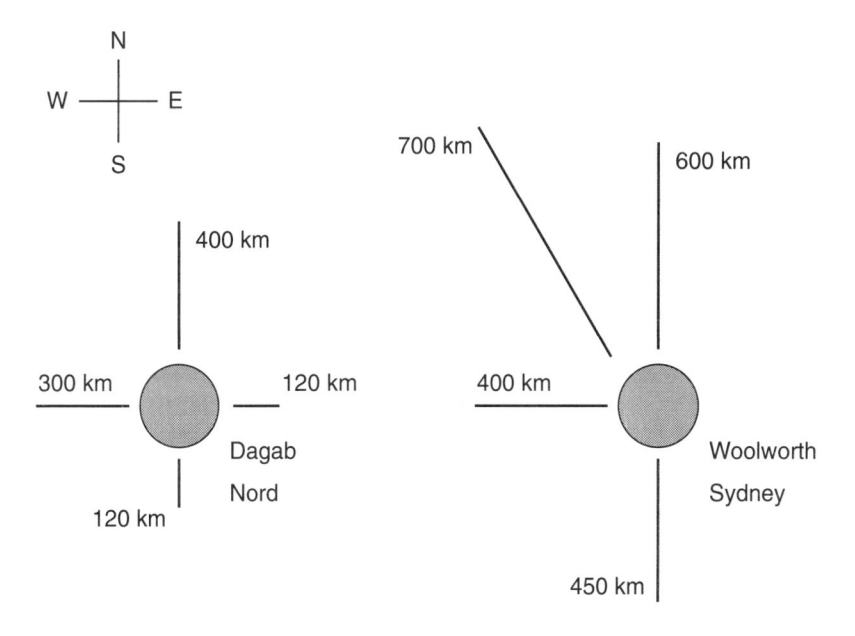

Figure 8.9 Area covered by the warehouses

[22] Dagab Nord and Yennora data from September, P&O data from November.

	Dagab Nord	**Yennora**	**P&O**
Throughput rate	59	57	93
Pick rate	150	130	270
Cartons per square metre	31	63	201

Source: Internal records

214 Achieving Service Productivity

- The Woolworths distribution centre covers a larger area than does Dagab Nord.
- Although a haulier's aim is to travel with a full truck in all directions, between 40 per cent and 50 per cent of travelled kilometres are, in fact, empty kilometres.

FACTORS INFLUENCING PRODUCTIVITY

External factors

Ownership

Both the type of ownership and the level of international ownership varies significantly between the two countries. In Australia the major retailers are public or private integrated chains, although a substantial part of the market is occupied by trade groups and independents using the retailer/wholesaler solution. Trade groups are joint organisations between independent storekeepers created in order to benefit from economies of scale in, for example, purchasing. In Sweden the major retailers comprise different forms of trade groups owned mainly by storekeeper or consumer co-operatives; they all operate using the retailer/wholesaler solution.

Type of ownership: 60 per cent of the Australian supermarkets and food stores are operated by three public or private integrated chains which operate

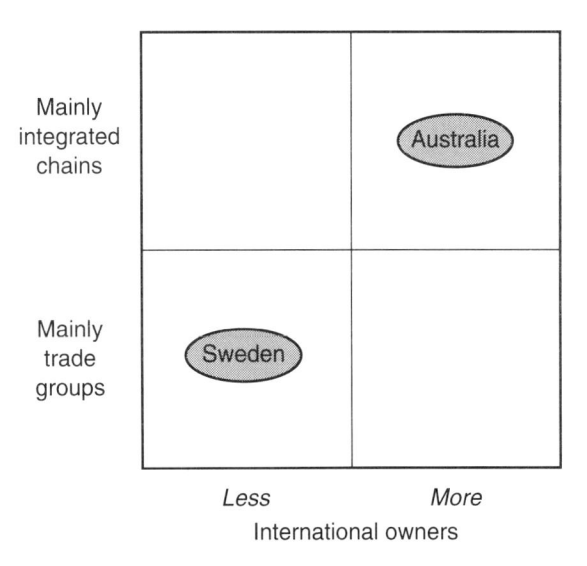

Figure 8.10 Type of ownership/international ownership

nationwide – Woolworths, Coles and Franklins. All the stores are linked together into a chain, adopting the same business concepts and purchasing organisation, and the company also operates the warehouse functions.

The remaining 40 per cent of outlets are operated by wholesalers and retailers, most of them linked in different trade groups. Each store is normally owned by the storekeeper, even though the wholesaler might own some equity in a few minor chains. The wholesalers are normally private companies or are owned by storekeepers.

The Swedish market is less fragmented.

- In Sweden, 90 per cent of supermarkets and food stores are operated by four groups – ICA, KF, the D-Group and Axel Johnson. They all operate using a wholesaler.
- In ICA the stores are owned by independent storekeepers, who also control their wholesaler ICA Partihandel through a co-operative. Rarely does each storekeeper own more than one store.
- In KF each store is owned by different consumer co-operatives, in which the consumers are members. These consumer co-operatives also own their wholesaler, KF Handel. Parts of KF are currently undergoing reorganisation designed to turn the company into an integrated operator without the traditional wholesale function.
- In the D-Group the stores are owned by independent storekeepers.
- Axel Johnson is a private company, owning a number of different chains. It also owns Dagab, which is the wholesaler used by the D-Group and the Axel Johnson stores.

Differences in the type of ownership can impact in two main areas – the adoption of common ideas and the magnitude of overheads.

- An organisation where the individuals have one common concept or vision can move together in one direction: this is necessary in order to achieve high productivity. The integrated chain facilitates the management of all the stores as one company making it possible to unite around one concept. By contrast, in the wholesaler/retailer solution, storekeepers tend to be more independent, making decisions themselves and having their own concepts for the store. In the case of ICA, 2,800 independent storekeepers each have their own concepts of how to do business. How likely is it that this kind of organisation can quickly unite around one concept in order, for example, to effect dramatic changes? The slow adoption of the discount store concept within ICA and KF proves a case in point. Not until it is obvious that the discount stores are in the market to stay will they gain market share.

216 Achieving Service Productivity

- Negotiation overheads tend to be less in the integrated chain. In the wholesaler/retailer solution there is a seller/purchaser relationship between the retailer and the wholesaler, the wholesaler and the manufacturer, and possibly between the retailer and the manufacturer. The storekeeper buys most items from the wholesaler, but can also buy directly from manufacturers or brokers. However, direct deliveries are mainly done by large retailers for high volume products. In the integrated chain all of these transactions are handled by a single seller/purchaser relationship, namely that between the integrated chain and the manufacturer. The store manager simply orders everything from the warehouse, purchasing is centrally controlled and selling is only undertaken by the stores. In essence, there is no duplication of overheads.

The discussion above indicates that the integrated chain can be more efficient than the retailer/wholesaler solution. The Australian case, however, shows that there are probably valuable benefits in both systems, and that the integrated chain and the retailer/wholesaler solution exist side by side. In Sweden this is not the case, and although changes are under way, the existing market structure has yet to be fully challenged by this concept.

In some cases the retailer/wholesaler solution is likely to be more efficient and flexible than the integrated chain. The strength of this type of relationship is that many decisions are made by independent storekeepers, who are typically close to their customers – decisions for example on the retail offer or whether purchases are made from a wholesaler, or directly from the manufacturer. By co-operating, independent storekeepers can also achieve economies of scale in purchasing, marketing and financing, which otherwise would be only possible for large chains.

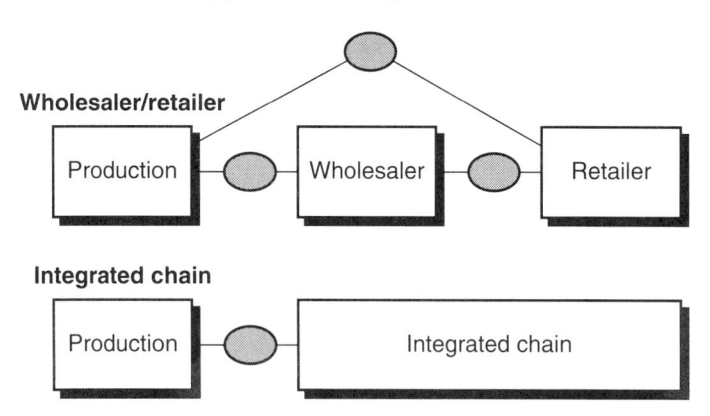

Figure 8.11 Points of negotiation in wholesaler/retailer versus integrated chain

One reason why the integrated chain seems to be successful may be the development of information technology and control systems. It is now possible to get information about store performance at very short notice, facilitating prompt action if necessary. When the current ownership structure in Sweden was developed, the information technology of today did not exist: a large number of independent storekeepers was therefore probably the most efficient solution. Today this is not necessarily true.

International ownership: The degree of international ownership throughout the process (from manufacturers to wholesalers, hauliers and retailers) is much higher in Australia than in Sweden. The most notable example is the US-based retailer K-Mart, who owns part of the major national retailer Coles. Another example is Franklins, the major discount chain, which is owned by Dairy Farm International – a multinational company. A large company in the transport sector is TNT, which has operations all over the world, while in the warehouse business, P&O, which originates from a UK-based company, is one of the major players. The greater variety in ownership than in Sweden also reflects the lower barriers to entry prevalent in Australia.

In Sweden there are no international owners among the major retailers, wholesalers or hauliers. However, among several of the new discount chains being introduced there are obvious links, such as franchising agreements, with foreign retailers.

Barriers to entry

High barriers to entry can impede productivity since it is hard for new entrants to enter the market. Access to sites, suppliers, wholesalers, manufacturers and imported products are all necessary to gain market share.

Access to sites: Access to sites for new stores is one of the most important strategic tools employed to gain or protect market share. However, in both Australia and Sweden site access and supply are effective barriers to entry for new entrants. Access to sites is regulated by urban planning authorities in both countries which determine how land is zoned into commercial, residential or industrial areas. Supermarkets and food stores are only allowed on commercial land.

In Australia the authorities have not had any power to decide what kind of commercial activity may take place on land designated for such use, with the result that supermarkets and food stores have been competing for new sites with other commercial activities, for example car dealers. The shortage of sites also reflects issues such as the size of available sites and the track record of the retailers.[23]

[23] Source: Price and Cartel Office 1986, Inquiry in Relation to Retail Prices of Food and Groceries.

Until recently the authorities in Sweden have not only been responsible for the zoning of land but they have also decided the specific sites on which supermarkets and food stores will be permitted. In order to establish a new supermarket or food store the operator must therefore have access to land designated for food trading and enjoy a good relationship with the authorities.

Access to suppliers: A new entrant at the retail end of the market needs to purchase supplies from either a wholesaler or directly from the manufacturer, domestic or international. Concentration among wholesalers and manufacturers is high in both countries but is greater in Sweden. The higher the degree of concentration, the harder it is for a new retailer to challenge the system and become established. A new entrant, approaching a manufacturer for direct delivery of supplies for example, may meet a reluctance from the manufacturer to do anything that would upset the wholesalers who are very important customers. The network of large wholesalers and manufacturers, who have developed these concentration trends in conjunction with each other, have a much more powerful position than the new retailer.

Access to wholesalers: There is little difference between the two countries in the number of wholesalers from which a new entrant can obtain supplies. In the areas where 70 per cent of Australians live there are at least two independent wholesalers, the same number as in the most populated part of Sweden.

Access to domestic manufacturers: A new entrant has a greater variety of domestic manufacturers from which to choose in Australia than in Sweden where the degree of concentration is higher. The food manufacturing sector provides examples.

- The three largest meat manufacturers account for more than 50 per cent of the market while farmers' co-operatives control almost 100 per cent of the Swedish milk market. In Australia there is no such concentration for either product.
- In the case of bread, the three largest manufacturers in Sweden account for about 80 per cent of the market compared to an Australian ratio of 50 per cent.

In both countries there remain legislative regulations regarding markets for products such as bread and milk, but in both, these laws are slowly breaking down.

The number of food processing establishments is much larger in Australia than in Sweden largely because Australia is a net exporter of food, while Sweden is a net importer. Thus the trend in Sweden is towards higher concentration, coupled with a declining number of establishments and increasing number of employees per establishment. Table 8.1 shows that in Australia the

Convenience Goods Distribution and Retailing 219

Sweden

38%

62%

Australia

59%

41%

■ 10 major manufacturers
□ Others

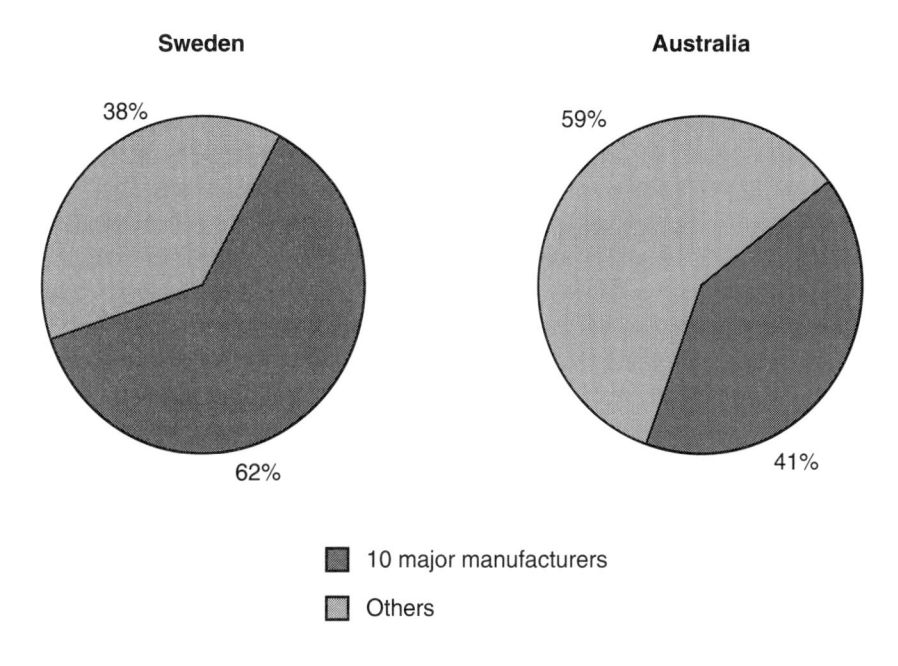

Figure 8.12 Market fragmentation

Source: Dept of Industry, Technology and Commerce, Australian Processed Food and Beverages Industry 1991, Sveriges Livmedelsindustriförbund, Livsmedelsindustrin i siffror 1992

opposite is true i.e. the trend is towards an increasing number of establishments but with fewer employees. Many new niche producers account for this trend.

Table 8.1 Food manufacturers in Australia and Sweden

	Number of establishments		Number of employees per establishment	
	1985	1989/1990	1985	1989/1990
Australia	3,400	3,700	48	46
Sweden	800	700	82	90

Source: Dept of Industry, Technology & Commerce, Australian Processed Food and Beverages Industry 1991; Sveriges Livmedelsindustriförbund, Livsmedelsindustrin i siffror 1992

Ownership concentration among manufacturers also characterises both markets. In Australia the majority of the market is controlled by private companies with domestic or international owners: farmers' co-operatives control a substantial part of certain industries, such as pineapples and sugar, but they are not important overall. Consumer co-operatives do not own any manufacturing. By contrast, Swedish farmers' co-operatives control almost 45 per cent of the manufacturing, consumer co-operatives about 10 per cent and the remaining 45 per cent is controlled by private companies.

There are two main reasons for the greater variety of food manufacturers in Australia. The first is the existence of high Swedish import barriers. Swedish manufacturers sell their products in the small and limited domestic market only. In Australia, import barriers for food are rare and the country is a net exporter of food. Secondly, the Australian market is about twice the size of the Swedish.

Access to imported products: In Australia, import duties and tariffs are unusual. Wholesalers and retailers can use the threat of imports as a tool to 'keep the manufacturers honest', i.e. if domestic suppliers are not up to standard there is always an alternative. However, wholesalers and retailers have a genuine preference for familar domestic suppliers offering more reliable and faster delivery with the avoidance of currency exchange risks.

As noted above, high import barriers in Sweden effectively keep imported products out of the country and also act as a shelter for domestic producers. This import policy forces wholesalers and retailers to look for supplies from domestic manufacturers.

Table 8.2, which details the import duties and tariffs for the items used in the food basket survey in this study, exemplifies these differences in national policies.

Table 8.2 Examples of import duties and tariffs

	Australia*	*Sweden**
Tomatoes	–	Duty: 10-17% (No duty between Oct. – March) Random sample fee: SKr0.0145 per kg Plant protection tax: SKr1.15 per 100 kg (minimum SKr115)
Frozen French fries	–	Agricultural fee: SKr1.85-2.05 per kg Random sample fee: SKr0.0145 per kg
Coca-Cola	Duty 5%	Agricultural fee: SKr0.33 per kg
Cream	–	Agricultural fee: SKr3-17.25 per kg Random sample fee: SKr0.027 per kg
Flour	–	Agricultural fee: SKr1.88-2.34 per kg Random sample fee: SKr0.0105 per kg
White bread	–	Duty: 5% Agricultural fee: SKr2.72-2.74 per kg
Rump steak	–	Agricultural fee: SKr20.25 per kg Random sample fee: SKr0.027 per kg
Tea	–	–

* Only fees that affect imported but not domestic products included. VAT or wholesale tax is not included.
Source: Customs authorities in Stockholm and Sydney. Average exchange rate 1992 was 1 SKr = 0.17 US$

The above has shown that the most important barriers to entry are access to sites and access to suppliers. Both are higher in Sweden than in Australia. What effect have these barriers had on the competitive conditions for companies already in business in the two countries? Are there any major differences in the factors affecting productivity?

Competition

In addition to differences in the macro environment, other factors affect the degree of competition in both countries. These include discount chains, house brands, generics and own labels and price setting mechanisms.

Discount chains: After a period of growth, the market share of discount chains in Australia has levelled out at around 27 per cent: in Sweden the comparable ratio in 1991 was 4.5 per cent and rising.

The discount chains in Australia focus on keeping prices low, stripping away any unnecessary costs. The growth of discount retailers in Australia is likely to be one of the reasons for the firm pressure on prices since the middle of the 1980s which, in turn, has probably forced retailers to become more cost-effective in order to sustain market share.

These stores concentrate on dry groceries, frozen food and dairy products, and are often located close to a butcher, greengrocer and a bakery to give the customer the opportunity of purchasing fresh food at the same time. The large national chains such as Woolworths, however, have managed to narrow, and in some cases eliminate, the price gap between themselves and the discount stores, which they see as their biggest competitors.

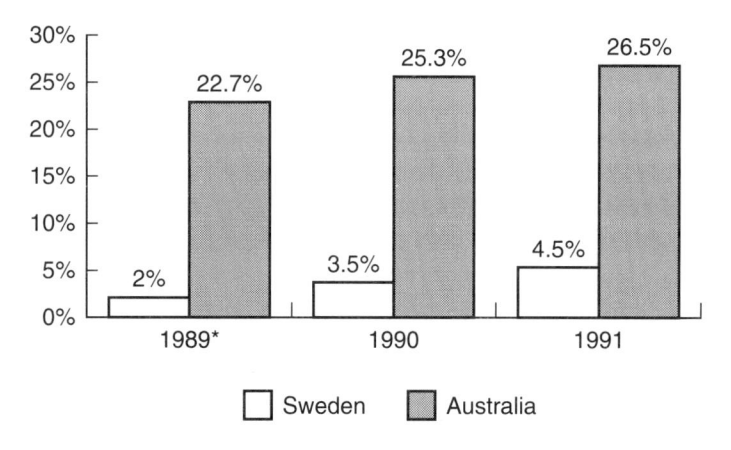

* The 1989 figure (2%) for Sweden is approximate.

Figure 8.13 The market shares for discount chains
Source: *Australian Supermarket News, Nielsen Grocery Trends*, April 1992; Svensk Dagligvaruhandel 1991–92.

222 Achieving Service Productivity

In Sweden the discount chains normally differ from the traditional supermarket on prices and product range; they generally offer dry groceries in addition to fresh food. Two reasons why discount retailing in Sweden has yet to capture a substantial part of the market are the ownership structure among the established operators in the market and the high barriers to entry discussed above.

House brands, generics and own labels: House brands, generics and own labels are products that are sold exclusively by one retailer. They are more common in Australia than in Sweden. One reason for introducing this kind of product can be to increase the negotiating power of the retailers/wholesalers in relation to suppliers.

House brands, generics and own labels are normally priced lower than branded products. In Australia the price difference may be up to 15 per cent.[24] In Australia house brands, generics and own labels are normally manufactured to retailers' specifications under competitive tendering by domestic manufacturers. In Sweden there is a mix of import and manufacturing in retailer-owned establishments.

These products can strengthen the bargaining position of the large retailers and wholesalers with brand name manufacturers. From a consumer point of view the presence of generics can also result in more competition, since they are one way of keeping prices down.

Price setting mechanisms: Price setting mechanisms are different in each country. In Australia prices tend to be market driven, whereas in Sweden prices traditionally have been driven by production costs.

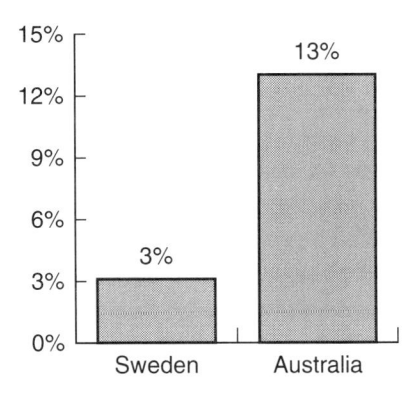

Figure 8.14 House brand/generics own labels segmentation shares in dry groceries

Source: *Australian Supermarket News, Nielsen Grocery Trends*, April 1992; ICA, KF and Dagab.

[24] Source: Price and Cartel Office 1986, Inquiry in Relation to Retail Prices of Food and Groceries.

Convenience Goods Distribution and Retailing 223

In Australia the retailer first assesses what price the market is willing to pay. The retailer then deducts the gross margin required to cover costs to arrive at a purchase price.

In Sweden the process typically starts when the supplier has calculated the production costs and added the necessary profit. The result is the price the supplier demands which, added to wholesalers' and retailers' gross margins, determines the final price in the store.

The key difference between the two methods is that in Sweden prices are based on the costs as they are in the system. The customer will pay the cost anyway, since consumer power is minor compared with that of the other parties in the process. Thus there is no real incentive to become more efficient. Swedish wholesalers and retailers use a percentage mark-up on products, which means they make more money per item, the more expensive the product. By contrast, the Australian way can imply that if a product turns out to be more expensive than the market is willing to pay, the parties in the system reassess the price, i.e. there is an incentive to be more efficient. Setting prices the Australian way requires a detailed understanding of the costs in the business, but using today's modern information technology, it is possible to set prices and perform profitability analysis for each item.

The situation is, however, changing in Sweden (and prices are becoming more of an issue) from a situation where a list of recommended prices was distributed to all stores in a region, regardless of their size, to more flexible methods of price setting. The changing situation is exemplified by the rising market share of the discount chains and the action taken by Hemköp to eliminate the sale price system, replacing it with 'everyday low prices, EDLP'.

Cost structure

A retailer's principal costs are those incurred in the purchase of goods, labour and premises. High labour costs might be an incentive to strive for high labour productivity. High costs for premises might be an incentive to strive for high floor area productivity.

Table 8.3 provides a breakdown of the major cost items for an average Swedish retailer and Woolworths. The figures for Sweden are restricted to the stores, but the figures for Woolworths include both the DC and the stores. Unfortunately, an exact comparison is precluded since information on the cost structure of the Swedish wholesaler is not available. The costs of the Swedish wholesaler are therefore included in the Swedish retailer's cost for purchasing. Summing up, the gross margin (all items in the table except the purchase of goods) for the Swedish store and wholesaler is higher than for Woolworths.

The figures in the table are averages, and variations for specific stores occur both upwards and downwards. VAT is excluded from the Swedish figures. Wholesale sales tax is included in the Australian figures for purchase of goods.

Table 8.3 Cost structure

	Swedish retailer (stores only)	Woolworths (DC+stores)
Purchase of goods	79.5%	78%
Labour costs	12%	12%
Premises	4%	4%
Others	3.5%	3%
Net profit margin	1%	3%
Total	100%	100%

Source: ICA-Förlaget, Butikskalender 1992; Woolworths internal records, 1992

In absolute terms the following facts are relevant.

- Labour costs for warehouse and retail employees are about 75 per cent higher in Sweden.[25]
- Premises costs are harder to compare. In Australia rent is often based on store revenue whereas in Sweden the rent is generally paid according to store size: revenue-based rents are also used, however.
- Transport costs are influenced by geography. However, although this is one of the commonly raised arguments for high costs in Sweden in comparison with Australia, the argument is not valid, rather the opposite. Distances in Australia are greater and hauliers move more tonnes.[26] Although, on the other hand, labour costs, road taxes and fuel each cost more in Sweden, it is likely that transport costs in Australia are equal to or higher than those in Sweden.

[25] Cost of labour for retail/wholesale staff is SKr195,000 in Sweden and A$111,000 in Australia. (Source: Australian Bureau of Statistics, 1992, *Year Book Australia 1992*; Statistics Sweden, Löner för arbetare inom privat sektor (AM57)).

[26] Average distance driven per truck, transported volume of food and transport work in million tonne km of food (Source: Australian Bureau of Statistics, 1992, Survey of Motor Vehicle Usage in Australia 1992; Australian Bureau of Statistics, 1989, Survey of Motor Vehicle Usage in Australia 1998; Statistics Sweden 1991, Varutransporter med lastbil och järnväg under 1990):

	Transport distance (km)	Transport work by trucks (million tonne km)	Transported volume (million tonnes)
Australia (1991)	18,600/76,100 (small/large)	14,207	77 (in year 1988)
Sweden (1990)	48,000	4,302	31

Internal factors

Goals and feedback

Productivity in companies is to a large extent created by the individuals within the organisation. The resolution of goals and the extent of feedback are therefore important in creating conditions for improved productivity. The Australian companies analysed break down goals in a more explicit way than their Swedish counterparts. Individuals and groups receive much clearer feedback of what they achieve and they are also given more information about what is expected of them. Technology supports this process and provides Australian companies with a better chance to improve productivity.

Long-range goals: Although, in general, communication and understanding of the corporate vision differs between companies, the level of communication among retailers tends to be good.

One obvious sign of this is that the employees in the supermarkets in Mora and Orange are all very proud of their company. The Hemköp (Mora) employees are proud of a company which is successful and is recognised as one of the most innovative retailers in Sweden: they also take pride in the environmental concern the company stands for. Co-operation between the unions and the management at Hemköp also exemplifies the successful communication of long-range goals.

Woolworths employees are also proud of being part of a company, which although it had a devastating drop in profits in 1987, is now successful. They are proud of being part of 'The Fresh Food People', a slogan that is painted on the trucks, displayed in the stores, used as a theme in commercials etc.

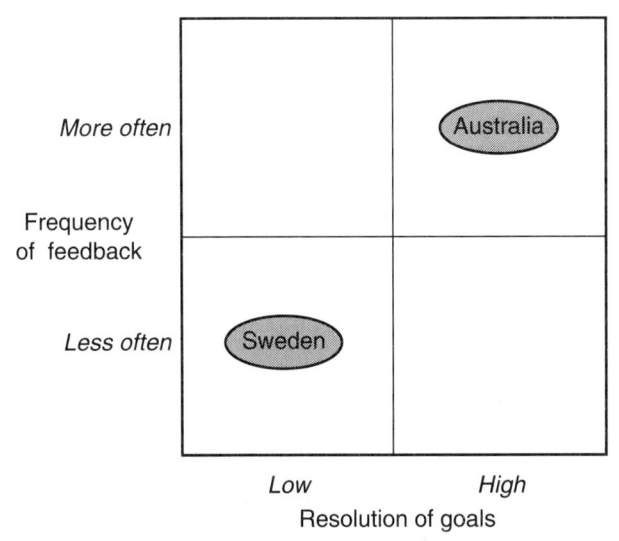

Figure 8.15 Frequency of feedback and resolution of goals

226 Achieving Service Productivity

Operational goals and feedback: In Swedish companies, goals are set and feedback received on a collective rather than individual level. This is a very Swedish way of operating. By contrast, in Australian companies goals are spread through the organisation and individual targets are more common. The time span between evaluation points is also different. Weekly targets are normal in Australia, whereas monthly targets are more common in Sweden.

More frequent evaluations enable the organisation to act on operational problems faster. A higher resolution of operational goals also creates opportunities for better understanding of company expectations on the performance of individuals and smaller working groups within the company. It is often necessary to develop and increase the usage of information technology in this process.

The budget is an important tool for setting goals in all organisations and supermarkets budget at a departmental level. At both Hemköp and Woolworths the store manager is responsible for the store profit. In addition, each departmental manager at Woolworths has responsibility for the gross margin of their department. This is not the case at Hemköp.

Both supermarkets report weekly on sales. The information collated at Woolworths is more detailed than at Hemköp but each is used for control and evaluation. At Woolworths, for example, the gross margin for all the fruit and vegetable departments in the state is reported on a weekly basis to the purchasers of fruit and vegetables. This enables the purchaser to make more accurate forecasts and fine tune pricing strategies.

Companies try to optimise the total cost for carrying stock. The traditional inventory optimisation model distinguishes between holding cost, order cost and stockout cost:

- holding cost is the cost of carrying stock such as interest and stockroom;
- order cost is the cost associated with ordering such as transport, ordering and receiving;
- stockout cost (not shown in Figure 8.16) is the cost of not being able to deliver goods due to shortage.

Figure 8.16 illustrates this model: the dotted line indicates optimal order quantity.

Although the model ignores many important factors and is very simplified, it is a useful tool for discussion. The integrated chain will try to optimise the total inventory cost for the combined function of the DC and the supermarket. In a less integrated retailer/wholesaler situation, however, there could be a risk that the retailer and the wholesaler will try to optimise

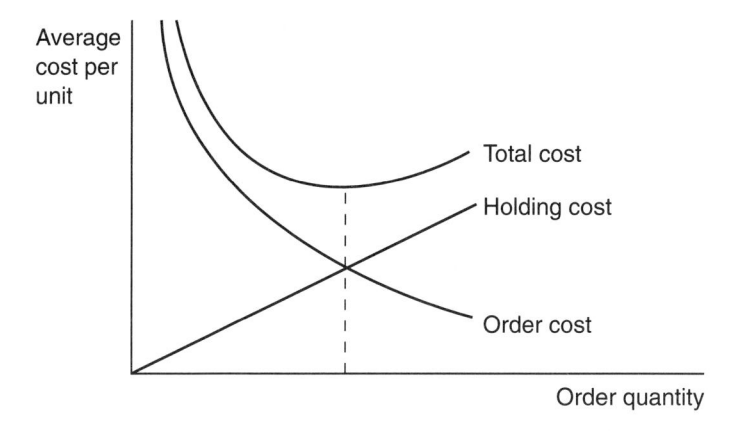

Figure 8.16 The economic order quantity model

their order routines individually, thereby generating a total cost that is suboptimal for the combined functions.

By maintaining a sufficient level of stock turnover the company can keep holding costs at a low level. The supermarkets in Hemköp must fulfil certain goals concerning turnover of stock: if they deviate from the goal the supermarket will be charged or credited for the difference, i.e. profit will be affected. This is not the case at Woolworths. Instead, they keep stocks low by frequent deliveries and splitting packages at the warehouse before delivery to the stores. (This is only done for products with high value and low turnover.) These different methods of operation are reflected in comparative annual stock turnover ratios; the ratio is 15 at Hemköp in Mora and 25 at Woolworths in Orange.

The role of Australian and Swedish distribution centres also differs. In Australia the distribution centres are dedicated warehouses and therefore are pure cost centres, i.e. they only have cost goals. Operations must not cost more than a certain percentage of store sales. To reach this goal costs must be kept under total control. This is possibly the reason why the Australian warehouses have such advanced information systems for cost evaluation.

In contrast, Dagab, which acts as a wholesaler, is a profit centre. Operations have sales and profit goals as well as goals related to minimising costs. The company is required to deliver a certain profit to its owner. This implies that they must be good at purchasing, selling, warehousing and transport. As a result corporate goals are rather varied, perhaps making it more difficult for the individuals to understand what the focus is and for the whole organisation to strive in one direction.

228 Achieving Service Productivity

Reward systems

Rewards play a key role in the process of building up employee incentive schemes. For example, Hemköp operates a progressive profit-sharing scheme involving all company employees. Each month 10 per cent of the net profit of each supermarket is added to the fixed income of the employees in relation to hours worked. The store managers work on a bonus scheme. Store and department managers at Woolworths are rewarded with an annual bonus if they reach, or surpass, their budget objectives.

Financial ratios

Financial ratios constitute a very important tool to achieving improvement. Such ratios enable individuals to see a clear link between their own tasks and the measure, while at a corporate level these measures can be used as tools for inter-company comparison.

In the supermarkets of Hemköp and Woolworths sales/hours worked and sales/m^2 are the two most important ratios. Both companies also study the number of customers, average purchase per customer and number of purchased items per customer.

The most important financial ratio that the wholesaler Dagab Nord uses is sales/hours worked, a critical measure since the company is not only warehousing, but also selling. For the warehousing function, Dagab uses a number of other measures such as number of cartons handled/hours worked.

The warehouses or distribution centres in the Australian companies also use a few well-defined measures. For example:

- number of cartons handled/hours worked;
- pallets received/hours worked;
- number of cartons picked/hours worked;
- number of pallets delivered/hours worked;
- number of cartons/pallet.

In the transport industry commonly used financial ratios are:

- capacity utilisation in the trucks;
- income/tonne;
- labour costs/km;
- income/employee;
- income/delivery.

Convenience Goods Distribution and Retailing 229

In addition some operators are introducing other measures broken down to the individual level including:

- number of km/driver;
- number of cartons/hours worked;
- number of km/hours worked.

Standards

In Australian companies a standard is defined by allocating a certain time for different parts of a work cycle. For the individual this can improve the measurement of goals, although on the other hand, rigid and detailed standards can have a negative impact on motivation.

The Australian companies work more actively with standards than their Swedish counterparts. At the Woolworths Yennora warehouse, standards and computerised terminals in the trucks are currently being introduced; each task is measured, a target set and individual performances are then evaluated against these standards. The system is computerised. The warehouse manager points out that the purpose is not to set goals too high, but to set realistic targets that everyone can strive for. The reason for introducing the new system is to improve performance, especially labour productivity, in the warehouse. At Dagab Nord this kind of individual evaluation is not undertaken. Evaluation is done on a more aggregated and collective level.

In the haulage industry, Refrigerated Roadways has introduced standards on a number of routes. In co-operation with the drivers, the company has developed a timetable, which shows how long different transport units may last. The drivers are paid for the standard time, not the real time. The result is that trucks tend to return to the depot faster, which has led to a higher utilisation of the vehicles.

Bilspedition in Sweden is also using standards but on a more collective level. Rather than allocate a time slot to each transport unit, the driver is paid a fixed amount regardless of stops on route.

Waste

Waste is traditionally categorised as known and unknown. Known waste comprises goods that break or become out of date. Unknown waste can occur when goods are stolen.

Whereas store operators strive to reduce unknown waste, the incentives to minimise known waste vary between a chain of stores and an independent storekeeper. The independent storekeeper can withdraw products for their

230 Achieving Service Productivity

personal use and will therefore accept a certain level of waste. In fact, in Sweden the storekeepers are automatically taxed for the fringe benefit of having 'free' food. This is not allowed in the integrated chain, however, which will work towards the elimination of known waste.

Traditionally, in both Australia and Sweden, a waste level of 2 to 3 per cent is accepted. To enhance control and thereby reduce waste (and prices) is, from a competitive point of view, important in both countries.

Woolworths is currently developing methods and tools to measure waste on individual items rather than on an aggregate value basis as was done previously, and which made it difficult to know where the waste actually occurred. The preliminary results of item-based control show that waste can be considerably reduced using these methods, and wastage of less than 1 per cent has been achieved.

Hemköp is not currently working with control systems for waste management.

Technology

Technology includes both information technology (IT) and automation. IT embraces the use of computers in order to benefit from scanner data, i.e. information collected from computerised cash registers. Automation is, for example, using conveyor belts in a warehouse instead of trucks or automated pallet storage facilities.

	Low	High
High (Level of automation)		P&O WW Yennora
Low	Dagab Nord Liljas Refrigerated roadways Hemköp (HK) HK Mora WW Orange	Bilspedition Woolworths(WW)

Usage of information technology

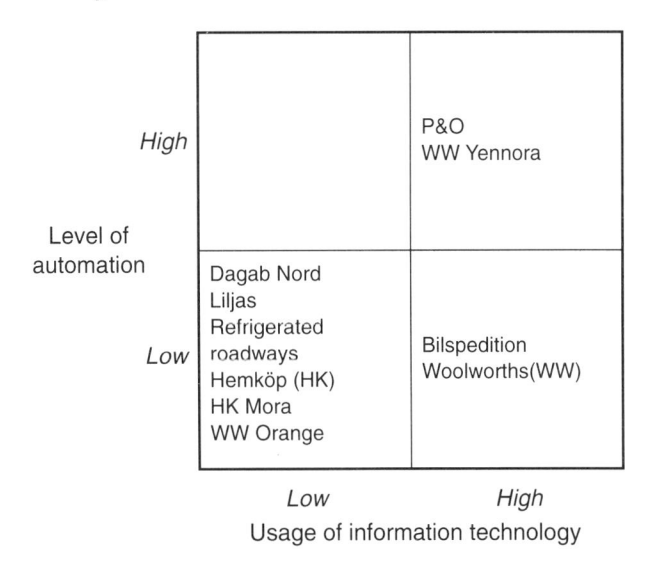

Figure 8.17 Comparative use of IT and automation

Convenience Goods Distribution and Retailing 231

The Australian companies utilise technology to a greater extent than the Swedish companies: Hemköp has made a strategic decision not to be in the front line in the use of IT and Dagab places less emphasis on this area. In contrast, Woolworths and P&O have invested heavily in IT and automation. The haulage sector provides an exception, however, in that Bilspedition is ahead of Refrigerated Roadways in the use of IT.

IT: The driving forces for the increased use of IT vary, but they generally include the desire for better planning, control, management and handling.

The use of IT is relatively similar in the supermarkets in Mora and Orange, although the latter derives greater benefits from the information generated via computerised scanning cash registers in the stores.

In Woolworths scanner information penetrates the whole organisation. The president, business area managers, store managers, department managers, warehouse managers and purchasers receive customised information about events in their company each week. Space management in the stores is, for example, effected using scanner data in order to optimise shelf space.

Hemköp place less importance on detailed information from scanner systems: total sales is the only measure analysed. In many ways it remains a small company although its rapid growth is likely to change this perspective.

Computerised ordering systems are used between Hemköp in Mora and Dagab, and between Woolworths in Orange and its distribution centres. The productivity gains resulting from a shorter order cycle are obvious. None the less, the individual employee makes the final decision as to whether a product should be ordered or not, based on the stock situation in the store. None of the stores have fully automatic order systems.

Automation: Automation is a traditional way of improving productivity by exchanging manpower for machine power. In this sector the opportunities for automation are most evident within the warehouse function. Opportunities within the stores and the haulage system are currently probably more limited.

All the distribution centres in the study are pallet based but the degree of automation is higher in Australia. The Dagab warehouse utilises a manual storing system, a computerised order pick system and radio communication between the truck drivers. This warehouse is not the most automated in Sweden. Woolworths' Yennora warehouse utilises a combination of a traditional warehouse and a fully automated one and the truck drivers use a computerised pallet control sytem.

P&O Cold Storage provide the most advanced warehouse system. Order picking is made for several orders at the same time using conveyor belts and each carton is labelled with a universal product code. These codes are later used to automatically sort the correct cartons for each customer, creating obvious gains in labour productivity.

Market intelligence

In order to ensure high productivity it is important to develop the ability to respond to changes in the marketplace. Companies must find ways of collecting crucial information from the market, analysing it and acting upon it.

Both retailers seem to be well aware of the attitudes and behaviour of their customers, although their market intelligence is gathered in different ways. Woolworths use systematic methods, often different kinds of market surveys, while Hemköp relies on a well-functioning internal network or 'marketing council' of store managers and top management; it rarely uses external sources.

Woolworths also have an internal network. However, even though top management spend a lot of their time in supermarkets, it is hard to maintain an acceptable level of market knowledge through this channel. The company is a giant, which makes it difficult to rely exclusively on these informal methods and its size is one reason why it has chosen to formalise market intelligence. Even though each store manager can pick up the phone and talk to decision makers at head office, the information and methodology need to be structured. Woolworths regularly undertake various external customer surveys as well as studies of their competitors, especially concerning prices and strategies.

9

LESSONS FROM THE BEST IN SERVICES

INTRODUCTION

The principal questions we have asked in this book are the following.

- What are the companies and organisations studied good at?
- Is it possible to measure productivity in service operations?

Combined strategies

To answer the first question, management textbooks ordinarily recommend that companies should choose one of two main strategies: either be a dominant producer possessing cost superiority, *or* a maker of exclusive or high-performance products for small customer segments that are not price-sensitive.[1] One interesting finding of our previous study was that the best companies in their respective fields of business try to achieve cost-effectiveness and innovation at the same time. For example, when new mobile telephones are developed, performance is improved at the same time as manufacturing costs are lowered. Even in a relatively mature sector like the paper industry, investments in new machines are made in such a way that the manufacturing cost is lowered at the same time as product quality improves.

New technology

One explanation for the fact that the combination of cost-cutting and performance-raising is possible is that certain technologies have effects in both dimensions. Technological advance can thus both raise the quality of a service and lower its production cost. We found several such examples in the payment transfer services provided by banks and postal giro systems. At the

---
[1] Our analysis of productivity in terms of cost-effectiveness and innovation is, of course, also an expression of this mind-set.

Henry Ford Health System, we also discovered that new technology made it possible to perform surgery at ambulatory care centres, resulting in both lower costs and fewer problems for patients.

The companies invest in technology that can be used to produce many different types of services. Woolworth's information system can be utilised not only to steer the distribution system, but also to make rapid changes in the product range as the wishes of their customers dictate. Relational databases with a broad range of information about customers and processes make it possible to offer services which are in demand, at just the right moment. The company is able to retain full control of product and customer profit calculations. Electronic communications systems have meant that the Postgiro's customers have been able to receive and follow up transactions more simply and quickly via a direct connection to their own financial systems. The cost compared to that of physical distribution is lower and furthermore, a greater portion of the processing lies with the customer.

Economies of scale in market intelligence

Several of the organisations we studied lower costs at the same time as they raise quality by segmenting their customers and adapting their services to better match customer needs. The company that possesses knowledge about the needs of its customers is strong on the market. In retail banking, Banc One and Credit Suisse have information systems that enable them to calculate the profitability of various services and customers. On the basis of such information, they can discuss whether to focus on certain segments. They can also price their services to correspond to their costs.

In the US, insurance brokers are in a strong position because they have acquired a large body of knowledge about and proximity to their customers via their sales channels. In Sweden, the insurance companies themselves have built up a similar network and the brokers are in a weaker position. Economies of scale with regard to access to information are of less importance if there is no competition. But examples to the contrary do exist.

We learnt from Banc One and Woolworths that it is important to conduct systematic customer and market analyses. Market knowledge determines which items are added to, or deleted from, the bank's standardised product range. We learnt that it is possible to combine standardisation with differentiation. The fact that a service is provided in a standardised and thus efficient manner does not necessarily mean that there is no room to give different customers different services.

Credit Suisse conducts profit analyses of its customers and customer groups. It had a small, profitable category of customers who have large deposits in the bank and a large group of customers with unprofitable transaction accounts. By designing different services for different customer segments, services can be adapted efficiently to match customer demand.

Co-ordinated autonomy

Banc One uses a system of co-ordinated autonomy. It decides centrally what products to sell, what quality norms to use, what earnings targets should be achieved and what information technology should be used. Locally, each Banc One affiliate makes decisions on, for example, what prices to charge for its services and what salaries employees should receive.

Modularisation of service components

The best organisations spell out their services clearly. Organisations that measure their operations get a better idea of what creates value-added for the customer. Through its computer system, Banc One has created a range of some 200 standardised services. The best service organisations thus resemble manufacturers who are very familiar with the performance and manufacturing costs of their products. Thanks to modularisation of program production, Ericsson has cut the lead times for the production of large software packages.

Measuring productivity

Turning to the second question, it is a common statement that productivity in service organisations cannot be measured. One argument is that their quality aspect is too difficult to evaluate in quantitative terms. Some scholars go further, arguing that it is almost offensive to measure the productivity of such public sector operations as hospitals and schools. The nature of these institutions is such that they are sustained by people's goodwill or sense of calling. Measuring their productivity would draw attention to non-essential dimensions and thus be incompatible with their operational concept. This attitude also crops up in certain private service-producing organisations. One example we encountered was the statement that underwriting at insurance companies is not a science, but an 'art'.

It is undeniably harder to measure productivity in services than in the manufacturing sector. Our studies of service companies nevertheless show that the best organisations are distinguished precisely by the fact that they are forerunners in being able to measure and manage their operations. The reason why not everyone has quantitative yardsticks for their services is not that they are hard to measure, but rather that some people feel no need to develop such instruments.

Another reason why some service-providing organisations do not measure and manage their operations as well as a manufacturing company, is that their operations can be highly diversified. For example, a bank branch performs a variety of different tasks, but its employees do not ordinarily record the time spent on each; only this would make it possible to estimate the costs of various services and of serving diverse customers. Similar examples are found in insurance companies and hospitals.

Quality measurement

Quality is not an objective concept. For instance, our researchers were surprised that the physical environment of the Crocker Middle School was so modest and had such obvious shortcomings. This is consistent with the view that quality is what the customer perceives as quality, not something that is measurable. This is not unique to service operations, however. The quality of certain products is also determined by customer perceptions of the product, rather than by measurable factors.

Employees at the Postgiro can monitor the number of calls at the switchboard via a display screen. When calls are coming in at intervals of 20 seconds or more, production workers help switchboard personnel to answer enquiries. One study would indicate that doctors are sceptical about the possibility of planning treatment times, claiming that these vary considerably from case to case. However, it transpired that operations for similar types of complaint took more or less the same amount of time.

Because banks, for instance, have failed to measure the costs of their services, there has not been any basis for correctly pricing these services. It has not been possible to weigh the bank's cost of providing a given service against its value-added to the customer. This has also been true of services provided by insurance companies, postal giro systems and letter delivery organisations. What we learnt from Banc One and Credit Suisse was that an extensive computer system that records costs and can sort them in different dimensions makes it possible to develop and price services in a way that is fair to customers and relevant to the bank.

Credit Suisse demonstrated that customer data can provide the basis for a segmentation of customers into groups, each with different requirements and with a different propensity to pay. Customers with the smallest balances in their account and only simple transaction needs can be offered standardised services. Customers with larger assets and investment-like transactions require more customised services.

In the Henry Ford Health System and at Princess Royal Hospital, full-paying private patients are found next to patients covered by insurance or even patients receiving free care. It is thus difficult to segment health care at a hospital, with the result that patients receive medical care of essentially the same quality.

PRODUCTIVITY MANAGEMENT

We studied two methods of improving productivity in services. The first is by measuring results. The second, by giving instructions that specify how the work should be performed in order to achieve the desired results. As mentioned above, one thing that typified the best companies was that they were forerunners in measuring and managing their work. For example, the Henry Ford and Princess Royal Hospitals have targets stating how many operations they should perform in one day. The Henry Ford Health System also has a target that specifies how many hours physicians should spend working with patients etc.

Underwriters in the Swedish insurance industry informed us that their work cannot be evaluated in the short term and perhaps not even in a one-year perspective. But at America's Home Insurance, the work of underwriters is managed by means of instructions and monthly follow-ups. After turning in three months of poor results, underwriters there can even be fired. Sweden's Trygg-Hansa insurance company has instructions, but relies mainly on the professional competence of the groups that handle each case.

'Services inventories'

It is customary to say that a service is produced at the same rate as it is consumed. This is only a qualified truth. In our studies we tried instead to view service production as a process, examining what happened from the time a customer came into contact with the company until the relationship ended. For example, what happens from the time a patient first visits a hospital until his or her treatment is completed? We discovered that, just as studies of manufacturing processes have found, value-added is created during a very brief period of the total business relationship. Thus, several months may pass from the date a customer calls to buy corporate insurance until the policy is issued. The period during which the company 'adds value' by calculating the insurance risks, typing out the documents etc. is only a few hours, i.e. only a tiny percentage of the entire processing period.

Effective process time

We can see two reasons why this processing time becomes unnecessarily long and drawn out. First, service-producing organisations do not perceive as clearly as manufacturing companies that capital is tied up in the services that are being processed. Secondly, the customer is often the one who pays for the waiting period. The crowds in hospital waiting rooms, and the long delays between diagnosis and treatment imply that patients' waiting time is not assigned any value or only low value.

238 Achieving Service Productivity

Process management

The banks that we studied have begun to examine their work in terms of processes that can be streamlined and managed in an effort to raise productivity and quality. Banc One, for example, has hired production technicians from industry to perform traditional flow and method studies. It has begun to design process descriptions that help it obtain better background material for analysing costs etc. Credit Suisse has begun segmenting its customer base, and comparing costs and revenues in ways that probably have never been done before in the banking world. Efforts are also under way at Sweden's S-E-Banken to obtain better background data for balancing the costs and benefits of services to different customers.

Measuring techniques

Our studies of successful companies show that they make continual measurements and evaluations of variables such as productivity, quality, profitability, behaviour and attitudes. Banc One goes out and takes a closer look at those branches that perform better than others. It studies what these top performers are actually doing, instead of trying to find reasons why others are not performing as well.

To enable banks to allocate their costs to different processes, customers, products and profit centres, banks must develop profitability management. Both Banc One and Credit Suisse and also Woolworths can calculate the profitability of individual customers, customer groups, products or product groups, as well as organisational units in both dimensions of the matrix structure.

Information technology

The two postal giro systems and Woolworths showed us the importance of advanced information technology. The principles are simple. Raw data on customers, accounts and transactions are relatively permanent, whereas procedures and compilations vary over time. The important thing is to build up a system that provides flexibility in using the database. Credit Suisse has been able to shift this kind of profitability management to the lowest organisational level, because unlike most other banks, it has stored raw data in a way that allows processing and compilations can be varied as needed.

Banc One places great emphasis on guiding all employees toward established goals. The company sets up sub-goals for different personnel categories; the common denominator for the sub-goals is that they are based on factors that the employee can influence. Managers of profit centres are evaluated on the basis of profitability goals, in terms of return on total assets.

These managers in turn evaluate their personnel according to behaviour or how well they perform certain tasks.

Both PTT in Holland and Sweden Post have comprehensive systems for measuring quality and productivity and each office is evaluated according to special models. Measurements show that both organisations have improved the quality of their services. However, these measurements are not based directly on the behaviour or attitudes of individual employees.

The students in the Swedish schools that we studied have the opportunity to influence their curriculum by means of regular assessments – the student is regarded as a customer. The asssessments made in Rödebyskolan in Karlskrona for instance are directly comparable to how companies investigate customer attitudes. In the American Crocker School, the school executive assesses both students and teachers. Here, the student is regarded as a product, which is refined through a process led by the teacher.

There is a clear connection between well-defined goals, continuous follow-up and evaluation, and productivity in the entire distribution chain of the food retail business. The Swedish food distributors often set up goals and give feedback for the group as a whole, rather than for the individual, whereas the goals in the Australian company studied were more stratified and focused on individuals. The frequency with which evaluations are made also varies between countries. In Australia, evaluation often takes place once a week, while companies in Sweden are content to make them once a month.

The Australian distribution centres are just warehouses and are regarded in-house as cost centres, thus they only have cost-orientated goals. Thanks to advanced information technology, the central offices can have full control of storage costs for individual products. In the warehouses at Woolworths in Australia, cost-orientated goals are broken down into small units; the number of pallets moved in and out of the warehouse per unit of time, for example. Every employee knows about the 'speedometer' and works all the time to improve the 'record'.

BENCHMARKING

Benchmarking represents a comparison of activities and processes; you could say that this study is in part a form of benchmarking, in fact. Sweden Post has developed its collaboration with the Dutch PTT, and between them the organisations are working to create a foundation for benchmarking.

The three banks studied are all trying to organise their activities in such a way that they will be able to upgrade performance continually. Activities in different departments are being scrutinised and compared to each other. This continuous benchmarking creates:

- greater motivation
- the possibility of learning from each other.

Banc One also uses traditional techniques for production management in order to study production and make flow charts. The bank has hired experienced production technicians to carry out this work. The purpose is to discover and eliminate or simplify complex flows and operations, both in the production and distribution systems. The bank is conducting frequency studies in a number of areas; every tenth minute employees note what they are doing at that particular moment in time. One purpose of this is to chart how long different activities take, another is to involve all the employees in the work of improvement.

Banc One also supports 'friendly, internal competition' between branch offices. A detailed, uniform system for monitoring profitability makes it possible to analyse and compare different units. Management demands that low achievement offices study the routines and methods of other, more efficient offices in order to take suitable steps. Through this and similar continuous improvements, the bank has been able to slim down its organisation, while all the time improving productivity.

In one of the S-E-Bank's regions, the managers for customer services have to submit reports about what activities they are planning for the coming two weeks and these reports are later compared to the outcome of these activities.

Quality

Postal services have fairly well-developed methods for measuring quality. One yardstick that has been used internationally for years is the percentage of first-class letters delivered overnight. Sweden Post earns a high score (96 per cent) in this respect. However, a large volume of letters are of such a nature that the corporate sender would prefer that they arrive on a certain day rather than overnight. This example shows that quality measurements must be based on current rather than past customer needs.

EXTERNAL FACTORS INFLUENCING PRODUCTIVITY

National factors

When we compare the findings of our two studies of productivity in leading companies, it becomes clear that external factors are more important in explaining the differences between service-producing organisations than differences between manufacturing companies. Service production often occurs within national boundaries because of the traditional and continuing obstacles to exports of certain services, such as bank deposit-taking. Most of the services we have studied are nationally regulated, making international comparisons difficult.

There appear, none the less, to be major differences in service sector productivity from one country to another. These differences can be estimated in various ways. One crude yardstick is to see how much labour is needed to fulfil a given function, for example preparing a certain type of insurance policy or performing a specific surgical operation. Another way is to compare the costs of specific services in different countries. Interest rate spreads at banks may thus show wide variations between countries, as may their operating costs as a percentage of interest income.

'Service nationalism'

Because of the lack of international competition in many service sectors, there may be very large differences in the costs of providing a given service from one country to another.[2] For example, the international expansion of banks has been limited, among other things, because it has not been possible to use the same systems in several countries. The marginal cost of international expansion has thus been higher in services than in manufacturing sectors.

When we studied the distribution of food products and other convenience goods, we found that the Woolworths chain in Australia had both higher productivity and lower costs than their Swedish counterparts. The same applied to PTT Post in The Netherlands compared to Sweden Post and the Crocker Middle School in California compared with the Swedish schools studied. The Henry Ford Health System, an American health maintenance organisation (HMO), admittedly had higher productivity in terms of numbers of patients treated than the Swedish hospital in our study, but as mentioned above, also a much higher cost level. America's Home insurance company also had higher productivity in volume terms but higher costs than its Swedish parent company Trygg-Hansa, as did Sweden's PostGirot compared with Norway's postal giro service.

Institutional factors

In some cases we found that other countries' rule systems were 'worse' than their Swedish counterparts, but that other organisations nevertheless

---

[2] 'Norman (1991) concludes that the EFTA countries should expect clear but moderate gains in most manufacturing industries from participating in the EC internal market, but the potential benefits from increased international competition in services are much larger.' *CEPR Annual Report*, 1992, p. 19.

managed to achieve high productivity. American rules governing insurance and hospitals are thus full of elements that we found counterproductive. In spite of this, Home and the Henry Ford Health System, respectively, were very efficient. For example, the American HMO performs a large number of surgeries per physician. Insurance policies are processed efficiently by Home, but carry premiums that are frighteningly high by Swedish standards.

Sweden has higher – much higher – costs for food product distribution, schools, bank deposits and first-class postage than the foreign companies we examined in these sectors. One reason is that compared to other countries, average Swedish pay levels in service production are very high.[3] In the Swedish labour market, the trend of wages in service sectors has largely followed wages in industrial companies. The only Swedish organisation we studied that could match its best foreign counterpart was PostGirot. Norway, the country used in the comparison, is not so different from Sweden in terms of wage levels in services.

Our study of food product and convenience goods distribution indicated that the percentage mark-up in the wholesale and retail stages was higher in Sweden than in Australia. In addition, prices in the food processing industry are about twice as high in Sweden as in Australia. Taken together, this explains why Swedish consumers must pay more than twice as much for their groceries as consumers in Australia.

In the service sectors there are plenty of 'national champions', but 'world champions' are more thin on the ground. The sectors and organisations we studied operate mainly in national markets and, in the case of schools and hospitals, their catchment areas are limited to local or regional markets, while letter delivery and postal giro services remain largely national. In recent years the most important service sectors that have begun to spread across national boundaries via multinational companies are insurance and, to some extent, food product and bank deposit-taking.

However, in other service sectors besides those we have studied, there are multinational companies. Some of these are extremely successful, for example the Swedish-owned IKEA furnishings chain and the American-based McDonald's fast-food franchise. These examples show that at least some types of service operations can become global, as in many manufacturing sectors. We therefore believe that more world champions may well emerge in service sectors, once they have gained access to international markets.

Another factor inhibiting globalisation is that many services are difficult or even impossible to export. International service operations often presuppose

[3] After Sweden abandoned its unilateral link to the European Currency Unit in November 1992, the exchange rate of the Swedish krona had fallen an average of nearly 19 per cent by April 1993.

on-the-spot service production, which may require heavy investments, not least in local market know-how. A less capital-intensive method that is increasingly being used in the service sector is franchising, i.e. granting the right to sell a given service to a locally active entrepreneur.

Because the organisations studied here are not necessarily world champions, they are not at the same level as the best companies in manufacturing industries that we earlier studied. To put it simply, we earlier were less impressed by what we discovered in the service sector. While companies are admittedly often the best in their fields, they 'play a gentler game' than the most productive manufacturing companies. One important reason is that service sector organisations operate under heavier regulation than manufacturing firms. One interviewee at America's Home insurance company put it this way: 'We are handling an inefficient system in an efficient way.'[4]

This study therefore singles out not only the good factors that improve productivity, but also those factors found to have a detrimental effect.

According to our model, companies strive for cost-effectiveness because they feel that their resources are scarce, while the degree of information complexity in their surroundings influences their ambition to innovate. The optimal combination is somewhere in the middle with regard to both factors. Classifying the organisations studied on the basis of their resource situation and information complexity, respectively, highlights differences between service sectors and between countries.

Hospitals in Britain, Sweden and the US work in surroundings characterised by fairly high information complexity, due to constant and rapid advances in medical science. At the same time, until fairly recently, hospitals in all three countries have had a relatively low degree of resource scarcity. One indication of this is that medical care costs have accounted for a growing percentage of gross domestic product.

Companies in convenience goods distribution and industrial insurance work in fairly dynamic surroundings. New products are constantly appearing, competitors are always making new moves and customer demand is not stable. Compared with their counterparts from other countries, Swedish companies in the study have had a smaller degree of resource scarcity, since they have not faced such stiff competition.

Until relatively recently, banks, postal services and schools have also operated in a fairly stable environment. At the same time, banks and postal services have not suffered from resource scarcity but have worked under conditions generally associated with bureaucratic organisations. Schools, on

---

[4] The American insurance system is greatly affected by the fact that such a large percentage of its claim disputes go to civil courts for final adjudication. The US has 5 per cent of the world's population but 70 per cent of its lawyers, according to former Vice-president Dan Quayle, himself a lawyer.

the other hand, have operated with fairly limited resources. This applies especially to the Swedish and Danish schools in our study, while the American school we examined is able to obtain extra money through fund raising. The Swedish schools can be described as having the worst external prerequisites: a combination of a low degree of information complexity and scarce resources. This provides little incentive for innovation, while there are insufficient resources for cost-effectiveness.

The sector that appears to have the best prerequisites is postal giro services, both in Norway and Sweden. Competition with the bank giro system places certain constraints on resources, while advances in information technology and constant demands by large corporate customers for faster payment systems, create a certain information complexity in their surroundings.

Factors at the industry level

Competition

Our case studies show that one key factor behind productivity differences between organisations in the same industry is that they work under different levels of competitive pressure. There are huge variations: from the strong rivalry prevailing in the American insurance market to the peaceful monopoly enjoyed by a Swedish compulsory school located in a small town.

There are about 800 US-based insurance companies, although due to state regulations the American market can instead be described as 50 local markets. In Sweden the market for industrial insurance is oligopolistic, with two major players and a few minor ones.

One important source of change in a company's surroundings is the behaviour of its competitors. In a market where there is competition, moves and countermoves will constantly occur. We found a clear example of this in our study of postal giro systems. In both Norway and Sweden, the postal giro system competes with the bank giro system, forcing each to launch technical innovations that make payments quicker, cheaper and more reliable.

The Henry Ford Health System has local competitors. It competes with other HMOs to land contracts with insurance companies, specifying that policyholders should use a given health care network when they need medical attention. Older patients who have no insurance but are covered by Medicare, a federally funded programme, can also choose their own provider.

American schools have no 'guaranteed' pupils. In principle, all pupils choosing the Crocker Middle School could attend another school. In Sweden, over the past year, certain municipalities have started allowing pupils to choose their own school, creating something of a competitive situation, but this option does not yet exist in Bräcke and Karlskrona.

In every country except Sweden, the post office still has a monopoly on delivering letters. In Sweden, this situation ended only in 1993. Despite the existence of such monopolies, however, the Swedish and Dutch postal services have shown good improvements in productivity, each undergoing a transformation from government agencies to business enterprises in corporate form.

But transforming a post office from a government agency into a business is no easy process. The new market situation requires greater flexibility and other new capabilities. At the same time, top executives want to maintain the high level of morale associated with the civil service spirit. PTT Post in The Netherlands and Sweden's PostGirot have largely drawn their new managements from the business sector.

The problem of shifting from non-profit status to more business-orientated operations also exists in hospitals. Well into the twentieth century, hospital work was something of a calling. Working hours were not regulated, and the wages of nurses and orderlies in particular were very low. After medical care came to be regarded as just another job, with regulated working hours and overtime compensation, labour productivity fell markedly.

Substitutes

In our study of Posten Brev, the letter-carrying business area of Sweden Post, it became clear how technical advances can create substitutes for services provided by monopoly companies. Due to the emergence of fax machines and electronic mail, the volume of letters in Sweden declined for the first time in 1991.

Because of advances in information technology, the deposit-taking operations of banks also face heavier competition. It has become possible for private individuals to invest in retail bonds or commercial paper issued by institutions other than banks. Such securities can be sold by telephone and it is no longer necessary to have a nationwide chain of offices in order to attract the savings of private individuals.

Customer/supplier contact

In our earlier study of manufacturing companies, we found that the presence of sophisticated customers was just as important as the existence of numerous competitors. The reason, quite simply, was that a sophisticated customer demands continuous improvement in productivity and can also judge whether this has been achieved.

The presence of demanding customers is a major force behind improved productivity in industrial insurance, postal giro services and even letter delivery. This is perhaps most apparent in the case of Home and Trygg-Hansa, which sell industrial insurance. Since large corporate customers in Sweden and independent insurance brokers in the US can make their own calculations of premiums and claim payments, Home and Trygg-Hansa are forced to be cost-effective and highly productive.

Barriers to market entry

Public sector regulation

All the service industries that we studied are subject to special public regulation. There are a number of reasons for this, past and present. One has been to ensure that everyone has access to a given service (mail delivery, postal giro payments and sale of convenience goods). Another has been the perceived need for public sector ownership in order to give all citizens the same quality of service (hospitals, schools). A third reason has been consumer protection (banking, insurance).

When we studied the historical evolution of these service industries, we saw that the need for public regulation changes over time. One instructive example is the letter-delivery monopoly, which was abolished in Sweden at the beginning of 1993. Because of technical advances, there are now alternative ways of delivering messages. In the banking sector, the economic and political integration of Europe has made the national regulation of the banking system increasingly irrelevant.

One example of a private sector regulation that directly impacts competitive conditions is the Swedish banks' ban on transferring money from and to bank accounts via the postal giro system. As technical advances encourage a growing proportion of direct debiting between accounts, the postal giro system's share of the transactions market will gradually erode and the bank giro system will see a corresponding increase.

Economies of scale

A somewhat surprising finding is that there are substantial economies of scale in many service sectors. One explanation for this is that service businesses handle a large volume of information, and unit cost falls, the larger the computer system. We saw this not only in banking, postal giro services and insurance, but also in convenience goods distribution.

In the insurance business, there are other clear economies of scale: a larger customer base improves the accuracy of risk calculations. In letter distribution, the main economy of scale nowadays is in delivery of letters to households. The emergence of a competitor to Sweden Post would probably mean that an unchanged volume of mail would be distributed by a larger number of letter carriers who would follow the same routes.

Price regulation

In our analysis of the letter, distribution postal giro and convenience goods distribution sectors, we found examples of how certain services subsidise others. Small customers pay too low a price, while large customers pay too high a price compared to the actual cost of each service. One effect of these cross-subsidies is to prevent or delay changes. At Posten Brev, two forms of cross-subsidies have recently been publicised. The first is that, to some extent, the postage income on corporate mail subsidises letter deliveries in rural areas: the high postage on corporate mail makes it profitable for competitors such as City Mail to focus exclusively on this market niche. The other example is electronic mail, where Sweden Post charges full postage for delivering the letters of its competitors, even though it does not need to ship and sort such letters.

INTERNAL FACTORS INFLUENCING PRODUCTIVITY

On the basis of our studies, it is not possible to say that all highly productive companies apply a certain type of model or method. Instead, it is more correct to say that they strive for efficiency and innovation, but that this effort can be manifested in many different ways.

Interaction with the surrounding world

It is not enough for a company to be subjected to actual competition and to face new demands. If resource scarcity is to result in higher efficiency and information complexity is to generate innovation, certain internal company conditions must be fulfilled. Primarily, employees must be aware of the resource situation and of changing demands.

Banc One conducts systematic customer surveys in questionnaire and interview form to find out what its customers want in terms of business hours and time-saving systems. Its branches also organise special activities in order to meet their customers and recruit new ones.

Banc One picks up ideas for improvements and innovation by encouraging its customers to complain if they are dissatisfied. The bank also uses inspectors disguised as customers, who report on the quality of the services the bank provides. Because of its customer-orientated perspective, Banc One has found it suitable to open branches inside other businesses. It also rents out space at some branches to businesses wishing to work in a bank setting.

One difference between goods and services is that the purchasing situation is not the same. We believe that service-producing organisations spend a smaller proportion of their time selling their product. Buying merchandise requires active customer participation, whereas certain services are bought more or less automatically. An insurance policy is renewed annually and a deposit account remains open until the customer closes it. Until now, a hospital or school in Sweden has not needed to worry at all about selling, since they have enjoyed a monopoly in their geographic catchment areas.

Willingness to change

It has been said that productivity is no mystery. In many respects, it is a question of mentality. The hard thing is to persuade employees to apply norms and methods that are well known. It therefore came as no surprise when we discovered that the best companies devote a great deal of care to personnel matters, or human resources management.

One of the most important lessons for Swedish organisations to learn from their foreign counterparts is how to formulate goals for individuals which correspond to collective or corporate goals as we saw in the Woolworths distribution chain. Another lesson is to use frequent feedback to control the service activities. The Henry Ford Health System receives its monthly financial reports within 24 hours, while it takes a couple of weeks for a Swedish hospital to obtain such material.

From Banc One we learned that managers with decentralised profit responsibility are monitored via business ratios for profitability. The salaries of these managers are related to a system of rewards which is entirely controlled by the business ratios and profitability in the individual units. In comparison with the average American bank, the profitability goals are high, which in itself can act as a strong incentive. Personnel at the various offices are evaluated by checking that different operations are carried out in the prescribed manner and salaries for non-managerial personnel categories are set locally by the office manager. This system of rewards differs from the traditional piece-work model of the manufacturing industry, where piece-work is a measure of performance and forms the basis of wages, while the salaries of the managers are based on subjective evaluations made by executives or board members.

At Banc One we also find that employees evaluate each other: via the 'WITTY-system' employees receive acknowledgement when they have done something out of the ordinary for a customer or colleague. The system creates a positive atmosphere among employees and also provides the recipient's immediate boss with another factor for use in his personnel evaluation.

The studies of Posten Brev and PTT show that it is hard to use piecework as a measure of productivity, since production volumes vary. The study of medical care also shows that reward systems related to time off are more likely to lead to reductions in productivity rather than improvements. In the American system, economic incentives are also used to improve the productivity of doctors. In Sweden, however, we use time in lieu, which inhibits productivity, at least according to comparisons with the time worked by doctors in different countries.

According to our model, employees must be motivated to strive for cost efficiency and optimum motivation is created through a well balanced mix of economic rewards, bureaucratic rules and team spirit. We found bonus systems in all sectors except in schools: in Banc One this is particularly pronounced, and both financial and non-financial rewards exist; the Crocker school, on the other hand, tried to attract teachers by offering them opportunities for further education; several successful companies were noticeable because they offered higher wages than their competitors. Individual employees are strongly affected by the fact that they are evaluated, which provides feedback and affects performance. This is clear in examples from the Postgiro. The feeling of belonging to a good or winning team also seems to have great significance for motivation. The employees of Woolworths are proud to belong to 'The fresh food people' and Hemköp employees in Mora, Sweden, have similar feelings about their company.

Rewards and motivation

One way of encouraging employees to change and become more efficient is by offering some form of performance-related pay. Especially in the best companies in countries other than Sweden, the compensation system is an important element of efforts to achieve higher productivity. Wages and salaries at these companies are based on performance to a greater extent than is true in Swedish companies.

For example, we learnt from Woolworths and Hemköp that managers with decentralised profit centre responsibility are monitored in terms of whether they achieve certain profitability ratios. Branch employees of Banc One are evaluated in terms of whether processes are being implemented in the prescribed way.

Competence

A number of studies have confirmed the existence of learning curves or unit cost declines that accompany larger production volume in a company. One explanation for this is that machines are fine-tuned and problems are corrected promptly. Another reason is that employees learn to use equipment better, resulting in fewer interruptions.

Unit prices fall at different rates in different sectors and there is a considerable difference between public and private services. For example, the cost of producing a certain type of insurance policy falls gradually as the company becomes more knowledgeable about a certain customer segment. In the same way, teachers become more expert at planning lessons. The difference is that the unit cost which the local council pays per student does not fall. In fact the reverse is true: it increases, since teachers' salaries are based on their experience. This is an example of how external factors, such as legislation, rules or lack of competition, can prevent the reduction of unit costs.

One way to discuss the matter of competence development in a service company is to use a soccer team as the basis for analysis. You can either invest large sums of money in buying good players from other teams or you can run an 'in-team' training centre in order to foster a good team in the long term. In the world of soccer it has turned out that a combination of both strategies is necessary. Successful service companies put a great deal of energy into developing personnel in competence-intensive areas, but also recruit professionals from rival companies in order to succeed more rapidly. Both Trygg-Hansa and Home invest a lot in training. Home follows up the development of its personnel very meticulously and recruits employees from rivals. The following statement from the very powerful CEO of Home demonstrates this strategy:

> The best companies in the 1990s will be those that have the best people, the best trained, best paid, most highly motivated people. Not only in New York but across the country in all field offices. People with knowledge, skill and authority to make decisions. There's no secret to having superior people. You hire the brighter people, you pay them more than your competitors, you train them in a technical way on a continuing basis, you bonus them if they beat specific business objectives, you truly reward those that make money for you and you dismiss those that can't or won't perform at a superior level. An organisation cannot rise above the level of its people.

The development of competence can be utilised both in order to enhance the knowledge of the employees and also to create motivation. This is demonstrated in two of the four successful schools in the study. The teachers at the Bräcke school are encouraged to acquire knowledge outside their own field, which has resulted in a more flexible organisation where teachers can support or replace each other if the need arises. Moreover, absenteeism due to illness has fallen dramatically and the need for supply teachers has been eliminated. 'The best school in the USA', Crocker Middle School, also uses further training for its teachers as an instrument to empower people.

Work which demands competence is a competitive tool which many successful companies use consciously parallel to and often in preference to salary incentives in order to attract the most competent personnel. The Henry Ford Hospital attracts specialists by offering the latest equipment and also the opportunity to earn money from private practice parallel to the job at the hospital.

One consistent difference between the best manufacturing companies and the best service-producing organisations is that their organisational pyramids have different shapes. Manufacturing companies have an executive management at the top, and then one or two levels of highly qualified managers and engineers. These are relatively numerous compared to the number of operators, who are the largest single employee category. At the bottom of the hierarchy is a fairly small number of workers with simple assignments. By contrast service organisations are more reminiscent of a typical pyramid with a very broad base.

Internal labour market

Individuals often show a natural resistance to change. The best companies have managed in various ways to make change seem less dramatic by carrying out small, frequent adjustments in the organisation and by maintaining a flexible internal labour market.

Job satisfaction is the result of concurrence between the goals of the individual and the company. There is no question that employees of the best companies feel proud of their companies. One interesting question is how the best companies have managed to create such a strong sense of community within their organisation. One answer is that success itself is an important component. It is more stimulating to work at a successful company than at a company with problems.

Organisational structure

Organising a company on a functional basis has the advantage of enabling it to achieve economies of specialisation. It also provides a clear division of labour. The disadvantage is that, especially in large corporations, such a structure easily becomes bureaucratic and slow-moving. In recent decades, the need to adapt products to customers' wishes has become more important. New manufacturing technology also makes it possible to widen the product range without affecting the cost of manufacturing. Adaptation to customers' wishes and flexible production presuppose the ability to make decisions quickly and across functional or departmental boundaries.

One disadvantage or risk in eliminating functional specialisation is that decisions may be of poorer quality and the work may not be performed as well. Another way of reducing the disadvantages of a functional organisation is to reduce the number of hierarchical levels. A number of the companies in our case studies used this method to speed up the decision-making process and move decisions closer to the operative level.

Technology

Many previous studies have shown that economies of scale and the economies that result from a large accumulated manufacturing volume are a major component of cost-effectiveness. This was also evident from our research.

One reason why the best companies operate in favourable segments of their industries is that they have invested in maintaining a technological lead. We found that Woolworths has a lead when it comes to using the latest information technology. One explanation for this may be that it is easier for an economically integrated chain to introduce technology than a chain of 2,000 independent merchants.

Top executives

The single factor that appears to be the most important in all the industries we have studied is undoubtedly the presence of dedicated, highly competent executives. What we found in our studies is that many service-producing organisations often work in a regulated environment with fairly weak or non-existent competitive pressures. In addition, the results of their operations are hard to quantify and fulfilment of goals is difficult to achieve. They consequently lacked the external pressure for change that is needed to stimulate employees to be efficient and provide incentives for them to learn to be more innovative. What we discovered is that in such organisations, good leaders were capable of replacing these vague external pressures for change with their own operational visions and goals. We found a clear example of this in the schools we studied, where the principals laid out a strategy and led the way through their own dedication. Their visions could be of various kinds. The most important thing seemed to be that such a vision existed.

Top executives are especially important when it comes to conveying the demands of the market to employees. The management of a company has the best overview of changing demands and the best grasp of resource scarcities. It is their responsibility to use this knowledge to formulate objectives and communicate this message to employees. In addition, through their behaviour, top executives underscore the importance of cost-consciousness. One of our consistent observations has been that the best companies, despite their high profitability, devoted a lot of effort to the search for even minor improvements.

Innovation

In principle, innovation in service organisations can occur in two ways. First, the production process is improved by new technology. In postal giro services, about half the improvement in productivity has been achieved through improved information technology. Secondly, new services can be developed. For instance, the Henry Ford Health System developed a system of day surgery at its ambulatory care centres. This new service raised productivity and was beneficial to patients, who no longer needed to be hospitalised. In the organisations we studied, innovation is not usually expressed in terms of product development but as quality improvement. More letters arrive within a specified time, the queues at bank branches become shorter etc.

One difference between service-producing companies and manufacturing firms is that it appears to be more difficult to commercialise innovation in services. This is because service producers do not obtain intellectual property rights on innovations. It is also relatively easy to imitate innovations in service industries. One example is insurance policies, which can easily be copied. The same is true of new kinds of bank accounts, since competing banks can offer their customers the same account terms. In markets with little price and product competition, such as bank deposit-taking, we found little differentiation between products from competing banks. There was therefore less reason for banks to devote a great deal of time to product development and marketing.

THE STEERING COMMITTEE'S PRACTICAL POLICY CONCLUSIONS FROM THIS STUDY

The seven service sectors represented by the companies and organisations in our study account for more than half of all employment in Sweden. Their share of the labour force in other OECD nations is similar. Obviously, then, productivity in the fields that we have studied plays a major role in the prosperity of these countries.

The purpose of our study has been to learn from good examples. Because we sought out leading companies and organisations around the world, the Swedish peer organisations that we compare them with may easily appear in a more negative light. Although not all of these Swedish companies and organisations can fully match the accomplishments of their foreign counterparts, we would describe them as highly capable considering their prerequisites. Some are close to the top international ranks or are moving towards this level.

Three overall findings from the case studies

- Competition is modest in some service sectors and non-existent in others. Disparities in the competitive pressures on different companies is one important reason why a service-producing organisation in one country may show higher productivity than in another.
- Services are often designed to conform with administrative or political rules, and the quality of these rule systems is another important factor behind the differences in productivity exhibited by the organisations we studied in various countries.
- There are major disparities in the costs and productivity of organisations producing the same service in different countries. For example, distribution of convenience goods is more than twice as expensive in one leading Swedish retail chain as in the best such chain in Australia. Cost per employee in the letter delivery unit of Sweden Post is 60 per cent higher than at its Dutch counterpart, PTT Post.[1]

Three overall recommendations

- Because we found that productivity in service production is so strongly dependent on positive external pressure for change, we would especially like to emphasise that the factors that need to be improved in Sweden are greater competitive pressure and the resulting increase in customer influ-

[1] These differences were measured before the exchange rate of the Swedish krona fell late in 1992.

ence. This can be achieved by means of sensible deregulation and more international competition.

- One important prerequisite if companies and organisations are to improve their own productivity is that they should measure and monitor their operations more thoroughly. Only then can they see what improvements they can make in order to generate greater value-added for their customers. Service organisations must also gather ideas for improvements by studying how other companies and organisations perform various tasks. Differences in productivity should not be explained away, but should instead be used as an incentive for improvement in their own operations.

- As greater deregulation encourages heavier international trade in services, differences between countries in terms of productivity and costs will generate pressures for change, which may lead to a major structural transformation in Sweden. We recommend that politicians, employer and employee organisations and the managers of service-producing organisations try to foresee how Sweden can best adapt to a situation of greater international trade in services and of international mobility among those who work in service professions.

Goods and services – different but often sold together

Goods and services are different in nature but are often sold together. It has become less and less relevant to draw distinctions between companies or organisations by labelling them as producers of either goods or services. Usually there is a combination of both. The physical production of goods occurs largely within the framework of scientific and technical laws, while services must be studied in a social context. In principle, the technical conditions governing the design of goods are the same for all manufacturers in the world. The products of manufacturing companies are ordinarily designed and defined according to a number of rather measurable dimensions and customers can generally choose among goods that can be inspected in advance. For example, a potential car buyer can read magazines that present automotive test results specifying the engine characteristics, acceleration and fuel consumption of each model, and sometimes their intangible qualities and resale value as well. Customers can often decide whether a price quotation is reasonable by comparing it with what competing companies are offering.

The design of service production in a given country is highly dependent on its social and political framework, which in turn is shaped very much by local customs. In their eagerness to ensure high quality, government agencies and politicians are inclined to intervene in the details of service production. One example comes from Sweden where, for many years, official food regulations prevented the restructuring of the convenience goods retailing system by prescribing that milk, meat and other groceries should be sold in separate premises. However, tradition and a wide variety of local prejudices also influence how services are produced.

Many services are 'designed' by politicians

Because services are performed in accordance with human rules rather than laws of nature, the availability of resources in service production can be expected to vary greatly from one country to another, since different political and institutional systems prescribe that a given service should be produced in different ways. In our case studies, we have seen numerous examples of how rule systems can lead to much higher costs for a given service in one country than in another, without any apparent significant differences in quality. Commercial insurance and medical care are thus far more expensive in the US than in Sweden, which offers more or less the same level of services. The American school that we studied, on the other hand, is an example of a service operation that has managed to achieve high quality at lower cost than a good Swedish school. As mentioned above, the Australian convenience goods retailing system has a lower cost level than its Swedish equivalent and also gives consumers rather high product quality in many cases.

International trade in services paves the way for economies of scale

Another conclusion is that the more we eliminate the differences between the legal and institutional systems regulating the shape of services in various countries, the better the prerequisites for efficient service production will be. Creating similar rules in many countries will open the way to greater international competition and will enable companies to take greater advantage of the economies of scale found in many service sectors. Politicians must realise that in much service production, the ground rules they formulate are what will determine the chances of improving productivity and will thus be beneficial to their national economy. When Sweden negotiates the terms of its harmonisation with the European Community, one goal is that countries with complex detailed regulation in their service sectors should emulate countries whose regulations are based on broad overall principles, not vice versa.

Productivity and public services

Productivity issues are especially complicated in the production of public services. In Sweden and many other countries, medical care, schools and postal services are examples of operations not directly controlled by the customers who pay the cost of the service. Instead, representatives of the 'public interest' make the decisions about there operations and establish their budget framework. Such a structure is necessary because these services are publicly financed or because customers are at a disadvantage in terms of their access to information.

We have found examples which demonstrate that over time, organisations increasingly adapt to the rules of these public sector representatives rather than to the needs and preferences of customers. The result may be sharp cost increases and burgeoning bureaucracies. One example can be taken from the school sector: When Swedish schools submit their budget requests, it has been easier for them to obtain resources for programmes aimed at pupils with special problems than for pedagogical development targeted to normal pupils. As a result, schools have been granted resources (for example in the form of immigrant native language teachers, therapists and special technical aids) not directly related to achieving their main teaching goals. Furthermore, it may be in the financial interest of the school to classify pupils as 'deviant', which naturally conflicts with their goal of turning young people into fully independent law-abiding citizens.

Customer influence and public services

One way of combating the lack of customer influence in public sector services has been to introduce various kinds of quality assurance systems. However, these programmes often tend to increase bureaucracy, reduce efficiency and thereby lower the quality of the service even more. In our opinion, the solution is instead to increase the ties between the customer and the service provider. The 'civil servant' that a customer deals with must be responsible to them for the delivery of complete and adequate service, whether that civil servant is a postman or a doctor. Like modern manufacturing companies, service-producing organisations must operate on the assumption that they work for their customers. For example, the task of the people above the postal workers in the organisational pyramid is to provide the services that postal workers need so they can genuinely fulfil their obligations to customers. This concept requires the establishment of simple systems that enable customers to articulate their needs. For example, one of the Swedish schools we studied had introduced an interesting procedure to ensure that the complaints of parents or pupils would receive rapid and serious examination. We also found examples of this philosophy in the retailing companies we studied.

Service companies are becoming smaller and more decentralised

In recent decades, the structure of service-producing organisations has evolved along approximately the same lines as that of manufacturing. Employees have become functionally specialised in order that their organisation could achieve economies of scale. Growing organisations have then required bigger and bigger bureaucracies to co-ordinate and manage their functional parts. Today manufacturing industry is changing, and we believe that service-producing organisations will follow suit. By delegating more responsibility for customer relations and giving greater authority over deployment of organisational resources to service producers who are close to the customers, administrative costs can be cut.

The tendency towards greater decentralisation and customer-orientation that we have seen in service-producing organisations is occurring a number of years after the corresponding change in manufacturing industry. In both cases, one factor behind the change is the development of new production technology: in service sectors, advances in information technology have made it possible to delegate decision-making in a way that was not previously possible. Another factor behind the increase in customer orientation is that the people who buy services demand or expect this change.

Productivity-raising measures in public service production

But how can we prevent customer demand for publicly financed services from leading to escalating standards and unreasonably high levels of service? The simplest solution, of course, is to link them up with markets, except in cases where this might lead to unacceptable consequences from a social welfare standpoint. Let the customers pay for the cost of these services, allow competition, and create better ground rules for this competition!

What can we do in sectors where it seems unreasonable to demand full payment from customers though? Schools can be regarded as one example of such a service sector. A number of mechanisms can be employed to a greater extent than previously:

- The right to market entry and competition. It should be possible to establish competing operations that can offer services to customers on the same basis as existing ones.

- The government grant system should be simple and should be designed in a way that provides incentives for cost-effectiveness and development of services that are better suited to the needs of customers. Paying a district health care centre a small capitation fee for each patient who registers there is one possible idea.
- Equal treatment of all individuals must be a strongly prevailing norm: everyone should have equal access to a given service regardless of financial and social position. Legislation may be required to establish this norm. To ensure that enforcement will not be too costly, norms must also assume a moral dimension, causing those who violate them genuinely to understand that such behaviour is not acceptable. Therefore we foresee a shift from detailed regulation by political bodies to more comprehensive public enforcement based on clear normative values.
- The development of mechanisms for influence (voice). Customers must become genuinely involved and active, as in Denmark's local school boards. Service-producing organisations must also become sensitive to the views of customers. If a customer receives bad service from a teacher or postman, steps must be taken to resolve this.
- Managers must be given greater latitude to take action, and their career success should depend on whether they deliver a good service. By all appearances, the outstanding schools that we studied owe their high status to their principals. Operative line managers in public sector operations must therefore have greater authority and should be rewarded more for the quality of the services that their organisation performs. How to apportion cutbacks in government grants to the school system must be determined by the administration of each school.

Major streamlining foreseen in service-producing organisations

Service-producing operations in most industrialised countries face a period of major streamlining that will result in the disappearance of many jobs in existing companies and organisations. Our case studies have shown that sharply improved cost-effectiveness can be achieved not only by means of increased – or rather, more efficient – use of information technology, but also by simplifying routines and processes. In some of the companies and organisations we studied, we noted that current and planned streamlining programmes will lead to very sharp cutbacks in the number of jobs. One example is the shift from traditional letter delivery to pre-sorted mail and electronic mail, which means that the need for mail-sorters will decline dramatically.

Waves of efficiency measures have previously swept over manufacturing sectors, but in many cases industry has been able to limit the number of lay-offs by producing more goods and by increasing sales in export markets. Service operations, which are more locally rooted, do not have the same potential for volume expansion. Despite the macroeconomic costs that the restructuring of service operations will bring about, we would advise against political regulation aimed at protecting them from this transformation. It is a sensible policy to make the transformation as smooth as possible by improving the conditions for establishing new service production.

The Swedish service sector is good, but very expensive

The one finding that caused us the greatest concern from our own national standpoint was that cost levels are generally so high in Swedish service production. Labour costs are high because Sweden's public sector – which is larger than in other countries – is financed to a great extent by income tax. Another explanation is that as a consequence of incomes policy, labour costs in the service sector are at approximately the same level as labour costs in highly productive export companies. In 1990, the pay level in Swedish retailing stood at 85 per cent of average pay in manufacturing. In the United States, on the other hand, wages and salaries in retailing are only 51 per cent of those in manufacturing. The question we must ask in Sweden is whether these differences in relative pay are due to higher skills and thus higher productivity in Swedish service-producing organisations than in other countries.

Preparing for stiffer international competition

The cost level in Swedish service production can remain higher than in other countries as long as it is not subjected to international competition. However, the 18-nation European Economic Area (EEA) treaty that will soon go into effect will lead to sharply escalating competition and GATT agreement in the services field area will further increase competitive pressures. Are Swedish service operations prepared for this? It is doubtful they are. We therefore consider it a matter of urgency that the Swedish government, in consultation with the employer and employee organisations, draws up a scenario of what might happen and discuss whether cost levels in the service sector can be lowered or productivity raised, and if so, how this can be accomplished. Otherwise there will be massive lay-offs and shutdowns in Swedish service production.

APPENDIX 1

Method and Model

INTRODUCTION

Productivity is an expression of how efficiently resources are being managed. In this study the productivity concept is defined as the ratio of the value of a given output to a corresponding input.[1] The values of outputs and inputs are thus a function of quantities and prices. As a result, productivity will also be determined by whether a company can improve the ratio between its quantity of output and quantity of input, as well as the ratio between the price of output and the price of input. Given this definition of productivity, it thus becomes important both to consume the least possible resources in relation to a given output and to achieve an output that is highly valued by the market.

The ratio between the quantity of outputs and inputs is often referred to as internal efficiency, while the ratio between the prices of outputs and inputs is called external efficiency. These labels are somewhat misleading, since they assume that a company cannot influence its internal efficiency by choosing cheaper input goods. We will instead use the label *cost-effectiveness* to denote the efficiency of internal resource consumption. Cost-effectiveness means the extent to which a company uses an optimal combination of resource inputs to provide a given service. An activity is cost-effective if it is not possible to supply more services of equal value, for example, by exchanging a certain sum of labour costs for the same sum of machine services and vice versa.

A company's ability to improve its output in such a way that it is assigned a higher value by the market is what we shall refer to as *innovative ability*.[2] This concept encompasses product development and product innovations, together with improvements in such fields as distribution and sales methods. Innovative ability is synonymous with a company's ability to design products and production processes that are a cut above the rest. Regardless of what labels are used, it is important to underscore once again that in this study, productivity is an expression of both effective use of resources and the capacity for innovation and self-renewal.

[1] Some authors speak instead of overall productivity, since the conventional definition of productivity refers to the ratio between the quantity of output and the quantity of input.
[2] The closely related term *differentiation* indicates that a company's product is sufficiently distinct from those of competitors that the market is willing to pay a higher price.

The purpose of this study is to learn from good examples. Can Sweden and Swedish companies learn anything from studying those companies that are considered to have the best productivity in the world? In light of the above, we felt that the study would be of greatest value if it could reveal the mechanisms that contribute to continuous (or incremental) improvement of productivity in successful companies. What is the internal and external environment of these companies like, and how have they taken advantage of their opportunities and avoided difficulties?

By external environment, we mean the forces that are common to companies in a given industry as well as institutional factors such as systems of taxation that are more or less uniform for businesses in a given country. The latter type of factors is especially interesting in a political perspective, because some of these institutional conditions can be shaped by political decisions. By internal environment we mean a company's organisational structure, its technological and human resource practices, plus its methods for communicating goals and expectations. These factors are important to executives and employees. In our judgement, both these fields are relevant to productivity. Achieving good productivity thus depends on the efforts of both governments and companies.

COST-EFFECTIVENESS

Greater cost-effectiveness means that a company manufactures and distributes a product at gradually declining cost. Such an improvement may be the result of using fewer inputs in the form of materials, labour or energy. Ordinarily, this is achieved when a company gradually learns to use more efficient manufacturing methods and an improved organisational structure. Increased production volume also ordinarily enables a company to lower unit costs by increasing the capacity utilisation of existing machinery or by obtaining larger, more efficient machines. By increasing the volume of operations, it is also possible to improve the ratio between performance and price of input goods. The explanation may be that a large-scale purchaser can gain a stronger position in price negotiations or more easily influence their suppliers' product development work.

Cost-effectiveness in service operations is achieved if a company uses the optimal combination of resources to supply a given service. In some cases, the problem of identifying cost-effectiveness is relatively simple. For example, this applies to such simple administrative procedures as invoicing and salary disbursement. Services provided by manual and more automated systems, respectively, are not so different. In other cases there is a great difference between production using manual or more automated systems. Examples are personal visits as part of municipal home-help services for the elderly, compared with telephone contacts with the elderly. Another example is a cash dispenser at a bank, which replaces a teller. The cash dispenser does not perform *exactly* the same service as the teller did. It is therefore not possible to determine cost-effectiveness *exactly* by studying the marginal production of a bank teller and a cash dispenser, respectively.

The above statements regarding productivity in service operations are based on service-producing companies in a competitive market. About half of all service operations in Sweden occur under public sector auspices, which means that these services are provided free or at regulated prices.

Granqvist (1990) has critically examined various available studies of productivity and efficiency in medical care. He discusses, for example, the difficulty of making objective statements about the efficiency of medical care, i.e. whether the medical care system is providing the right services. Unlike goods production, a medical clinic can produce different kinds of services by using its employees and equipment. For example, an orthopaedic clinic can treat athletic injuries *or* perform hip replacement surgery. In the absence of market pricing of these services, it is not possible to determine whether one clinic is more efficient than another in a macroeconomic sense.

Granqvist maintains that in manufacturing, it is possible to study productivity without knowing who will consume the product. By excluding all manufacturing methods that are lower in productivity, we have in no way limited the chances of distributing our goods production among consumers. We have merely chosen the manufacturing method that creates the largest pie to divide up.

In the production of medical care services, the above situation is not so self-evident. In services, production and consumption are linked. In the medical care system, determining what care a given patient should receive is an important part of the production process. Thus medical care cannot first be produced, then distributed among patients. Granqvist points out that deciding *which* patients should receive medical care is no less important than deciding whether the clinic is using the smallest possible resources for the medical care it actually provides.

Granqvist believes that the match between medical care and needs can be analysed both in static and dynamic terms. The former refers to how a given supply of services is distributed among consumers, while the dynamic analysis refers to how supply is adapted to suit consumers better. In the short term, establishing priorities between athletic injuries and hip replacement surgery is thus a difficult problem. In the long term, however, the system can be reshaped and adapted in such a way that it better matches the need for medical care.

Despite the great difficulty of matching supply and demand in this field, Granqvist does not say that the productivity of medical care cannot be analysed. He suggests two strategies. One is to study types of care in which the matching process is relatively easy. This applies to cases where a diagnosis is fairly easy to make. One such example, perhaps, is dental care. The second strategy is to study performance in subsectors where the matching aspect can be left entirely out of account, for example the 'hotel' function in institutional care.

INNOVATION

Like greater cost-effectiveness, innovation leads to better resource utilisation, but by producing something to which the market assigns a higher value. Innovation is often associated with new products or processes. If it results in a product with new or improved qualities, the price can be set higher than otherwise. Innovation in the form of product development does not necessarily lead to higher prices, for example if competitors carry out equivalent improvements at the same time. If the price cannot be raised in such cases, innovation has not boosted productivity. On the other hand, if the company had *not* innovated, perhaps it would have had to lower the price of its product.

Innovations that improve a product are considered more beneficial to a company's competitiveness than price reductions[3] This is because being first with a product enhancement may help to strengthen a company's brand name or reputation. The company may thus benefit from its innovation even after competitors have made equivalent improvements. Cost-cutting measures may also be easier for competitors to imitate, and unlike product improvement the advantage also ceases when competitors have reached the same level. One important exception, however, may be far-reaching innovations in manufacturing technologies, which may prove very difficult to imitate and may thus give a company long-term competitive advantages.

Innovation occurs in service production if the organisation can adapt its services so that they better address the needs of customers. Certain qualities can be measured in terms of improved 'performance' while others are difficult to measure. As in the case of improved goods, improved services can be assigned a value under certain conditions by studying how much the market is willing to pay.

[3] Porter (1990), p. 581f.

CONTINUOUS IMPROVEMENT AND ONE-TIME PRODUCTIVITY ENHANCEMENT

A productivity-raising measure normally has no permanent value. Some measures, such as obtaining new machinery, may be followed by additional improvements and effects based on learning, thus enhancing the initial gain in productivity. Other measures lose their value with time because of changing circumstances. A functioning market is a mechanism that selects the best solutions and assigns them higher value. The other side of this coin is that established positions are constantly being questioned and challenged by:

- new demands and market prices;
- changes in the performance of competitors;
- new technology and new institutional conditions.

Such changes in prerequisites lead to a continuous reassessment of productivity. The interesting question in our study is therefore how a company adapts or renews itself in such a way as to increase the value of the above-mentioned ratio. An understanding of how companies achieve change is consequently the key to understanding why some companies can remain highly productive over a long period.

MEASURING PRODUCTIVITY IN SERVICE OPERATIONS

It is difficult to define productivity in practical operations. The question, then, is how to measure productivity. We will not become deeply involved in this issue, because our purpose is not to rank the organisations under study in terms of productivity. We are primarily interested in studying what factors lead to high productivity. For two reasons, however, we cannot disregard the measurement issue. First, we must carry out measurements in order to ascertain that the organisations we are studying actually have high productivity. Second, we assume that a company's ability to measure productivity is one important reason why it manages to achieve high productivity.

What makes it hard to measure productivity in services is that the quality of output is open to question.[4] The solution to this problem varies, depending on whether the services are being produced in a competitive market or not. The problem is smaller in cases where services are being sold in a competitive market. This is because the sales figure can then be used as an indicator of the value of production. In the case of public services that are

---

[4] For a discussion of this, see for example Mellander-Ysander (1990), Berg (1989), Edvardsson-Thomasson (1991).

provided free or at regulated prices, productivity must be analysed by using some form of indirect estimate.[5]

In markets with smoothly functioning competition, the profitability or value-added of service operations is likely to be closely correlated with the relative efficiency of companies at a given point in time. However, we cannot expect the trend of productivity over time to have any correlation with the trend of profitability. If the trend of productivity in a given industry is uniform for all companies, competition will prevent a general increase in profitability. We can thus only expect a difference in profitability to indicate relative differences in the efficiency of companies in a given industry at a given time, not changes in productivity over time. But if competition functions smoothly in a market where production is difficult to measure, perhaps we can abstain from measuring productivity.

As for measuring productivity in services where there is no functioning competition, we can use various yardsticks depending on whether quantity or quality is measurable. In the simplest case, quality is homogeneous and quantity can be measured, as in the letter delivery operations of Sweden Post. In such cases we can measure productivity by comparing volumes.

When we cannot separate quality and quantity, for instance if the products are unique, the measuring problems are 'almost insurmountable'.[6] One example is research and development operations. In such cases we must rely on some kind of indirect yardsticks, for example follow-up evaluations (peer reviews) used in assessing university departments. Such evaluations are performed by outside experts who are well-acquainted with the activities to be examined. In other cases, there may even be differences of opinion on what constitutes good quality. This may be true of assessments of day-care centres, in which case the problem of measuring productivity is even greater.

Hjalmarsson (1991) states that if production in one country assumes the form of a monopoly, it may be valuable to make international comparisons at company level. He also points out that it is often more difficult to measure the costs of various services than to measure the volume of services. Especially in the public sector, it is difficult to pin down the costs of a particular service, for example a university course.

MODEL

The purpose of our study is to learn from good examples. We do this by studying the external and internal prerequisites of these companies and organisations and what methods they have used. On the other hand, we will not evaluate or rank them on the basis of actual results achieved, since this is

---

[5] Granqvist (1990) discuss this problem in measuring the productivity of medical care.
[6] Hjalmarsson, 1992/1, in 'Expertrapport nr 1 till Produktivitetsdelegationen', Stockholm 1991.

Appendix 1 267

Industry characteristics and domestic market conditions
- Barriers to market entry
- Competition
- Customers
- Substitutes
- Suppliers
- Strategic groups in the same industry
- Production factors in the home country
- Institutions

Organisational factors
- Institutions
- Technology
- Organisational model
- Owners

CONTINUOUS IMPROVEMENT OF PRODUCTIVITY

Cost-effectiveness

Productivity
- Actual results
- Productivity management

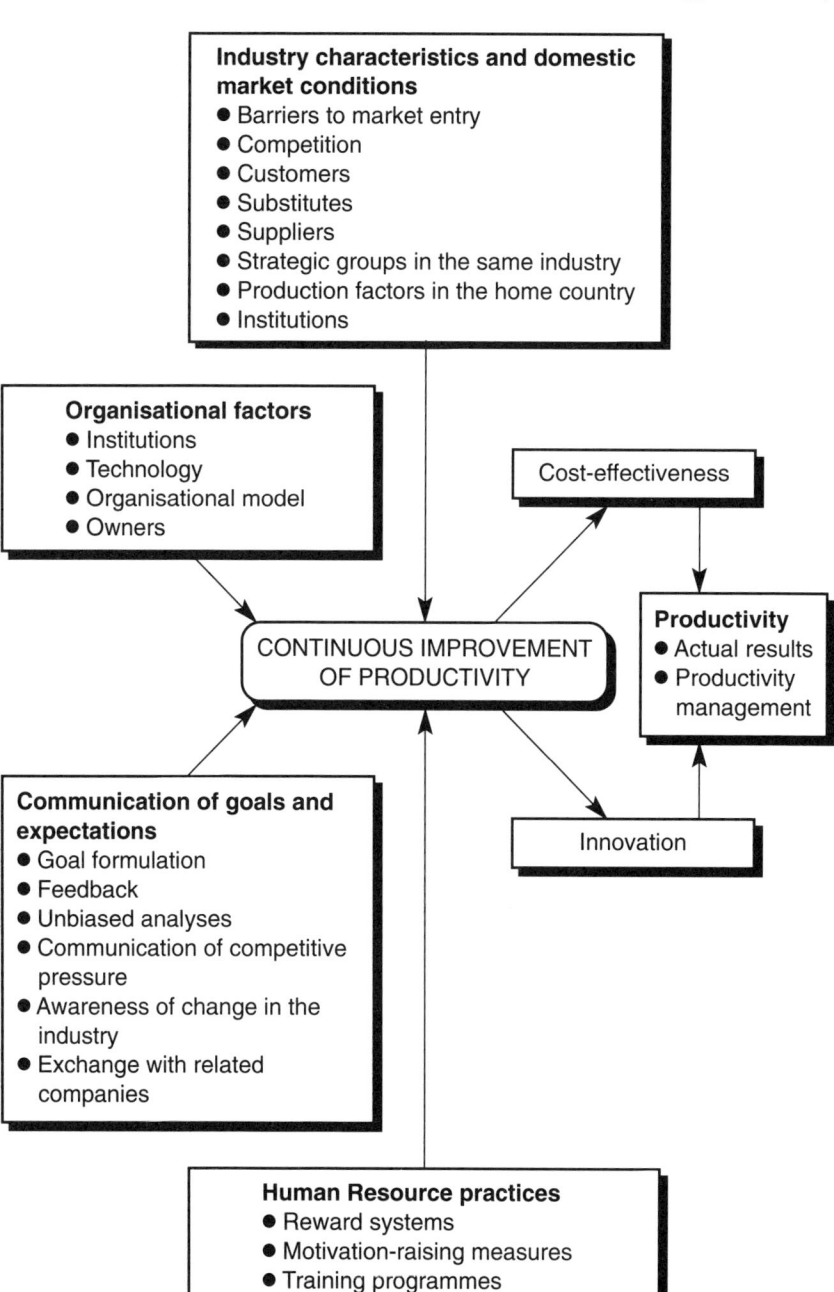

Innovation

Communication of goals and expectations
- Goal formulation
- Feedback
- Unbiased analyses
- Communication of competitive pressure
- Awareness of change in the industry
- Exchange with related companies

Human Resource practices
- Reward systems
- Motivation-raising measures
- Training programmes

Figure 1 The path to productivity

268 Achieving Service Productivity

a treacherous task. In Figure 1 the process by which a company achieves cost-effectiveness is called *continuous improvement*. A company achieves this if its employees strive for cost-effectiveness and at the same time learn or are trained to be capable of innovating products and processes.

The study assumes that continuous improvement of a company's productivity is dependent on both external and internal factors. It thus has both a macro- and microeconomic perspective. The former includes *external factors*. We begin by studying factors more or less specific to companies in a given sector or a particular product area. The macroeconomic perspective also includes factors at the national level that may explain or influence a given company's opportunities and incentives to improve its productivity. The case studies then adopt a microeconomic perspective to explore three categories of *internal factors* that influence productivity: first, a company's organisational structure and technology; second, internal communication of goals and expectations; and third, development and *management of human resources*. These factors are presented in Figure 1 and are described briefly in the following paragraphs. In addition to the questionnaire, our researchers also used an interview guide containing comments and instructions on the various questions.

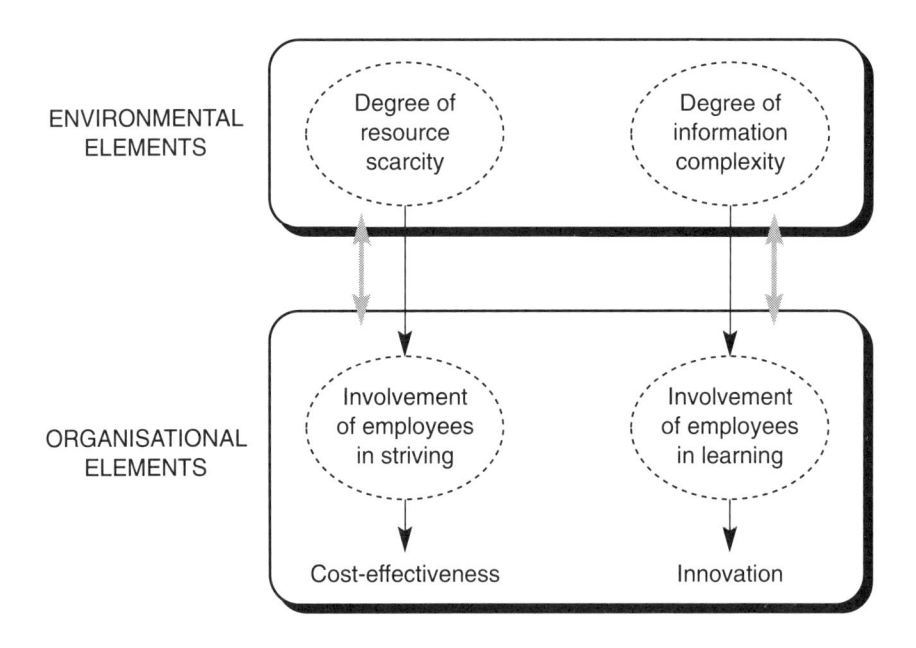

Figure 2 Main correlations in the model

Productivity is studied in a long-term perspective. It encompasses both cost-effectiveness and the ability to improve current operations efficiently and to develop new services. In order for the employees of a service company to be cost-effective, they must be *motivated*. In order for them to contribute improvements, they must be *professionally competent*.

According to our model, high productivity in a company presupposes external pressure for change. This, in turn, is created by two circumstances: the degree of resource scarcity and the changeability of the company's surroundings. Resource scarcity is an incentive for the company to operate efficiently, while the changeability of its environment helps create pressure for a company to adapt and renew its operations.

If pressure for change is to result in higher productivity, via employee motivation and competence, certain internal mechanisms in the company must also function. These are its organisational structure and technology, human resource management and communication of goals and expectations.

The explanatory factors in this study are taken from the theory of industrial organisation (in the case of external factors) and organisational theory (in the case of internal factors). The theory of industrial organisation and organisational theory are not ordinarily associated with analyses of productivity. But in their book *Renewing American Industry*, Lawrence and Dyer made an attempt to formulate a bridge between these two theories by using the concepts of *resource scarcity* and *information complexity*.[7]

Resource scarcity and efficiency

A company's resource situation influences its efforts to achieve cost-effectiveness. *Resource scarcity* is an expression of a company's difficulty in ensuring sufficient resources for its survival. The most important factors here are customer demand for the company's products and the behaviour of competitors in obtaining the same resources. Other factors include government actions and the state of markets for input goods, and the credit and labour markets. A company can influence its own resource situation by means of the quality and cost of its products. If its resources are not scarce or are not perceived as scarce, a company has no especially strong incentives to improve efficiency. If, on the other hand, its supply of resources is scarce, the company must allocate internal resources to coordinate and streamline its operations and thereby safeguard its continued existence. If the resource situation becomes too scarce, the company may find itself in a situation where it can no longer allocate enough internal resources to improve its efficiency. The conclusion of this description of the correlation between resource scarcity and efficiency is that efficiency is highest somewhere between extremely high and extremely low levels of resource scarcity. [8]

[7] Lawrence, P.R. and Dyer, D., *Renewing American Industry*, The Free Press, Macmillan, New York, 1983.
[8] As Lawrence and Dyer point out, this kind of 'inverted U-shaped' correlation is problematical, because it is hard to specify how it could be measured and tested.

Information complexity and innovation

The *information complexity* of a company's external environment influences its need to adapt and also to pre-empt expected changes. Information complexity can be calculated on the basis of variables in the company's immediate surroundings, including the wishes of customers, the actions of competitors, technological developments in its field and changed rules. Among the surrounding conditions which may indicate a slow pace of change in an industry are monopolies, single technologies and only one type of customer.

The relationship between information complexity and innovation may also be assumed to form an inverted U. Low information complexity with few changes requires little innovation in companies. For example, if competitors do not launch new products and technology in the industry does not develop, a company has no reason to devote itself to product development. On the other hand, if changes are very large and occur over a long period, it is hard for a company to build up the professional competence which is a prerequisite for innovation. For example, if the government changes its energy policy from one year to the next, the result may be that process industries abstain from investments in new plants with long depreciation periods. Excessive information complexity can therefore have a detrimental effect on the chances of innovation. The best conditions for innovation are therefore somewhere between the extremes of complete stability and turbulence.

External factors

Industry and domestic market conditions

By using the theory of industrial organisation, it is possible to analyse both the resource situation and information complexity of an industry. Our selection of explanatory factors is largely based on Michael Porter's books *Competitive Strategy and Competitive Advantage of Nations*. The first of these books deals with the interplay of factors at the industry level and a company's competitive advantage. The second book includes a model of factors in the domestic markets of companies that influence the competitiveness of various industries. Our study examines to what extent the groups of factors presented below contribute to resource scarcity or to information complexity in the companies and organisations under study. The information complexity of an industry such as truck manufacturing affects all manufacturers in a fairly similar fashion. On the other hand, the resource situation may vary substantially from one company to another in the same industry. This is because the resource situation is influenced to a greater extent than information complexity by a company's own actions.

As Lawrence and Dyer point out, companies will try to improve their resource situation and reduce information complexity by dominating their environment. In other words, they will try to create a monopoly position by such means as product development, vertical integration and alliances. But at the same time, forces around the company help create greater insecurity and make this company less dominant. These forces include new competitors, technologies and input goods. The interesting question then becomes: in the long term, can a company remain in the comfortable middle zone in terms of having a resource situation and information complexity that promote efficiency and innovation?

Our study looks at the role of differences in conditions from one country to another. Do the best companies enjoy especially favourable conditions in their domestic markets, compared with companies in other countries? Of special interest in this context are institutional conditions that prevent or possibly promote adaptation and innovation. Some institutional conditions are easily influenced and can be changed through political decisions, while others, that have their roots in culture, religion and tradition, change only over a very long period.

After having studied conditions at the industry and domestic market level, we switch to a microeconomic perspective and study three kinds of factors inside companies that we assume will influence their incentives and ability to continuously improve their productivity. Connections exist between the external and the internal factors in the model. The internal factors, such as the design of reward systems and the type of organisational model, should be tailored to the external factors that determine a company's resource situation and the information complexity around the company. Because we assume that the prerequisites for continuous improvement of productivity are best in a middle position in terms of resource scarcity and information complexity respectively, it follows that we expect highly productive companies and organisations to display internal prerequisites that match this middle position.

Internal factors

Organisational structure, institutional conditions and technology

One way of characterising a company's organisational model is by looking at whether it emphasises *integration* or *differentiation*. Integration gives top priority to coordination and stability, while differentiation means that specialisation and decentralisation are considered the most important. The choice of organisational model depends on both the resource situation and the information complexity surrounding the company. A rapid pace of change combined with a fairly good resource situation – as found in industries characterised by fast-growing demand – requires an informal, flat, decentralised organisation. Such a differentiated organisation may have good innovative ability. The disadvantage is that it may be less efficient. A more static environment that requires higher standards of efficiency, such as a mature engineering company, might be better served by an integrated organisation based on rules and strong leadership. Because we assume that the most productive companies occupy a middle position in terms of their information complexity and resource scarcity, it follows that these companies should have an organisational model that is neither purely integrated nor purely differentiated, but has elements of both.

Under the heading of institutions, we raise questions concerning labour union activity, workplace norms, attitudes toward work and its social role. These conditions conceivably influence a company's ability to achieve high productivity in two ways. First, the desire for efficiency may spring from such feelings as duty and dedication. If these norms are absent, the result is naturally the opposite. Second, institutional conditions may influence the chances of making changes. Strong norms and organisations ordinarily act as obstacles to change, but this does not always have to be the case.

Many previous empirical studies of productivity in manufacturing companies have focused on technological factors, such as economies of scale, learning advantages, simplification of production, inventory reduction and various pay systems. During the 1980s there were numerous studies of the distinguishing features of highly productive Japanese manufacturing operations. These studies report how Japanese companies use *lean production, simultaneous* or *concurrent engineering*, management of information and components so that everything arrives just when it will be used (*just-in-time*) and other recipes for success. These studies are interesting, among other things, because they show that a number of traditional assumptions are no longer valid. Examples of the concepts now being challenged are that long production runs result in lower manufacturing costs that more than justify higher inventory costs, that high quality and fewer defects in a product can only be achieved at higher costs and that shortening product development time is more expensive and leads to poorer results.

Communication of goals and expectations

The demands of the market and changes in the environment stimulate companies to innovate and increase their cost-effectiveness. But in order for external pressure to influence a company's operations, there must be mechanisms that convey relevant external information into the company. This can be done in a number of ways. One important task of management is to communicate goals and expectations clearly and systematically to employees. There should be as little ambiguity as possible about the company's fundamental strategy, structure and working methods. Another method of disseminating an awareness of the outside world is to forge business relationships with customers and suppliers noted for superior quality and levels of technological development. In connection with innovations, it may be useful to have a network of contacts with companies in related fields. This is because there are many examples of innovations that are created by combining technologies or approaches from different places into one potent solution. We therefore expect highly productive companies to be open to seeking new customers and markets that demand high standards and provide incentives for change.

In the conclusions of his study of *Competitive Advantages of Nations*, Michael Porter wrote that once a company has achieved advantages, it can only preserve them by constantly searching for other and better ways of making things and by modifying the behaviour of the company within the framework of an overall strategy. The need for constant change conflicts with the organisational norms of most companies. Especially in successful companies, it is difficult to change strategy. Earlier behaviour becomes institutionalised in budgeting and planning processes and in the management systems that executives use. Special facilities are created. The company recruits people it believes will fit in, etc. Its strategy almost becomes a religion and it is difficult to challenge. When an organisation matures, it seems as if its need for stability increases.

Strong forces are required to counteract such rigidities. These forces rarely come from inside the organisation. Companies rarely change voluntarily. Instead, outside threats force the pace of change. A company must subject itself to outside pressures and stimuli that motivate and govern activities. The difficulty of creating change from within is one explanation for the fact that outsiders are often the ones who bring innovations.

Human resource management

The personnel of a company or organisation is generally regard as its central productive resource. One prerequisite for continuous improvement in productivity is that employees are motivated to strive for greater efficiency and have sufficient skills to renew their company's operations. Our study deals with two main personnel issues. One concerns human resource management mechanisms such as reward systems and other incentives. The other is how companies continuously enhance the professional competence of their employees by means of advanced training and other programmes.

Reward systems are generally assumed to be able to influence the desire of employees to achieve efficiency. A company's reward system includes, first of all, its salaries, wages and other direct compensation for work performed. We examine the type of pay system that is used, for example the existence of bonuses, piecework and individual salaries. What is the connection between performance and compensation? How large a percentage of pay is dependent on performance? We also look at the issue of the overall pay range in the company and in selected categories of employees. Financial rewards can be expected to have more impact on efficiency the scarcer the resource situation and the greater the information complexity around a company. The reward system also includes more indirect rewards such as promotion, travel and scholarships.

Financial rewards are harder to use in encouraging innovation activity. Here, social incentives are assumed to fill a more important function. These may range from the intrinsic status of a job at a development laboratory to the sense of community engendered by being a team member. Management plays an important part as a creator of social incentives and as a role model. Through its actions and emphasis on certain portions of operations, management defines what is important.

The professional competence of employees is important to their ability to achieve high efficiency, but especially for a company's ability to innovate. In our study, we therefore asked questions about the size of company training programmes on an annual and per-employee basis. We asked what training programmes the companies have for their newly hired employees and for employees wishing to advance in the company.

Productivity management

Although we are not primarily interested in measuring productivity in companies and organisations, we examine how they measure or estimate their own productivity. Companies can measure productivity in many different ways and with varying levels of ambition. The differences reflect variations in technology and organisational structure but also depend on what internal control mechanisms a company chooses to apply. Internal cost accounting systems rarely provide a good basis for decisions related to productivity management.

Appendix 1 275

On the other hand, data from accounting systems provide historical information on actual financial outcomes. Productivity management requires other criteria or rules of thumb that do not need to be expressed in monetary terms. We began with the hypotheses that highly productive companies and organisations have internal productivity criteria that are:

- clearly formulated;
- well understood and accepted as valid by employees;
- related to employee reward systems; and
- difficult to manipulate.

AN EARLIER STUDY OF PRODUCTIVITY MANAGEMENT IN SERVICE PRODUCTION

Measuring productivity is part of the task of guiding operations toward higher productivity. As mentioned earlier, one of our hypotheses is that successful companies and organisations are good at measuring their productivity. Voss *et al* (1990) conducted a study of nine service-producing companies and tried to see whether the successful companies used other yardsticks in productivity management than less successful companies. The study employed a 'process-based model'. It assumes that each service can be regarded as the result of one or more processes. Each process can be analysed and measured in five respects.

1. *Is the process carried out in accordance with the specification?* The first step in providing services is to design and specify the process behind the service. One way of managing operations is therefore to check whether the process has been designed in accordance with a specification and then whether this task has been carried out in the prescribed manner.
2. *Productivity.* Every process is viewed as a transformation from inputs to outputs. The important input factors are labour and the capital invested in facilities and equipment. Standard levels of labour productivity and capital productivity can be established and measured.
3. *The input of the process.* It is possible to measure the quality of the labour and the material that go into the process. For example, measurements can be made of how recruitment occurred, what training was provided to those who were hired, etc.
4. *The output of the process.* The output of the process can be specified by hard or soft variables. These can then be measured by the company or the customer (see Figure 3).

Characteristics of the service \ Measurement by means of	The company	The customer
Hard	• Number • Time required	• Ask the customer to rate the service
Soft	• Mystery shoppers	• Ask the customer to rate the service • Degree of satisfaction • Complaints

Figure 3

5. *Yardsticks from the financial reporting system.* Data from the accounting system can also be used for management. There are three kinds of yardstick:

(a) costs;

(b) profitability or margins; and

(c) prices.

Each type of yardstick can be applied to the whole company, a department of the company or a given service.

The following were among the findings of the nine case studies.

If the process is specified, then performed accordingly, no further measuring is neeeded. What characterised the best companies, and was therefore labelled *best practice*, was

- specification and measurement of the process; and
- specification and measurement of output or service level. (Especially the use of customers to measure a given output or service level.)

What characterised the worst companies (*bad practice*) was that they based their management exclusively on productivity and financial yardsticks.

The researchers also commented that companies made little use of a potentially good yardstick: measuring the customers' needs and expectations.

METHOD OF THE STUDY

The results of a case study may be difficult to interpret, since an individual piece of data does not tell us very much unless there is something to compare it with. Researchers thus ordinarily try to evaluate their findings on the basis of existing theory or by comparing them with other studies. In this study, we decided that for each company or organisation we examined, there should be a Swedish reference company in the same industry.

In selecting reference companies, we also looked for good examples. The primary purpose of the comparison between the best company and the reference company is to study differences between countries in terms of management, organisational structure, institutional prerequisites, etc., and also to see whether there is room for more than one successful solution in the same industry. It is thus not a question of comparing a good and a bad company. In some cases, our reference companies were so good that the difference in the level of continuous improvement of productivity of the more respected company and the reference company was not very large or could even be questioned.

Selection of companies and organisations

The selection of companies and organisations as topics of our study began with a compilation of possible candidates. A questionnaire asking for suggestions was sent to Swedish scientific and technological attachés worldwide as well as to the members of the Royal Swedish Academy of Engineering Sciences (IVA) in Sweden, members of IVA's Industrial Council and about 70 of IVA's foreign members. A list of nearly 100 suggested companies resulted from the questionnaire.

We gathered annual reports and articles covering a large percentage of the suggested companies and organisations. We also studied information on prizes and distinctions that had been awarded to companies in certain countries for their high quality or productivity. Using interviews and inquiries, we tried to ascertain the reputation of these companies in their industries. We asked about the path of their development during the 1980s. It was nevertheless impossible to rank the suggested companies on the basis of this information alone. Instead, we concluded that most of the suggested companies appeared sufficiently interesting to be included in the study. The question was then what selection criteria should be applied.

The final selection of companies and organisations took into account the following criteria:

- representation from sectors of interest in a Swedish economic policy perspective;
- a broad range of countries;
- to enable us to complete the study within a very tight time frame, in some cases we allowed our researchers' previous experience of various industries to determine the choice of company.

An obvious additional criterion is that companies and organisations must be interested in participating. A few of the companies that we initially contacted declined to take part. The group we finally selected must therefore not be viewed as a listed of 'the very best', but instead as a representative selection from a larger group of companies and organisations with very good earnings and very good reputations. It remains our hope that our final selections can provide answers to the question: What can we learn from leading companies and organisations?

Implementation

We conducted our case studies simultaneously, all using the same questionnaire and interview guide. We largely used the same set of questions as in our previous study.

(a) First, the researchers gathered material about the service sector and the country in question. This included articles, research studies and official statistics.

(b) Interviews were undertaken and data gathered at the companies and organisations. Interviews were conducted with top executives, department heads or the equivalent, marketing managers, personnel managers and trade union representatives. The number of interviews varied from about ten to more than forty per study.

(c) Additional written questions were sent to the companies and organisations.

(d) Reports, consisting of 100-250 pages per case study, were compiled.

(e) The reports were analysed and summaries compiled. This task was done by each respective research group. To keep the presentation from being weighted down by footnotes, only a minimum of references to sources were included in this book.

(f) The summaries were discussed with contact people at the companies and trade union representatives. It should be emphasised that these reference people are responsible neither for the facts nor the conclusions in the chapters.

Background data

There were severe time constraints on our assignment. This meant that we had to base our study of intra-company conditions on information that was mainly provided through interviews. This information was evaluated by the research associates, and where possible, information from different people was compared. The material we present is thus essentially a reflection of the companies' own perceptions of the important factors behind their improvement in productivity.

Our primary purpose has been to study the conditions that enable companies and organisations to improve their productivity. We wanted to identify both internal and external factors. It is, of course, always possible to object that we could never know for sure which factors were important, since we could not conduct any quantitative analysis of causal connections. To double-check our conclusions on these connections we subsequently discussed the reports with individuals including labour union representatives who were familiar with each respective industry we studied.

Our time perspective is largely the 1980s. To determine what role such factors as the educational system play in determining productivity, we should have gone even further back in time. It is also true, of course, that the factors that were important to productivity improvements during the 1980s will not necessarily be important a decade later. It was a period that included an unusually long economic expansion.

References

Assarsson, B., 'Kvalitetsförändringar och produktivitetsmått' ('Changes in quality and yardsticks of productivity'), in *Hur mäta produktivitet?* (*How Should Productivity be Measured?*), expert report no. 1 to the Swedish Government's Productivity Delegation, Allmänna förlaget, 1991.

Berg, P.-O. 'Kvalitet i det postmoderna samhället – från egenskap till koncept' ('Quality in post-modern society – from trait to concept'), in Edvardsson, B. and Thomasson, B. (eds), *Kvalitetsutveckling i privata och offentliga tjänsteföretag* (*Quality Trends in Private and Public Sector Service Companies*), Natur och Kultur, 1989.

Bäst i världen – vad kan vi lära av världens ledande företag (*Best in the World – What Can We Learn from the World's Leading Companies?*), expert report no. 6 to the Productivity Delegation, Allmänna förlaget, 1991. (Available in a somewhat abridged English version as Hörnell, E., Improving Productivity for Competitive Advantage: Lessons from the Best in the World, Pitman, London, 1992.)

Edvardsson, B. and Thomasson, B., Kvalitetsutveckling – ett managementperspektiv (*Quality Development – a Management Perspective*), Studentlitteratur, 1991.

280 Achieving Service Productivity

Eliasson, G., *Produktivitet, vinster och ekonomisk välfärd – hur ser sambanden ut? (Productivity, Profits and Economic Welfare – What are the Connections?)*, Industrins Utredningsinstitut, 1991.

Granqvist, R., *Effektivitet och produktivitet i sjukvården (Efficiency and Productivity in the Medical Care System)*, Department of Business Administration, University of Stockholm, Publication R, 1990:1.

Kaplan, R.S. (ed.), *Measures for Manufacturing Excellence*, Harvard Business School Press, 1990.

Lawrence, P.R. and Dyer, D., *Renewing American Industry*, The Free Press, Macmillan, New York, 1983.

Magnusson, P.-O., 'Produktivitets- och kvalitetsutveckling i hotellbranschen' ('Productivity and quality trends in the hotel industry'), in *Produktivitet i vissa tjänstesektorer (Productivity in Selected Service Sectors)*, expert report no. 2 to the Productivity Delegation, Allmänna förlaget, 1991.

Mellander, E., Ysander, B.-C., 'Analyzing Productivity and Efficiency in the Absence of Output Measures', in Carlsson, H. and Larsson, B. (eds), *Problems of the Mixed Economy. Cooperation, Efficiency and Stability*, Elsevier Science Publishers BV, North Holland, 1990.

Porter, M.E., *Competitive Strategy. Technique for Analyzing Industries and Competitors*, The Free Press, New York, 1980.

Porter, M.E., *The Competitive Advantages of Nations*, The Free Press, New York, 1990.

Spechler, J.W., *When America Does it Right. Case Studies in Service Quality*, Institute of Industrial Engineers, Norcross, Georgia, 1991.

Voss, C., Johnston, R., Fitzgerald, L. and Sylvestro, R., 'Patterns of measurement of service performance: empirical results,' in Teare, R., Moutinho, L. and Morgan, N. (eds), *Managing and Marketing Services in the 1990s*, London, 1990.

APPENDIX 2

Steering committee

Mrs Antonia Ax: son Johnson, Chairman
Axel Johnson AB, Stockholm, Sweden

Dr Martin Leimdörfer, Managing Director
Industri-Matematik AB, Stockholm, Sweden

Dr Martin Lundberg
Särö, Sweden

Professor Pierre Guillet de Monthoux
Department of Business Administration, Stockholm University, Stockholm, Sweden

Professor Johan Myhrman
Stockholm School of Economics, Stockholm, Sweden

Dr Björn Sprängare, President
Chairman of the Steering committee
Trygg-Hansa SPP Holding AB, Stockholm, Sweden

Professor Bengt Stymne
Stockholm School of Economics, Stockholm, Sweden

Dr Carl Johan Åberg, Managing Director
The National Swedish Pension Fund
First, Second and Third Fund Boards, Stockholm, Sweden

APPENDIX 3

Research associates

RETAIL BANKING

Credit Suisse, Switzerland
S-E-Banken, Sweden
Banc One, Columbus, USA

Dr Eric Giertz, Associate Professor
The Royal Institute of Technology
Stockholm, Sweden

Mr Erik Grenmark, MBA
Royal Swedish Academy of Engineering Sciences (IVA)
Stockholm, Sweden

COMMERCIAL INSURANCE

The Home Insurance Company, USA
Trygg-Hansa International Insurance, Sweden

Mr Alarik Arthur, MBA
RCM Consulting AB
Norrköping, Sweden

Mr Fredrik Lennartsson, MBA
Institute for Management of Innovation and Technology
Stockholm School of Economics
Sweden

POST: LETTERS

PTT Post, The Netherlands
Sweden Post/Posten Brev, Sweden

Mr Claes Fritsch, MA, Chief Administrator
The Royal Institute of Technology
Stockholm, Sweden

Mr Sven Söderberg, Manager
INDEVO Proudfoot
Stockholm, Sweden

Swedish Postal Giro
Norwegian Postal Giro

Mr Michael Grindfors, MBA
The Boston Consulting Group
Stockholm, Sweden

Mr Dan Johnson, MBA
The Boston Consulting Group
Stockholm, Sweden

Mr Mikael Lövgren, MBA
The Boston Consulting Group
Stockholm, Sweden

Mr Andreas Regnell, MBA
The Boston Consulting Group
Stockholm, Sweden

SECONDARY SCHOOLS

Rødeby School, Sweden
Bräcke School, Sweden
Rønnebær Allé School, Denmark
William H. Crocker School, USA

Dr Jan Löwstedt, Associate Professor
Institute for Management of Innovation and Technology
Stockholm School of Economics
Sweden

Mr Martin Rogberg, MBA
Institute for Management of Innovation and Technology
Stockholm School of Economics
Sweden

Cand. merc. Birthe Ryberg
Århus School of Economics
Denmark
Professor Rami Shani
California Polytechnic State University
USA

284 Achieving Service Productivity

Professor Bengt Stymne
Institute for Management of Innovation and Technology
Stockholm School of Economics
Sweden

HEALTH CARE

Henry Ford Hospital, USA
Princess Royal Hospital, UK
Uddevalla Hospital, Sweden

Professor Bengt Jönsson
Centre for Health Economics
Stockholm School of Economics
Sweden

Dr Clas Rehnberg, Assistant Professor
Centre for Health Economics
Stockholm School of Economics
Sweden

FOOD DISTRIBUTION AND RETAILING

Hemköp, Sweden
Woolworths, Australia
Dagab Nord, Sweden

Mr Peter Blomqvist, MBA
Anderblom Handel AB
Stockholm, Sweden

Mr Anders Ferntoft, MSc
CEPRO AB
Stockholm, Sweden

Mr Mats Graffman, MSc
Expressen
Stockholm, Sweden

Mr Michael Spencer
Brunswick Hill Consulting Services
Victoria, Australia

APPENDIX 4

Executives' commentaries

We asked the companies analysed in this book to comment on our findings. The selected quotations below therefore serve as fitting conclusions to the study.

John A. Russell, Chief Communications Officer, Banc One

We believe there are three areas critical to the survival and success of banks in the 1990s. They would work in nearly any industry since they are that simple and universal, and we follow them at Banc One. The first is to maintain a consistent strategy. We try to remind ourselves of this requirement every day. As a matter of fact, we call it sticking to the 'nuts and bolts'. The second is our strong commitment to technology, which allows us to retain high profitability levels, offer efficient quality service and maintain a cutting edge in product development. And third, as we expand our franchise, we choose our partners carefully.

We maintain our culture by never acquiring a bank that is more than one-third of our combined size. Our objective is to never dilute earnings through acquisitions, not even in the first year. We invest about 3 per cent of our profits in technology research and development. This has allowed us to invest in computer software that will provide customers with the most advanced banking services available anywhere.

The most significant challenges to banks include continuation of growth, retention of customers, and maintaining momentum. Banks that have well-defined and consistently-practised strategies are best positioned for success. We think we are one of the institutions that will continue to succeed if we do not take all the nice things people say about us too seriously, and if we do stick to the 'nuts and bolts'.

Mr Lars-Göran Nilsson, Director, Trygg-Hansa SPP/Home

The insurance industry today is experiencing a dramatic restructuring covering all lines of insurance. These substantial changes are due to the impact of the following three factors: deregulation of the European markets; weak growth in the industry; and significant loss developments. These factors, in addition to poor financial performance, are forcing the industry to restructure.

Two major movements are developing. First, at the industry level, is a major contraction of the number of companies and employees in the industry. The ultimate consequence for the end consumer will be reduced overall transaction costs.

Further, and geared to internal corporate productivity, insurance companies and intermediate functions, such as brokers, are being forced to substantially improve efficiency levels by eliminating the functional organisation of companies and replacing that with a leaner, process-orientated, organisation where basically all previous back-office functions are expedited at the front end of operations.

The consequences for the industry and the consumer are major, and it is most likely that the overall transaction costs of the industry will be reduced by at least 50 per cent over the next decade. In addition, the quality of the industry's output will significantly improve.

Mr A. J. Scheepbouwer, Managing Director, PTT Post BV

What keeps us moving is performance through the eyes of our customers. With this in mind, there is still a lot of work to do, not least because our (business) customers expect more of us tomorrow. Both companies, Sweden Post and PTT Post of The Netherlands, respond to this by raising quality standards and levels and changing their technical infrastructure to meet new demands.

In each product-market combination (PMC) in which PTT Post is operating we have to face *de facto* competition. Dedicated competitors give more alternatives to our customers than ever before. The liberalisation process going on within the European Community will give support to more open and competitive markets. PTT Post must be ready for this. We have to stay alert by improving our performance and reducing our costs. The developing of new business must also contribute to our results in the future.

Our strategic planning for the year 2000 will create many changes in our postal business, in our services, in our infrastructure and management and so on. We are not yet ready and never will be.

Mr Christer Malm, President, PostGirot Sweden

The successful growth of a business is predicated on the eagerness of its employees to make a whole-hearted contribution.

PostGirot's vision and focus on three concrete goals – profitability, customer satisfaction and employee fulfilment – have been key guiding principles.

Yet most important of all is the ability of managers to communicate the trends in our surroundings, goals and standards and expectations related to their own units. At the same time, each manager must express the fundamental values of PostGirot – an interpretation of the company's soul.

Management must focus on liberating the organisation from internal threats and ensuring that its work and attitudes are thoroughly positive. Managers must project constructive attitudes to all employees. In other words, it is a matter of creating a climate that liberates energies and stimulates greater diversity and a broad sense of commitment.

If this mental and physical training of the organisation is to succeed, we need managers at all levels who are rather like coaches in the world of sports: managers who can present information about values and provide guidance.

Ms Marilyn Lushin-Miller, Superintendent, Hillsborough City School District

Creative thinking, keen intellectual curiosity, personal dedication to life-long learning, and individual commitment to the collective good are the essential goals necessary to prepare students for a future replete with unknown challenges and opportunities. Understanding that the responsibility for achieving these goals is a collaborative effort among all members of the Crocker community is the foundation of our school's success. Students, staff, parents and community members work together, communicating frequently to establish and to clearly understand the concepts and processes necessary to achieve the aforementioned goals.

Mr Gail L. Warden, Chief Executive Officer, Henry Ford Health System

The focus for improving productivity has been at three key levels within the organisation.

- Strategic level: this refers to the broadest set of mission, goals and key objectives of the organisation. At this level HFHS has prepared a ten-year strategic plan. Each year operating divisions prepare a three-year rolling plan for approval by the system leadership. This process of top down long-term planning and bottom up yearly planning allows the system to focus on key strategic objectives of the organisation.

- Clinical effectiveness: most health care resources are ordered by physicians, namely laboratory, radiological and other diagnostic tests. At HFHS, we have established a Centre for Clinical Effectiveness to work with our physicians and nursing professionals to develop clinical protocols and pathways for care. These protocols have been developed using the principles of continuous quality improvement (CQI) and have enabled us to reduce length of stay and resource consumption.
- Operational level: at this level we have targeted three key important factors, namely: improving the skills of our workforce, improving the system support including information systems and management support systems, and employee effort and motivation. Today over 100 employee teams are working on improving operational efficiency within the system.

Mr David Sandbach, Chief Executive, The Princess Royal Hospital

In conditions where the volume of sickness is likely to reduce, the successful 'ill health' manager of the future will:

- be more demanding in terms of cost benefit analysis of new techniques;
- pursue labour substitution strategies by replacing skilled personnel with semi-skilled, and by increasing automation. In addition, job demarcation between professional and non-professional staff will be reduced and capital invested in existing personal and group productive capacity;
- seek to centralise high cost facilities and run these for 18 to 24 hours rather than eight to 10 hours per day;
- seek financial deals which makes money more productive;
- reward and encourage personnel who can redefine how things can be done for a reduced unit cost of production and maintain or increase quality;
- monitor more closely the productivity performance of competitor hospitals and clinics.

In short, the hospital manager of the future must learn the lessons taught to manufacturing organisations during the 1980s.

INDEX

AIG, 63, 71, 72, 77
Australia, food distribution and retailing, 201–4
  Woolworths, 201–2, 204, 205–32

Banc One, USA, 4, 13–17, 27–38, 234–49 *passim*, 265
banking, 4–52, 243
  Banc One, 4, 13–17, 27–38
  Credit Suisse, 4–5, 13–17, 38–44
  customers, 18, 22, 32, 50–1
  economies of scale, 20–1, 22, 35, 51–2
  information technology (IT), 7–8, 23–7
  organisation and management, 16–21, 30–1, 38–9, 44–6
  personnel, 8–9
  rewards and motivation, 33, 40
  pressure for change, 22–7
  processes, 10–12
  productivity, 7–9, 15–16, 21–2
    comparative, 15–16
    factors influencing, 21–2
    monitoring of, 32–3
  profitability, monitoring, 9–13, 18–19, 25–7
  quality, 18, 19–20, 46
  regulation, 16, 21, 246
  revenues and costs, 6–9
  S-E Banken, 5, 13–17, 44–52
  sector, 5–6
  barriers to market entry, 246–7
  food distribution and retailing, 217–21
Belgium giro post, 127–8
benchmarking, 239–40
Bilspedition, 205, 229, 230–1
Bräcke School, Sweden, 148, 151–2, 153–5, 157–69, 250–1

Canada giro post, 127–8
Chubb, 72
Citymail, 86, 99
Coldsped, 205
competence, 250–1
competition, 1, 244–5
  food distribution and retailing, 221–3
  giro post, 131–2

insurance, 67–8
letter post, 99, 119
convenience goods distribution and retailing *see* food distribution and retailing
coordinated autonomy, 30–1, 38–9, 44–6, 235
cost–effectiveness, 2–3
Credit Suisse, Switzerland, 4–5, 13–17, 38–44, 234–6, 238
Crocker Middle School, USA, 148, 151–2, 156–69, 236–51 *passim*, 267
customers, 245–8, 257–9
  banking, 18, 22, 32, 50–1
  giro post, 133, 138, 141–3
  health care, 191–2
  letter post, 99–100

Dagab, 204, 205, 208, 210, 212, 213, 215, 227, 229, 230–1
Denmark, schools, secondary, 148
  Ronnebaer Allé School, 148, 151–2, 155–6, 157–69

economies of scale, 246–7
  banking, 20–1, 22, 35, 51–2
  giro post, 125–9
  insurance, 53, 68–70
  letter post, 117
  and market intelligence, 234–5
education *see* schools, secondary
environment, 2–3
European Community (EC), 68
  postal services, 97
European Economic Area (EEA), 68, 260
executives *see* leadership

food distribution and retailing, 201–32, 243
  automation, 230–1
  competition, 221–3
  costs, 223–4
  entry barriers, 217–21
  financial ratios, 228–9
  goals and feedback, 225–7
  Hemköp, 201–2, 204, 205–32
  information technology (IT), 201–2, 230–1
  market intelligence, 232

ownership, 214–17
personnel, 225, 228
processes, 206
productivity, 207–32
  comparative, 210–11
  factors influencing, 214–32
  measurement of, 207, 211–14
sector, 202–5
standards, 229
waste, 229–30
Woolworths, 201–2, 204, 205–32
Ford Motor Company *see* Henry Ford Health System
France:
  giro post, 127–8
  insurance, 54

Germany:
  banking, 9
  giro post, 126, 127–8
  insurance, 54
giro post, 120–47, 243–4, 246
  competition, 131–2
  customers, 133, 138, 141–3
  economies of scale, 125–9
  efficiency, 126–7, 134
  information technology (IT), 129
  internationalisation, 144–6
  organisation and management, 135, 141–3, 146–7
  personnel, 124, 135
  Postgiro, 120–47
  PostGirot, 120–47
  processes, 134–7
  productivity, 120
    comparative, 135
    factors influencing, 125–46
  profitability, 124
  quality, 137
  sector, 121–4
Greenberg, Hank, 71

health care, 170–200, 243
  customers, 191–2
  expenditure, 171, 172
  Henry Ford Health System, 170, 178–9, 180–200
  hospital services, 173–5
  information technology (IT), 195–6, 200
  insurance, 175–7, 183–8
  monopoly, 199
  organisation and management, 195–9
  personnel, 192–5

Princess Royal Hospital, 170–1, 178–200
processes, 189
productivity, 176–7, 181–200
  barriers to, 199–200
  comparative, 181–2
  factors influencing, 182–99
  regulation, 182–3
  sector, 171–7
Uddevalla Hospital, 171, 178–9, 180–200
Hemköp, Sweden, 201–2, 204, 205–32, 249
Henry Ford Health System, USA, 170, 178–9, 180–200, 234–53 *passim*, 267–8
Home Insurance Company, USA, 53, 57–62, 237–50 *passim*, 265–6
hospitals, 173–5
  see also health care

information technology (IT), 238–9
  banking, 7–8, 23–7
  food distribution and retailing, 201–2, 230–1
  giro post, 129
  health care, 195–6, 200
  insurance, 81, 83
  letter post, 97
innovation, 2–3, 253
insurance, 53–83
  competition, 67–8
  economies of scale, 53, 68–70
  efficiency, 62–7, 72–3
  health care, 175–7, 183–8
  Home Insurance Company, 53, 57–62
  information technology (IT), 81, 83
  leadership, 71–2
  organisation and management, 81–2
  ownership, 75–6
  personnel, 73–5
  processes, 55–62
  productivity, 62–83
    barriers to, 76–83
    factors influencing, 62–76
  regulation, 54, 66–7, 76–7, 82–3
  sector, 54–7
  Trygg–Hansa SPP, 53, 57–62
internationalisation, 256
  banking, 23
  giro post, 144–6
Italy, giro post, 127–8

Japan:
  giro post, 126, 127–8
  insurance, 54

leadership, 252–3

Index 291

insurance, 71–2
letter post, 118
schools, secondary, 162–5, 168
letter post, 84–119, 243–4, 245
  competition, 99, 119
  costs, 88–9, 102–3
  customers, 99–100
  economies of scale, 117
  efficiency, 90–1
  information technology (IT), 97
  leadership, 118
  licences, 86–7
  monopoly, 87, 115
  organisation and management, 106–10, 117–18
  personnel, 94–5
  Posten Brev, 84, 87–8, 90, 93–119
  processes, 101–2, 111–12
  productivity, 90, 97–119
    barriers to, 115–19
    comparative, 112–15
    factors influencing, 97–112
    measurement of, 112–15
  profitability, 96
  PTT Post, 84, 87–8, 90–119
  quality, 90, 99–100, 103–6, 116
  regulation, 97
  sector, 85–91
Liljas, 205, 230
litigation USA, 54, 77–8, 200
Lushin–Miller, Marilyn, 267

Malm, Christer, 266–7
Meenaghan, Jim, 71, 72, 74

Netherlands:
  giro post, 126, 127–8
  letter post, 84, 86, 90, 97
  PTT Post, 84, 87–8, 90–119
Nilsson Lars-G_ran, 71, 72, 265–6

Norway:
  banking, 9
  giro post, 120–47

organisation and management, 251–2
  banking, 16–21, 30–1, 38–9, 44–6
  giro post, 135, 141–3, 146–7
  health care, 195–9
  insurance, 81–2
  letter post, 106–10, 117–18
  schools, secondary, 150–1, 162–5, 169

P&O Cold Storage, 205, 212, 213, 230, 231
personnel, 248–9
  banking, 8–9, 33, 40
  competence, 250–1
  food distribution and retailing, 225, 228
  giro post, 124, 135
  health care, 192–5
  insurance, 73–5
  letter post, 94–5
  rewards and motivation, 249
postal services, 84–5, 243–4
  giro post, 120–47
  letter post, 84–119
  Posten Brev, Sweden, 84, 87–8, 90, 93–119, 245, 247, 249
  Postgiro, Norway, 120–47, 234, 236, 241, 249
  PostGirot, Sweden, 120–47, 266–7
Princess Royal Hospital, UK, 170–1, 178–200, 236–7, 268
processes, 237–8
  banking, 10–12
  food distribution and retailing, 206
  giro post, 134–7
  health care, 189
  insurance, 55–62
  letter post, 101–2, 111–12
productivity:
  banking, 7–9, 15–16, 21–2
  external influences on, 240–7
  food distribution and retailing, 207–32
  giro post, 120, 125–46
  health care, 176–7, 181–200
  insurance, 62–83
  internal influences on, 247–53
  letter post, 90, 97–119
  management, 237–9
  measurement of, 235–6
  public services, 256–9
  schools, secondary, 157–69
  PTT Post, Netherlands, 84, 87–8, 90–119, 239–49 *passim*, 266

quality:
  banking, 18, 19–20, 46
  giro post, 137
  letter post, 90, 99–100, 103–6, 116
  measurement of, 236, 240
  schools, secondary, 165–7
Quayle, Dan, 77

Refrigerated Roadways, 205, 229, 230–2
regulation:
  banking, 16, 21, 246

health care, 182–3
insurance, 54, 66–7, 76–7, 82–3
letter post, 97
public sector, 246
resources, 1
Rödeby School, Sweden, 148, 151–3, 157–69, 239
Ronnebaer Allé School, Denmark, 148, 151–2, 155–6, 157–69
Russell, John A., 265

Sandbach, David, 268
Scheepbouwer, A.J., 266
schools, secondary, 148–69, 243–4
  Bräcke School, 148, 151–2, 153–5, 157–69
  costs and quality, 165–7
  Crocker Middle School, 148, 151–2, 156–69
  education sector, 149–51
  environment, 159–62
  leadership, 162–5, 168
  organisation and management, 150–1, 162–5, 169
  productivity, 157–69
    barriers to, 167–9
    comparative, 157–9
    factors influencing, 159–65
  Rädeby School, 148, 151–3, 157–69
  Rønnebaer Allé School, 148, 151–2, 155–6, 157–69
services:
  banking, 4–52
  food distribution and retailing, 201–32
  giro post, 120–47
  and goods, 255
  health care, 170–200
  insurance, 53–83
  letter post, 84–119
  productivity (*q.v*), 235–53
  schools, secondary, 148–69
Skandia, 54
Skandinaviska Enskida Banken (S-E Banken), Sweden, 5, 13–17, 44–52, 238
Spain, banking, 7, 8, 9
supermarkets, 211–12
  see also food distribution and retailing
Sweden:
  banking, 7–9
  food distribution and retailing, 201–4, 208–10, 219–23
  giro post, 121–47

health care, 171–7
insurance, 53–4
letter post, 84, 86–7, 90
schools, secondary, 149–51
see also companies etc. by name
Sweden Post, 84, 86–7, 92, 94, 239–41
see also Posten Brev
Switzerland:
  banking, 7, 8–9
    Credit Suisse, 4–5, 13–17, 38–44
  giro post, 126, 127–8

technology, 233–4, 252
  banking, 7–8, 23–7
  food distribution and retailing, 201–2, 230–1
  giro post, 129
  health care, 195–6, 200
  insurance, 81, 83
  letter post, 97
transport, food, 212–14
see also food distribution and retailing
Trygg–Hansa SPP, Sweden, 53, 57–62, 237–50 *passim*, 265–6

Uddevalla Hospital, Sweden, 171, 178–9, 180–200
United Kingdom (UK):
  banking, 7, 8–9
  giro post, 127–8
  health care, 171–7
  Princess Royal Hospital, 170–1, 178–200
  insurance, 54
United States of America (USA):
  banking, 7, 8–9, 29
    Banc One, 4, 13–17, 27–38
  giro post, 127–8
  health care, 171–7
    Henry Ford Health System, 170, 178–9, 180–200
  insurance, 53–4, 58, 66–7, 234, 244
    Home Insurance Company, 53, 57–62
  litigation, 54, 77–8, 200
  schools, secondary, 148
    Crocker Middle School, 148, 151–2, 156–69

Warden, Gail L., 267–8
warehouses, food, 212–13
see also food distribution and retailing
Woolworths, Australia, 201–2, 204, 205–32, 234–52 *passim*